NINETEENTH CENTURY AMERICAN POETRY

THE
MAGILL
BIBLIOGRAPHIES

Other Magill Bibliographies:

The American Presidents—Norman S. Cohen
Black American Women Novelists—Craig Werner
Classical Greek and Roman Drama—Robert J. Forman
Contemporary Latin American Fiction—Keith H. Brower
Masters of Mystery and Detective Fiction—J. Randolph Cox
Restoration Drama—Thomas J. Taylor
Twentieth Century European Short Story—Charles E. May
The Victorian Novel—Laurence W. Mazzeno
Women's Issues—Laura Stempel Mumford

NINETEENTH CENTURY AMERICAN POETRY

An Annotated Bibliography

PHILIP K. JASON
Professor of English
United States Naval Academy

SALEM PRESS

Pasadena, California   Englewood Cliffs, New Jersey

∞The paper used in these volumes conforms to the
American National Standard for Permanence of Paper
for Printed Library Materials, Z39.48-1984.

Library of Congress Cataloging-in-Publication Data

Jason, Philip K., 1941–
    Nineteenth century American poetry / Philip K.
    Jason.
        p.   cm. — (Magill bibliographies)
    ISBN 0-89356-651-9
    1. American poetry—19th century—History and
criticism—Bibliography.   2. American poetry—19th
century—Bibliography.   I. Title.   II. Series.
Z1231.P7J37   1989
[PS316]
016.811 ' 309—dc20   89-10804
                                                          CIP

CONTENTS

CONTENTS

EDITORIAL STAFF

NINETEENTH
CENTURY
AMERICAN POETRY

INTRODUCTION

With notable exceptions, the history of nineteenth century American literature, poetry in particular, is the history of adapting the traditional literary uses of the English language to the special cultural conditions of the new nation. We must remember that as the nineteenth century opened, the United States of America was not yet three decades old. Poets born in the early years of this century were living in a nation that had yet to develop a distinct literature, though a strong beginning had been made. The country itself was changing rapidly, and the whirling processes of geographical expansion, technological innovation, and swift advances on the world political and economic stage did not create—until the later decades—a sense of a settled national identity. Surely, shared principles were articulated over and over again. Yet those principles were always being tested by new, often unexpected circumstances.

The poetry of the nineteenth century reflects this newness and this dynamism in many ways. Bryant and Emerson are usually presented as founding fathers of an American aesthetic in poetry. Emerson in particular, in his essays and journals, fashioned ideas about the nature of poetry and of the poet that influenced his contemporaries and generations to come. In his role as the foremost spokesman of the Transcendentalist movement, he also developed the intellectual framework for American individualism. Thoreau—in his poetry, his other writings, and his style of life—was Emerson's first and most complete student. Holmes is seen as foreshadowing the traditions of realism while simultaneously looking back to eighteenth century models. He is best remembered as a poet of wit. Longfellow, whose reputation was second to none during his lifetime, has undergone extreme devaluation, and some come close to calling him a plagiarist. However, he was in the forefront of those who discovered a usable past that could be embodied in an accessible, popular poetry. He helped put American literature on the world map while showing American writers how to benefit from the knowledge of European literature. Lowell "the natural aristocrat" and Whittier "the militant Quaker" also are noted for their attempts at an accessible poetry based on regional and national themes.

The list of prominent poets quickly reminds us that for most of the nineteenth century, American literature was the literature of New England. Poe and Lanier represent the South; Whitman, Crane, and Melville New York (though Melville spent much time visiting Hawthorne in New England). Bryant, Emerson, Thoreau, Holmes, Whittier, Lowell, Longfellow, and Dickinson were citizens of New England (as were the lesser-known Tuckerman and Very) and looked to Boston as the classical world looked to Athens. It was the seat of culture. Dunbar is the lone midwesterner. The New England writers, Tuckerman and Dickinson excepted, knew one another, and their careers had many points of intersection. They met to discuss a wide range of issues, not only literary ones. As a group, they were highly conscious of a shared responsibility: the building of a national literature.

Some, Whittier and Longfellow in particular, tried to shape American folklore and history into a shareable body of work that would help bond the young nation. Holmes and Lowell looked to commemorate significant moments, to mark our history as it unfolded. Their "occasional poems," along with those of Emerson, are literary monuments to our ongoing national story. Lowell's work in Yankee dialect celebrated and immortalized native American types in their own speech patterns. Bryant, Emerson, and many others worked to save in poetry what was unique in the American landscape. They built an America of the imagination, although it was an America that looked very much and sounded very much like the area around Cambridge and Concord.

The two southerners, Poe and Lanier, are significant as prosodic theorists as well as experimenters in versification. Both, but Lanier in particular, were enchanted by the affinities between poetry and music. They tried to find in the auditory and rhythmic properties of language parallels to the affective communication of musical compositions. This tendency is squarely in the Romantic tradition, the starting point for all nineteenth century poetry, but Lanier tried to develop a scientific system based on correlations between the two arts. To various degrees, the other major voices were experimenters, too. Emerson's remarks on poetry and his own attempts at a free-verse line look forward to Whitman and to our own time.

In Whitman and Dickinson we have our most public and most private poetic voices. Both writers forged highly personal, innovative styles. Whitman's sweeping cadences, in which rhyme is abandoned and meter overwhelmed by the rhythms of speech and oratory, are a form of free verse that has had enormous influence on twentieth century poets. His transcendent and variegated "I" plays the central role in a drama that is both democratic and cosmic. Dickinson's rhythmic hesitations and daring off-rhymes break down and reconstruct traditional prosody into a highly personal instrument. The drama of her personae is simultaneously domestic and otherworldly. Whitman would seem to be speaking—shouting, almost—to every-one. Dickinson's listener seems most often to be another aspect of her self or her deity. Many of Dickinson's poems are among our most sophisticated religious lyrics. Indeed, devotional poetry constitutes a large part of what was written by our best poets, though much of it is unorthodox and unsettling. Whittier's vigorous hymns, the metaphysical strain in Very, Emerson's insistence on the spiritual nature of reality, Holmes's militant Unitarianism, and Whitman's pantheistic reveries represent various colors in nineteenth century America's religious spectrum.

Whitman and Dickinson are also linked by their concern with building larger structures out of sequenced elements. Whitman's *Leaves of Grass* was one of the first sustained experiments in designing a book of poems in which individual items are ordered to create a work that can be read as a multipart long poem. Dickinson's manuscript fascicles hint at a similar intention. The untitled poems that make up Stephen Crane's collections, especially the first one—*The Black Riders*—may be understood as stemming from this same impulse. Melville's *Clarel*, a long poem with a continuous narrative line that connects it in some ways with the traditional story poems as Americanized by Longfellow, is fashioned in curious patterns of generically distinct subdivisions that allow us to consider it, too, as a version of the sequence poem.

It is curious that there are so very few studies directly focused on nineteenth century American poetry. The sweep of studies on American poetry tends to be either broader or narrower. Of course, the major poets are included in general studies of the century or one or another of its major segments. Still, few critics or historians have seen the body of poetry produced by American writers during this century as a topic in and of itself. Perhaps the absence of inclusive theses about this material is testimony to the great variety of work produced.

As is common in literary history, the canon of nineteenth century poetry has undergone significant revaluations over the course of time. By the end of the century, critics and anthologists had enshrined Bryant, Emerson, Longfellow, Whittier, Poe (somewhat reluctantly), Holmes, Lowell, Whitman (tentatively and with apologies), Lanier, and Bayard Taylor. Other poets, now long forgotten or yet to be resurrected, were extremely popular.

In our own century, Poe's achievement as a poet remains a question, while Whitman is considered by many to be the foremost poet this country has produced. Almost any shift or innovation in critical fashions discovers an aspect of Whitman that deserves further examination. Emily Dickinson is considered by some his equal, and rarely takes less than second place. Feminist critics in particular have swelled the body of materials on Dickinson, much of their work published only in the last decade. The gulf between these and the rest is enormous. In fact, for many of today's scholars, only Whitman and Dickinson are true poets of genius, all the rest having only historical importance. In recent decades, Melville's poetry, virtually neglected in his own time and through the first half of this century, has received concentrated scholarly attention. Bayard Taylor has disappeared from view while Jones Very, Frederick Goddard Tuckerman, Stephen Crane, and Paul Laurence Dunbar have been granted access to the halls of fame, albeit limited access.

The purpose of this volume is to help the student of nineteenth century American poetry locate those secondary materials needed for coursework, background reading, research, and independent study. The listings are not meant to be comprehensive. The items included here are books, portions of books, and—much more selectively—articles in periodicals. The periodicals cited most frequently are *American Literature*, *Studies in the American Renaissance*, *Emerson Society Quarterly*, (abbreviated as *ESQ*) and *American Transcendental Quarterly* (abbreviated as *ATQ*). For the vast body of interpretive literature available in periodicals the student must turn to specialized author bibliographies, to the authoritative bibliographical essays published annually in *American Literary Scholarship*, and to the listings in the *PMLA Bibliography*. Students should know about such specialized journals as the *Walt Whitman Review*, *Dickinson Studies*, and other journals dedicated to single authors. Articles in these journals have not been cited here.

The first section of the bibliography is devoted to general treatments of nineteenth century American poetry; this is followed by sections on individual authors (in sequence according to date of birth). Each of these individual sections begins with a listing of general studies of the author at hand, followed by a listing of studies keyed to specific works (arranged alphabetically by title except in the case of Emily Dickinson, where poems are cited by first line and number in the sequence established in Thomas H. Johnson's definitive edition of *The Poems of Emily Dickinson*, published in three volumes in 1955). For Very, Thoreau, and Dunbar, where there is a relative scarcity of commentary devoted to individual works, the listings are limited to general studies.

The section listing "General Treatments of the Period" includes a wide variety of materials. The student of nineteenth century American poetry, or the literature of any period, will soon discover that literature is not created in a vacuum. For this reason, many works that discuss the literature of the period broadly, many that discuss it thematically, and many that provide historical and cultural background are included. As noted above, few works isolate nineteenth century American poetry as a topic in itself. The tendency has been to treat the literature of the century as a whole (broken into two pieces by the Civil War), with little concern for genre development, or to treat the genre in wider purview, going back to the Puritans or forward to the modernists or both.

Fruitful study most often requires a movement from general to specific, from context to text, and then back again. A general consideration of an author's life and the nature of his writing can inform one's approach to a specific work. Thus, the first entries under each poet are such biographical, career, and critical studies that explore characteristic themes, methods, or other features of the poet's work as a whole rather than individual works. In the case of Whitman, this distinction is compromised by the special nature of *Leaves of Grass*—a specific, multipart work developed over many years in many published versions. There is little of Whitman's poetry that can be considered outside *Leaves of Grass*, and yet the individual "leaves" have lives of their own.

Our group of writers includes many who wrote in genres besides poetry. Indeed, some are best-known for their essays (Emerson, Thoreau) or their fiction (Melville, Crane). In selecting among the responses to their work, I have chosen to be inclusive. Much of the poetry of Emerson and Thoreau, for example, is in the service of ideas which are elaborated in their prose works. A number of critical studies of those ideas that do not pay attention to the poetry have nevertheless been included, for the student can make effective application of such information. Likewise, the comments of these writers on art, esthetics, and poetry itself have obvious relevance to how we approach their poems. Similarly, thematic studies of Crane's fiction, as well as stylistic studies that pay attention to how he handles imagery in his prose, may well be useful to the student of Crane's poems and are therefore included.

For most of the poets, as noted above, annotations on writings about particular poems have also been included. The intention here has been to provide access to the commentary on frequently anthologized poems. These commentaries range from reprinted articles and chapters of books to much shorter discussions. Though the references cited and annotated here should take students a long way into almost any project in nineteenth century American poetry, this guide is in no way meant to be comprehensive. It will suffice for the researches of most high school and undergraduate students, but it is only a starting point for the more specialized needs of advanced English majors, graduate students, and professional scholars.

General Treatments of the Period

Aaron, Daniel. *The Unwritten War: American Writers and the Civil War*. New York: Alfred A. Knopf, 1973.
Aaron surveys the great number of literary works of all kinds inspired by the Civil War. He argues that the essential issues of the war seemed ready-made for literary treatment. Among the important nineteenth century poets whose works engage the war to a greater or lesser degree are Lowell, Holmes, Melville, Lanier, and Crane. Aaron also treats a number of minor poets as well as writers in other genres. In a supplement, he briefly traces the impact of the war on Emily Dickinson's work.

Abel, Darrel. *The Literature of the Atlantic Culture*. Vol. 2 of *American Literature*. Woodbury, N.Y.: Barron's Educational Series, 1963.
Part of a three-volume study guide, this volume covers the major nineteenth century movements and writers, including most of the poets treated in this bibliography. Bryant is in volume 1. Though reliable, these discussions are basic and introductory: useful for background reading but not for incorporation into a paper. Surprisingly good on Melville's poetry as well as that of Holmes and Lanier.

Allen, Gay Wilson. *American Prosody*. New York: American Book, 1935.
Chronological treatment of the theory and practice of American poetic technique measured against its English background. Explores how various writers conform to or declare independence from that background. A primer on prosody and scansion as well as an introduction to the technical virtuosity and innovations of masters like Poe, Whitman, and Dickinson. Includes separate chapters on these three figures as well as the more conservative Bryant, Emerson, Whittier, Longfellow, Holmes, Lowell, and Lanier. Scattered passages speculate on a distinct American tradition.

Anderson, Quentin. *The Imperial Self: An Essay in American Literary and Cultural History*. New York: Alfred A. Knopf, 1971.

Asserts that there is an "absolutism of the self" in major nineteenth century American writers. Claims that Emerson, Whitman, and James managed to escape constraining social concerns in their art: "their imaginative work ignores, elides, or transforms history, politics, heterosexuality, the hope for purposeful change." Anderson wonders if this stance is essentially American. Each writer asserts an imperial power over the flood of sensations that threaten to divide attention and in so doing divide the self.

Arms, George. *The Fields Were Green: A New View of Bryant, Whittier, Holmes, Lowell, and Longfellow with a Selection of Their Poems*. Stanford, Calif.: Stanford University Press, 1953.
Arms observes that "American poets of the last century occupy a paradoxical place. They have unequaled currency in the national mind and their poems constitute a large part of the formal study of American literature. Yet critical response to them is generally nonexistent, or if expressed, antipathetic. My belief is that there has been a failure to do justice to these poets and that in dealing with them as it does criticism is either inadequate or wrongheaded." Arms revalues these neglected "schoolroom poets," giving us fresh reasons for admiring their work.

Barbour, Brian M., ed. *American Transcendentalism: An Anthology of Criticism*. Notre Dame, Ind.: University of Notre Dame Press, 1973.
Selections represent the backgrounds and central ideas of Transcendentalist philosophy. Topics include the relationship of Transcendentalism to German philosophy, Jacksonian democracy, Unitarianism, and the writings of John Locke. Three essays consider the importance of Emerson. Barbour's introduction stresses the centrality of this subject to any study of nineteenth century American culture and its literature.

Bickman, Martin. *The Unsounded Centre: Jungian Studies in American Romanticism*. Chapel Hill: University of North Carolina Press, 1980.
An application of the psychological system developed by Carl G. Jung to the literature of the period. This system is seen as "another formulation . . . of the confluence of traditions that shaped American Romanticism." A chapter on methodology is followed by a series of interpretive applications. Extensive discussion of Emerson. Separate chapters on Whitman and Dickinson.

Blasing, Mutlu Konuk. *American Poetry: The Rhetoric of Its Forms*. New Haven, Conn.: Yale University Press, 1987.
Establishes four tropes with corresponding strategies to differentiate the major nineteenth century poets. Poe is defined by allegory, Emerson by analogy, Whitman by analogy, and Dickinson by irony. Each part of this study begins with a treatment of one of these masters and then explores two later poets

whose strategies are related. An alternative to the single- or dual-tradition approaches that dominate poetry criticism.

Bloom, Harold, ed. *American Poetry to 1914*. New York: Chelsea House, 1987.
A selection of what Bloom calls "the best criticism available upon American poetry from its inception . . . through the era that ended with our entry into the First World War." Three essays each on Whitman and Dickinson, two each on Bryant, Melville, and Lanier. Other poets addressed in single essays. Most selections are book excerpts, but a number are periodical pieces collected here for the first time. Solid introduction by Bloom.

Boswell, Jeanetta. *Spokesmen for the Minority: A Bibliography of Sidney Lanier, William Vaughn Moody, Frederick Goddard Tuckerman, and Jones Very, with Selective Annotations*. Metuchen, N.J.: Scarecrow Press, 1987.
These lists of secondary sources are alphabetically arranged by author. Boswell not only includes books, chapters, and periodical articles, but also brief references to these authors in comprehensive works or works about their contemporaries. There is a separate subject index for each poet as well as an index of coauthors, editors, translators, and illustrators.

Brenner, Rica. *Twelve American Poets Before 1900*. Reprint. Freeport, N.Y.: Books for Libraries, 1968.
First published in 1933, this study treats, in separate essays, ten of the poets included in this bibliography (Bryant, Emerson, Longfellow, Whittier, Poe, Holmes, Lowell, Whitman, Dickinson, Lanier). Brenner attempts, following the temporary dominance of realism in American letters, to reestablish interest in the "classic" American poets through "a background of biographical and critical information." Brenner is concerned with the historical significance of these poets as interpreters of the American spirit. Eugene Field (1850-1895) is a surprise inclusion.

Brooks, Van Wyck. *The Flowering of New England, 1815-1865*. Rev. ed. New York: E. P. Dutton, 1937.
An analysis of "the New England mind" as revealed in the efforts of the region's major cultural figures. Brooks sees the major writers emerging from vigorous communities, each conscious of participating in a "collective impulse" of imaginative and artistic awakening. This "flowering" was the peak of a culture cycle and necessitated a settled, self-confident society. Poets and prose writers are discussed together in this landmark study of American cultural dynamics. Longfellow, Emerson, Thoreau, Holmes, and Lowell are the poets given most attention.

——————— . *New England: Indian Summer 1865-1915*. New York: E. P. Dutton, 1940.

Brooks's sequel to *The Flowering of New England* continues his cultural exploration of the region whose energies radiated from Boston and Cambridge. Aside from treatments of Howells and James, this volume is notable for its examination of the cities themselves, the political and intellectual climate following the Civil War, and the phenomenon of Emily Dickinson. The "Indian Summer" metaphor suggests an afterglow following a period of growth and first harvest. This was a period of reminiscence, but also one in which our foremost academicians and artists traveled abroad for inspiration and renewal.

——————— . *The Times of Melville and Whitman*. New York: E. P. Dutton, 1947.

A companion to the New England volumes listed above, this study concentrates on the careers of writers outside the New England orbit. New York, Philadelphia, the Middle West, the South, and San Francisco are the cultural settings Brooks explores. Includes major discussions of Lanier and Whitman. There is also a section on the lure of Europe.

Buell, Lawrence. *Literary Transcendentalism: Style and Vision in the American Renaissance*. Ithaca, N.Y.: Cornell University Press, 1973.

"The purpose of this book is to survey the literary art and criticism of the American Transcendentalists and to contribute in the process to a better understanding of the relationship between style and vision in all nonfictional literature." This study is organized by the broad concerns of spirit, nature, and man. The major figures treated are Emerson (most prominently), Thoreau, Ellery Channing, Very, and Whitman.

——————— . *New England Literary Culture: From Revolution Through Renaissance*. Cambridge, England: Cambridge University Press, 1986.

Discusses this region's centrality in America's early decades of nationhood, its sense of itself, its print culture, and its developing traditions. Special chapter on poetics (treats Emerson and Dickinson) and oratory (Emerson). Regards Puritanism as a historical factor and as an imaginative moral landscape. "Pilgrimism" is explored as a cultural and literary fashion. Chapters on "Neoclassical Continuities" and "The Village as Icon."

Cameron, Kenneth Walter, ed. *Contemporary Dimension: An American Renaissance Literary Notebook of Newspaper Clippings on Alcott, Emerson, Whitman, Thoreau, Hawthorne, Longfellow, Lowell, Holmes, Poe, Bryant, Irving, Whittier, and Others*. Hartford, Conn.: Transcendental Books, 1970.

A copious gathering of reviews, interviews, essays, news items, and obituaries drawn principally from Philadelphia, New York, and Boston newspapers. Cameron provides a comprehensive index to publications (periodicals), proper names, places, and subjects (such as "abolitionism").

Canby, Henry Seidel. *Classic Americans: A Study of Eminent American Writers from Irving to Whitman*. New York: Russell & Russell, 1959.
Originally planned to be a history of American literature viewed against its social and intellectual backgrounds, this volume concentrates instead "upon the great writers who are the essences of their times." Emerson, Thoreau, Melville, Poe, and Whitman are among those treated. Canby sees American literature as "the adjustment of a European, and generally a British, culture by new men to a new environment." His essays explore just what "new" means with regard to these writers. Begins with a long essay on the colonial background.

Carter, Everett. *The American Idea: The Literary Response to American Optimism*. Chapel Hill: University of North Carolina Press, 1977.
Demonstrates the relationship "between the idea of America and literary forms." Most of Carter's examples are drawn from nineteenth century writers in such chapters as "Nineteenth-Century Styles of Affirmation," "Romantic Defense of the Idea," "and "Varieties of Rejection." References to Bryant, Longfellow, Holmes, Emerson, Thoreau, Whitman, and Poe. These writers are discussed on the basis of their attitude toward "the way their culture made sense of the universe."

Carton, Evan. *The Rhetoric of American Romance: Dialectic and Identity in Emerson, Dickinson, Poe, and Hawthorne*. Baltimore: Johns Hopkins University Press, 1985.
Part 1 treats "the dialectics of romance by examining the concepts of nature, selfhood, authenticity, and language in Emerson, Dickinson, and Poe." Only Dickinson is treated as a poet. The writers are discussed together, rather than in separate chapters. Key issues are "Originality and the Self," "Integration, Detachment," and "The Power of Words."

Chai, Leon. *The Romantic Foundations of the American Renaissance*. Ithaca, N.Y.: Cornell University Press, 1987.
A detailed examination of how the various components of European Romanticism worked their way into the culture and literary texts of early nineteenth century America. Focal figures are Poe, Emerson, Hawthorne, and Melville. Chai draws upon a wide range of disciplines.

Connor, Frederick William. *Cosmic Optimism: A Study of The Interpretation of Evolution by American Poets from Emerson to Robinson*. Gainesville: University of Florida Press, 1941.

Examines pre-Darwinian currents as they are reflected in Emerson, Poe, and Whitman, then discusses the largely negative reactions of Bryant, Longfellow, Lowell, and Lanier to Darwin's theories. A difficult, stiffly written work on an issue of great importance. Chapter on Holmes, a man of scientific training, especially useful. No references to Dickinson. Good on close of century, with brief comment on Crane.

Dangerfield, George. *The Awakening of American Nationalism: 1815-1828*. New York: Harper & Row, 1965.
Though not a literary study, this book can be useful to students exploring nationalistic themes in the poetry of this period. Dangerfield examines the contest between the economic nationalism expounded by Henry Clay and John Quincy Adams and the democratic nationalism exemplified by the partisans of Andrew Jackson. Reviews the major political and economic events at home and abroad that cast shadows over the rest of the century.

Donoghue, Denis. *Connoisseurs of Chaos: Ideas of Order in Modern American Poetry*. 2d ed. New York: Columbia University Press, 1984.
Treats the quest for order in American poetry beginning with Bryant and Poe in the earlier nineteenth century through chapter-length discussions of Whitman, Tuckerman, Melville, and Dickinson. These are Donoghue's springboards toward analyses of major moderns: Robinson, J. V. Cunningham, Robert Lowell, Frost, Stevens, and Roethke. Stevens is the presiding figure whose notions of poetic order inform Donoghue's readings of the other poets.

_____ . *Reading America: Essays on American Literature*. New York: Alfred A. Knopf, 1987.
This collection of essays and reviews traces the central dynamic of the American enterprise—the imperatives of a powerful national past versus the subversions of an irrevocably anarchic spirit. Early chapters treat Emerson, Thoreau, Whitman, and Dickinson. The chapter called "America in Theory" is a useful overview of approaches to American literary culture and civilization.

Duffey, Bernard. *Poetry in America: Expression and Its Values in the Times of Bryant, Whitman, and Pound*. Durham, N.C.: Duke University Press, 1978.
This study places "the value assumed in poetic composition at the center of attention" and is thus less concerned with persons and reputations than with the means of literary expression. Describes three phases of development: celebration, contradiction and question, and "private sophistication of feeling and thought." Issues include "the fiction of coherence," "poetic piety," and "the idyllic imagination." All major (and some minor) nineteenth century poets treated.

Elliot, Emory et al., eds. *Columbia Literary History of the United States*. New York: Columbia University Press, 1988.

This comprehensive, multi-author survey is intended to supersede Spiller's *Literary History of the United States*, coming forty years after the first edition of that work. American writers discovered or rediscovered since the 1960's are integrated into a revised vision of America's literary heritage. Part 2, covering 1810-1865, includes an essay on Bryant and the Fireside Poets, another on Poe and the Old South, and individual treatments of Emerson, Thoreau, Whitman, and Melville—whose poetry is given significant attention. Dickinson receives her own chapter in part 3. Very receives only a paragraph, Tuckerman a mention, Stephen Crane's poetry is unacknowledged, and Lanier does not make the index.

Feidelson, Charles, Jr., *Symbolism and American Literature*. Chicago: University of Chicago Press, 1953.

Considers the "unified phase of American literature" that runs from Poe through Whitman as essentially a symbolist movement, though not consciously so. The distinctive quality of major nineteenth century writers is their "devotion to the possibilities of symbolism." Treats Emerson, Poe, Whitman, and such topics as "The Symbolistic Imagination" and Puritan traditions of expression. Stresses fiction more than poetry.

Foerster, Norman. *Nature in American Literature*. Reprint. New York: Russell & Russell, 1958.

First published in 1923, this study presents the nineteenth century as America's adolescence, a period during which a "gospel of nature" had particular appeal. Through being responsive to nature's expressiveness, man could find ideals for his moral, social, and aesthetic conduct. An intellectual curiosity about scientific facts mixed with "an ardent devotion to nature because of her beauty or divinity." Chapters on Bryant, Whittier, Emerson, Thoreau, Lowell, Whitman, and Lanier sort out their similarities and differences in responding to nature.

Foster, Edward Halsey. *The Civilized Wilderness: Backgrounds to American Romantic Literature, 1817-1860*. New York: Free Press, 1975.

Explores "popular attitudes towards landscape and the aesthetic and moral values which wilderness landscapes in particular were supposed to have." Also considers the attempts to "resolve the tension between nature and civilization" in American Romantic literature and thought. Touches on Bryant, Poe, Emerson, Thoreau, Holmes, Lowell, Longfellow, Whittier and others, but deals more with prose than with poetry. An important thematic issue.

Freeman, John, and Gregory Green. "A Literary Cul-de-Sac: The Sonnet and the Schoolroom Poets." *ATQ*, no. 42 (Spring, 1979): 105-122.

This study surveys and assesses the uses of the sonnet by Longfellow, Lowell, Bryant, and Whittier. These poets used the popular European form for translations, as cultural postcards, for eulogies, for religious themes, for treatment of mutability, and for patriotic issues and American values. All in all, the sonnet was more often used to convey European values than to affirm those of the new democracy. American experience was too raw, of too much magnitude, to be handled in such cramped quarters.

Fussell, Edwin. *Lucifer in Harness: American Meter, Metaphor, and Diction.* Princeton, N.J.: Princeton University Press, 1973.
Attempts a theory of American poetry that can "accommodate Poe and Whitman" into a continuity with the major moderns. Emerson, Bryant, and Lowell are also discussed. Fussell examines the ways in which major American poets either politely wear or rebel against the "harness" of English tradition. Searching for an embracing theory, Fussell takes particular interest in the theories of his subject poets. Also useful for students of modern poetry.

Gelpi, Albert. *The Tenth Muse: The Psyche of the American Poet.* Cambridge, Mass.: Harvard University Press, 1975.
Examines "the poet's mind as part of his psyche" to determine what "quality of imagination, voice, form, and technique . . . could be called American." After a short chapter on the artist in America, Gelpi provides separate analyses of Edward Taylor, Emerson, Poe, Whitman, and Dickinson. For each, he explores "the elusive connection between the cultural situation and the psychological situation." Gelpi's method centers on the myths of Eros and Psyche.

Gura, Philip F., and Joel Myerson, eds. *Critical Essays on American Romanticism.* Boston: G. K. Hall, 1982.
A huge collection of documents that form an embracing, complex discussion of what Transcendentalism grew out of, what it was, and how it influenced American culture in and beyond the nineteenth century. The essays explore various strains of Transcendentalism as well as its theological and literary implications. The editors' introduction includes an excellent bibliographical essay. Probably the most useful, most comprehensive such collection available.

Harding, Brian. *American Literature in Context.* Vol. 2, *1830-1865.* London: Methuen, 1982.
Designed for students, this book provides an introductory essay followed by a series of chapters on representative writers. Some of these writers are not strictly literary figures, but thinkers and historians. Each chapter begins with an excerpt from a representative work that is analyzed and related to the author's work as a whole. An engaging approach that leads to especially vivid treatments of Poe and Whitman.

Hoff, Rhoda. *Four American Poets: Why They Wrote*. New York: Henry Z. Walck, 1969.
Treats Dickinson, Longfellow, Poe, and Whitman. For each, Hoff provides a short essay that assesses the poetry and offers reasons for the choice of a poetic career. A selection of the poet's work follows each essay. The explanations are usually superficial. Dickinson's poetry was the result of a broken heart. Longfellow wrote to profess, Poe to survive his griefs and morbid fantasies, Whitman to give America its poetic voice.

Hoffman, Daniel G., ed. *American Poetry and Poetics*. Garden City, N.Y.: Doubleday, 1962.
A representation of American poets, most of whom are major nineteenth century voices, is followed by a series of theoretical and interpretive essays. Many of these are by the poets themselves. Bryant, Poe, Emerson, Whitman, and Dickinson are included. Hoffman's introductory essay, "Tradition and Invention in American Poetry," is an excellent analysis of the conflicting tendencies in the American stance toward and practice of poetry.

Horton, Rod W., and Herbert W. Edwards. *Backgrounds of American Literary Thought*. 2d ed. New York: Appleton-Century- Crofts, 1967.
Provides a simplified account of the complex "historical and intellectual materials necessary to the fuller understanding of the leading American authors." Unitarianism, Transcendentalism, expansionism, industrialism, evolutionism, pragmatism, Marxism, and naturalism are among the nineteenth century cultural currents discussed. A fine source for preliminary research on poets and poetry that touches these issues. Sources for further reading follow each chapter.

Hubbell, Jay B. *Who Are the Major American Writers?* Durham, N.C.: Duke University Press, 1972.
A study of how the American literary canon was formed and how it has changed. About half of the book treats nineteenth century figures, recording the lines of argument that shaped their reputations and the shifts in those reputations. Considers the roles of editors, reviewers, anthologists, and English departments. Treats Emerson, Thoreau, Poe, Melville, Whitman, and Dickinson. European recognition is considered. Presents the results of polls.

Jones, Peter. *A Reader's Guide to Fifty American Poets*. Totowa, N.J.: Barnes & Noble, 1980.
Among the fifty are Bryant, Emerson, Longfellow, Poe, Thoreau, Melville, Whitman, Dickinson, and Stephen Crane. These treatments, which average about eight pages, establish the essential contribution each writer made both in absolute and in historical terms. Jones provides thumbnail biographies, illus-

trated discussions of thematic and stylistic features, and summaries of influence and reputation. Poems are generously quoted, and key critical statements are judiciously excerpted.

Justus, James. H. "The Fireside Poets: Hearthside Values and the Language of Care." In *Nineteenth-Century American Poetry*, edited by A. Robert Lee. Totowa, N.J.: Barnes & Noble Books, 1985.
This overview of topics and vocabularies in Lowell, Whittier, Longfellow, and Holmes describes how these poets transformed cultural values into art. Justus finds that "the story that these poets tell is not that of subordination of private purpose to the constituent values the larger culture endorsed, but of the convergence of personal and public history, of private prerogative and the public weal."

Kazin, Alfred. *An American Procession*. New York: Alfred A. Knopf, 1984.
Woven out of seminars, lectures, reviews, essays, and introductions, this comprehensive overview considers the "literary century" that began with Emerson's founding of a national literature in the 1830's. The first two of its three parts divide the nineteenth century, covering Emerson, Thoreau, Poe, Whitman, Dickinson, and Crane. Kazin considers Henry Adams, whose life spanned most of this period, its greatest historical thinker, and thus he uses Adams as a presiding intelligence throughout. The work ends with the fulfillment of modernism in the 1920's.

Kindilien, Carlin T. *American Poetry in the Eighteen Nineties*. Providence, R.I.: Brown University Press, 1956.
Surveys the literary scene in the last decade of the century and then explores the continuing elements and new ingredients in American poetry. Chapters include "The Poet-Critics of Society and Religion," "Whitman and The Vagabondians," and "Poetic Form in the Nineties." In this decade, most of the seeds of modernism in American poetry were sown. Sets discussion of Stephen Crane in a valuable historical context.

Kramer, Aaron. *The Prophetic Tradition in American Poetry, 1835- 1900*. Rutherford, N.J.: Fairleigh Dickinson University Press, 1968.
Finds a strong current of prophetic utterance "in all of its relevant manifestations: visionary, admonitory, denunciatory, inspirational, martial." Combines references to the works of major and minor poets, dividing his treatment into touchstone subjects: the Mexican war, the mistreatment of the Indian, the fugitive slave problem, mobbism, and the Spanish-American War. The prophetic stance in American poetry immediately influenced by the English Romantic poets. Moral fervor essential to poetic greatness.

Kreymborg, Alfred. *Our Singing Strength: An Outline of American Poetry (1620-1930)*. New York: Coward-McCann, 1929.
A highly personalized and colorful journey through the subject matter, written with a poet's sensibility. Kreymborg summarizes the minor movements and personalities while giving the nineteenth century masters chapter-length discussions. Especially useful on Emerson and Lowell. A lively, respectable, but not totally reliable forerunner to the studies by Pearce, Waggoner, and Shucard.

Kuntz, Joseph M. *Poetry Explication: A Checklist of Interpretation Since 1925 of British and American Poems Past and Present*. Rev. ed. Chicago: Swallow Press, 1962.
The listings are alphabetically arranged by poet and poem. There are seven pages of entries on Dickinson's poems, three pages on Poe's, four on Whitman's, and at least several entries for each of the other major nineteenth century poets. This reference omits commentaries on poems of more than five hundred lines as well as materials found in critical studies of single authors. Extremely useful, but long out of date.

Lee, A. Robert, ed. *Nineteenth-Century American Poetry*. Totowa, N.J.: Barnes & Noble Books, 1985.
An intriguing assortment of essays written especially for this volume. Contains two essays on Whitman, one each on Dickinson, Poe, Emerson, and Melville. Other poets and issues discussed in "The Fireside Poets" (Whittier, Holmes, Longfellow, Lowell) and in "Imaging America: Paintings, Pictures and the Poetics of Nineteenth-Century American Landscape." Prepared in England, with most of the contributions by British scholars.

Lenhart, Charmenz S. *Musical Influence on American Poetry*. Athens: University of Georgia Press, 1956.
A chapter on America's musical background is followed by treatments of the seventeenth, eighteenth, and nineteenth centuries. The last three chapters treat, in turn, Poe, Whitman, and Lanier. Connects the science of musicology to the interest in relationships between the arts. Relates each poet to the theories, terminologies, and forms commonly known in his day. A remarkable synthesis with many new insights.

Lewis, R. W. B. *The American Adam: Innocence, Tragedy, and Tradition in the Nineteenth Century*. Chicago: University of Chicago Press, 1955.
Examines the place of the Genesis myth in the development of American literature from 1820-1860. The American Adam is a new personality on a new adventure in new land. He is freed from history and ancestry, undefiled, and without guilt or shame. He is "self-reliant and self-propelling." Examines the recurring "vision of innocence and claim of newness" in American culture and

letters beginning with Emerson. Discussions of Holmes, Whitman, and Melville are the most telling extensions of Lewis' thesis.

Marder, Daniel. *Exiles at Home: A Story of Literature in Nineteenth Century America*. Lanham, Md.: University Press of America, 1984.
Argues that the enthusiasm for a new American culture left many writers disillusioned and disinherited of any comforting traditions. In various ways, significant American authors found themselves misplaced persons, exiled by the religious, political, and technological revolutions going on around them. These include Dickinson and Poe, whose degrees of self-absorption suggest a pushing away from the material and social environment.

Matthiessen, F. O. *American Renaissance: Art and Expression in the Age of Emerson and Whitman*. New York: Oxford University Press, 1941.
Tries to explain why so many American masterpieces were written in an "extraordinarily concentrated moment of expression." Considers the shared understandings of the major mid-nineteenth century writers on "the function and nature of literature" and how their masterpieces fused form and content. Explores "patterns of taste and aspiration" that include a kinship felt by Emerson, Thoreau, and Melville for the seventeenth century metaphysical writers. Diction and rhetoric primary concerns.

Miller, Perry. *The Raven and the Whale*. Reprint. Westport, Conn.: Greenwood Press, 1973.
First published in 1956, this lively study examines literary and cultural politics of the period. Discusses who the tastemakers were and how literary reputations were made, lost, or otherwise manipulated. Pays special attention to societies and clubs at which influence was brokered. New York City is the central scene. Impact of publishers, magazines, and newspapers seen as crucial to the fortunes of Melville and Poe.

——————, ed. *The American Transcendentalists: Their Prose and Poetry*. Garden City, N.Y.: Doubleday, 1957.
This anthology presents the views of the key players in the Transcendentalist movement in their own words. Chapters on "History and Doctrine," "Naturalism," "Religious Radicalism," "Literary Aspiration," "The Poetic Endeavor," "Politics and Society," and "Future Reference." Good background material for the student of the Transcendental vision in American poetry.

Moore, Rayburn S. "Antebellum Poetry." In *The History of Southern Literature*, edited by Louis D. Rubin et al. Baton Rouge: Louisiana State University Press, 1985.
The achievement of Southern poets between 1830 and 1860, excluding Simms

and Poe, was modest—as was that of poets in the North. Figures who claim our attention include Thomas Holley Chivers, Alexander Beaufort Meek, Philip Pendleton Cooke, and James Mathewes Legare. Characteristically, Southern verse is written for the ear and is closely related to song. As a whole, though, this body of work "seldom breaks the mold of British tradition." The Southern love of the human voice talking, singing, and orating is apparent.

_____ . "Poetry of the Late Nineteenth Century." In *The History of Southern Literature*, edited by Louis D. Rubin et al. Baton Rouge: Louisiana State University Press, 1985.
Abram Joseph Ryan, Paul Hamilton Hayne, and Margaret Junkin Preston receive attention here. Hayne was the Southern laureate during this period. He was particularly accomplished as a writer of sonnets and nature lyrics. His work is "unabashedly in the Anglo-American tradition, and he is Southern to the core in his celebration of the land he loves, in his pride in his state and the virtues of the Old South, and in the natural melody of his lyrics." Moore also treats Irwin Russell, John Bannister Tabb, and Sidney Lanier.

Myerson, Joel, ed. *The American Renaissance in New England*. Vol. 1 of *Dictionary of Literary Biography*. Detroit: Gale Research, 1978.
This survey contains biographical sketches of ninety-eight New England authors who participated in the American Renaissance, including Dickinson, Emerson, Holmes, Longfellow, Lowell, Thoreau, Whittier, and Very. The major essays (Very gets a minor one) begin with career chronologies after which come life and career summaries that include discussions of major works and reputation. Bibliographical materials conclude the portraits.

_____ . *Antebellum Writers in New York and the South*. Vol. 3 of *Dictionary of Literary Biography*. Detroit: Gale Research, 1979.
Among the sixty-seven authors treated are Bryant, Melville, Poe, and Whitman. The format is the same as in *The American Renaissance in New England* (above). These volumes are attractively illustrated, often with reproductions of the authors' handwritten letters or drafts of important works. This volume contains a list of further readings that pertains to both volumes.

_____ . *The Transcendentalists: A Review of Research and Criticism*. New York: Modern Language Association, 1984.
This series of essays in critical history begins with broad coverage of the movement, its historical context, its relationship to Unitarianism, to experimental communities, and to periodical literature. Next comes a group of essays on the individuals who were at the core of the movement, including a major essay on Emerson. The final section treats the reactions of Dickinson, Melville, Poe, and Whitman.

Onderdonk, James L. *History of American Verse (1610-1897)*. Chicago: A. C. Mc-
Clurg, 1901.
One of the earliest backward glances that brings us through the nineteenth cen-
tury, Onderdonk's study includes chapters in which writers are grouped by
affinities—usually a number of minor poets along with one or two major ones.
The chapter on "Humor and Satire" provides a revealing context for comments
on Holmes and Lowell. Other poets treated are Bryant, Emerson, Longfellow,
Poe, Emerson, and Whitman. Many poets now long obscure are noticed here.

Parrington, Vernon Lewis. *Main Currents in American Thought*. Vol. 2, *The Romantic Revolution in America 1800-1860*. New York: Harcourt, Brace, 1927.
This is the bible of American intellectual history to which all later studies pay
homage. Excellent overview of cultural developments in the South and West as
well as the growing urban centers along the Atlantic coast. Sections or comment on Emerson, Thoreau, Holmes, Lowell, Poe, Longfellow, Bryant, and
Whittier. More important for treatment of forces like liberalism, southern
expansionism, and Transcendentalism.

——————. *Main Currents in American Thought*. Vol. 3, *The Beginnings of
Critical Realism in American Thought 1860-1920*. New York: Harcourt, Brace,
1927.
Unfinished at Parrington's death, this volume was completed to 1900, with
notes for the first decade of the twentieth century. Treats the Gilded Age,
industrialization, the developing Midwest, the rebuilding South. Includes a
section on Whitman and notes on Lanier.

Paul, Sherman, ed. *Six Classic American Writers*. Minneapolis: University of Minnesota Press, 1970.
A series of introductory essays on writers who have shaped American's sense
of itself. Among the six are Emerson, Longfellow, Thoreau, and Whitman.
Each essay stresses the continuing relevance of the writer's vision. Little explication or evaluation, but a carefully measured case for how each is a cultural
landmark. Extensive bibliographical material.

Pearce, Roy Harvey. *The Continuity of American Poetry*. Princeton, N.J.: Princeton
University Press, 1961.
Chapters 4 and 5 review the American Renaissance, with brief sections on Poe,
Emerson, Whitman, Dickinson, Bryant, Longfellow, Lowell, Holmes, Whittier, and Lanier. These treatments are parts of a sweeping history whose
argument is that the achievement of American poets reflects the style and spirit
of American culture. The poet's compulsion to justify himself and the terms of
that justification provide clues to societal values, as does the poet's adversary
stance to certain of those values.

Pease, Donald E. *Visionary Compacts: American Renaissance Writings in a Cultural Context*. Madison: University of Wisconsin Press, 1987.

The major writers of the early nineteenth century "searched for forms of cultural agreement more lasting than the mere opposition to the past sanctioned by the Revolutionary mythos." The frictions that led to the Civil War called for either conflict or accommodation. Rather than justifying conflict, these writers created "visionary compacts" that would restore relations. These compacts stressed shared national ideals. Discusses Poe, Emerson, Melville, and Whitman.

Phelps, William Lyon. *Howells, James, Bryant and Other Essays*. Reprint. Port Washington, N.Y.: Kennikat Press, 1965.

First published in 1924, this collection includes introductory essays on Whitman, Thoreau, and Lowell as well. Each poet gets a career study, an appreciation, and a partial analysis of representative passages. Each is placed in the larger perspective of nineteenth century Western literature. Phelps updates Stedman's late Victorian assessments in these readable, sensible overviews only partially damaged by time. "Bryant is the poet of Autumn, as Whittier is of Winter, and Lowell of June."

Rees, Robert A., and Earl N. Harbert, eds. *Fifteen American Authors Before 1900*. Rev. ed. Madison: University of Wisconsin Press, 1984.

Includes bibliographical essays on Bryant, Dickinson, Holmes, Longfellow, Lowell, and Whittier. Each essay is written by an expert on that particular author, and each provides a chronological survey of bibliographies, editions, manuscripts and letters, biographies, and criticism. The treatments are both descriptive and evaluative. These are reliable summaries that can be supplemented with the annual volumes of *American Literary Scholarship* published by Duke University Press.

Reynolds, David S. *Beneath the American Renaissance: The Subversive Imagination in the Age of Emerson and Melville*. New York: Alfred A. Knopf, 1988.

A response to F. O. Matthiesen's *American Renaissance* (see above), this study sets the major literature in the context of a broad range of lesser-known works. "American literature was generated by a highly complex environment in which competing language and value systems, openly at war on the level of popular literature, provided rich material which certain responsive authors adopted and transformed in dense literary texts." Many major writers began in popular modes and styles, then, in later works, developed a refined synthesis.

Richardson, Robert D., Jr. *Myth and Literature in the American Renaissance*. Bloomington: Indiana University Press, 1978.

Examines how the major "nineteenth-century writers from Emerson to

Melville dealt with the problem of myth." Not concerned with theories of unconscious myth formulation, Richardson limits his discussion to the purposeful use of myth and to the concepts of myth available to those writers. He looks for both their common assumptions and their personal understandings. Whitman's poetry is given a separate chapter. Useful approach for more detailed analyses of individual poems.

Ruland, Richard. *The Rediscovery of American Literature: Premises of Critical Taste, 1900-1940*. Cambridge, Mass.: Harvard University Press, 1967.
Ruland tells the story of an emerging "American criticism" developed in the earlier decades of the twentieth century that reassessed the achievement of the American writers of the nineteenth century. He finds much of this critical work as self- consciously nationalistic as the literature it addresses. Particularly useful is the chapter on F. O. Matthiessen's *American Renaissance*. Available through the index are comments on the critical fortunes of most of the major poets.

Scholnick, Robert J. *Edmund Clarence Stedman*. Boston: Twayne, 1977.
Stedman (1833-1908) was the best critic of American literature working at the close of the nineteenth century. A minor poet, he was particular sensitive to the aspirations and achievements of his predecessors and contemporaries. Stedman was the first to tell us who the major poets of the century were. The impact of his practical criticism and his work as an anthologist is still with us. Scholnick treats Stedman's theory of a native American poetic tradition, his aesthetic views, and his judgments of individual writers.

Sherman, Joan R. *Invisible Poets: Afro-Americans of the Nineteenth Century*. Urbana: University of Illinois Press, 1974.
At least 130 black men and women published poetry in America during the nineteenth century. Sherman provides biographical and career profiles as well as critical assessments of twenty-six of these writers. The work of each is viewed within its historical and cultural setting. An introductory chapter examines the shared circumstances and characteristics of these poets, setting forth criteria for evaluation and discussing the reasons for their neglect. Various appendices provide data on poets not treated in the main text.

Shucard, Alan. *American Poetry: The Puritans Through Walt Whitman*. Boston: Twayne, 1988.
Describes the emergence of a distinctly American tradition by examining the early Puritan verses expressing nationalist ideals and following that impulse through the nineteenth century. Chapter on "The Nineteenth Century: Romanticism in American Poetry" touches upon Bryant, Longfellow, Holmes, Lowell, Whittier, Tuckerman, Lanier, and Melville. Each writer is viewed as

one fulfillment of this tradition. Emerson, Poe, and Whitman receive separate chapters. A basic introductory survey presented in a lucid style.

Spiller, Robert. E. *The Cycle of American Literature*. New York: Macmillan, 1956.
A handy overview of American literature from its beginnings to the middle of the twentieth century. Various chapters in part 1, "The First Frontier," treat Bryant, Emerson, Thoreau, Melville, and Whitman. Dickinson is discussed in the second part. Spiller views these writers as partaking of and reflecting social and intellectual currents that first formed an Eastern seaboard culture and later a continental culture. Special concern with discovering the place of the artist in American society. Good introduction to major issues and trends surrounding the careers of representative major writers.

Spiller, Robert E. et al., eds. *Literary History of the United States*. 3d ed., revised. New York: Macmillan, 1963.
This is the standard one-volume treatment of the broad field. It is accompanied by a bibliography volume. All major and minor movements are discussed, as well as all major authors and most minor ones. An unparalleled group of scholars was assembled to contribute essays to this monumental work. See references to specific sections under author listings.

Stauffer, Donald Barlow. *A Short History of American Poetry*. New York: E. P. Dutton, 1974.
Not really that short, but a rather generous overview marked out in chronological and thematic chapters. Five chapters cover the nineteenth century. The author does not attempt to support any generalizations about American poetry, though he recognizes them in passing. His goals are to see how each poet is related to his times while yet discovering the uniqueness of each.

Stedman, Edmund Clarence. *Poets of America*. Reprint. New York: Johnson Reprint Corporation, 1970.
A landmark early estimate of the shape of American poetry. Stedman's study, first published in 1885, attempts to define an American school and the problems of writers in a new nation with a rapidly changing culture. Stedman was one of the first to shape the American canon. Individual chapters treat Bryant, Whittier, Emerson, Longfellow, Poe, Holmes, Lowell, Whitman, and Bayard Taylor. Some sense here of how the nineteenth century looked at itself.

Steele, Jeffrey. *The Representation of the Self in the American Renaissance*. Chapel Hill: University of North Carolina Press, 1987.
Steele examines "psychological mythmaking" and the literary strategies that allow us to glimpse self-consciousness. "At issue will be those privileged figures and rhetorical strategies through which writers during the American

Renaissance disseminate their sense of the mind." Emerson, Thoreau, and Whitman receive separate chapters. Another chapter explores the situation of women, while yet another, called "Materializing the Psyche," considers Poe, Hawthorne, and Melville.

Strong, Augustus Hopkins. *American Poets and Their Theology*. Philadelphia: Griffith and Rowland, 1916.
This early study is a useful reminder of the degree to which our major poets were people of religious conviction. A great deal of the work of Emerson, Lowell, Bryant, Longfellow, and certainly Whittier is a religious poetry. Poe, Holmes, and Lanier are also included. Strong examines the commonly held religious notions of the principle nineteenth century poets as well as the individualizing elements. Pays attention to the role of religious education in the background of each writer.

Sutton, Walter. *American Free Verse: The Modern Revolution in Poetry*. New York: New Directions, 1973.
Examines the theory and practice of representative figures and groups of poets from the early nineteenth century through the revolution in the modern period. The early chapters treat Emerson, Whitman, and Stephen Crane. Sutton argues that, except for Crane, the later nineteenth century poets did not further the development of free-verse modes and that more significant innovation was taking place in prose fiction. Primarily a study of modern poetry, Sutton's book provides a useful glance at the roots of the dominant modern style.

Vendler, Helen, ed. *Voices and Visions: The Poet in America*. New York: Random House, 1987.
These essays on thirteen major American poets are companion pieces to the Public Broadcasting System television series of the same name. The concerns of both are to illustrate the ways in which a distinctly American poetry came into being and to give a sense of the poet's place in American culture. The essays are responsive to these questions: "what they inherited, what they were fostered by, where they found their language, what they created in the way of forms." Whitman and Dickinson represent the nineteenth century. Illustrated.

Wager, Willis. "The Work of Art, Closed and Open: Poe to Whitman." In his *American Literature: A World View*. New York: New York University Press, 1968.
Wager examines the sweep of American literature within the context of larger trends in Europe, including the impact of Asiatic culture on the West. Nineteenth century American poets partook of and accelerated a movement away from containment and toward freedom. Bryant, Emerson, Longfellow, Lowell,

and Whittier are treated. Many of these poets show an awareness of their place in the contemporaneous world scene, not just their roles as American writers.

Waggoner, Hyatt H. *American Poets from the Puritans to the Present*. Boston: Houghton Mifflin, 1968.
This sweeping history provides seven chapters covering the nineteenth century poets, both major and minor. The study uncovers "Emerson's centrality in our poetry" and traces the unorthodox religious attitudes that run through so much of this literature. Reviews attitudes toward literary standards, the poetic process, and the relationship between poetry and the national life. Clear, distinctive judgments on the achievement of each poet.

Walcutt, Charles Child, and J. Edwin Whitesell, eds. *The Explicator Cyclopedia*. Vol. 2. Chicago: Quadrangle Books, 1968.
This collection of items reprinted from the first twenty years of *The Explicator* covers "Traditional Poetry: Medieval to Late Victorian." Included are brief items on individual poems by Bryant, Emerson, Holmes, Lanier, Longfellow, Lowell, Melville, Poe, Thoreau, and Whittier. Vol. 1 (1966), "Modern Poetry," includes Stephen Crane and Dickinson. These items, too brief to summarize here, are often very useful and sometimes the seeds of major reinterpretations.

Walker, Robert H. *The Poet and the Gilded Age*. Reprint. New York: Octagon Books, 1969.
Examines the late nineteenth century "in the light of the verse produced by its citizens." Walker is concerned with the social role of poetry. Thus, his chapters cover such issues as the frontier, the city, progress and protest, statesmanship, women's issues, immigration and minorities, science, and materialism. Mostly minor writers treated, but there are several references to Stephen Crane. First published in 1963.

Weirick, Bruce. *From Whitman to Sandburg in American Poetry: A Critical Survey*. Reprint. New York: Biblo and Tannen, 1967.
First published in 1924, this was one of the earliest historical surveys to acknowledge Whitman as "our greatest poet." Weirick begins with a detailed appreciation of Whitman and then moves on to assess "his influence, and his point of view as democrat, mystic, and poet." Sees late nineteenth and early twentieth century poetry as participating in the drift away from New England's "derivative and sterile culture." Chapters include "The Poetry of the People," "The Period of Reconstruction," and "Fin de Siecle, Vagabondia, and Nationalism."

Wells, Henry W. *The American Way of Poetry*. Reprint. New York: Russell & Russell, 1964.
First published in 1943, this study explores the question of whether the national

qualities of American poetry are "trivial, modestly significant, or of primary importance." Selects sixteen poets as representative, but the selection process and balance of attention subordinate those whose work is more derivative than indigenous. Melville, Emerson, Whitman, and Dickinson get fullest attention. Distinguishes between earlier sectional traditions and a new and true nationalism that was a much later development.

Westbrook, Perry D. *A Literary History of New England*. Bethlehem, Pa.: Lehigh University Press, 1988.
The New England mind as revealed in literary endeavor from the beginning of the colonial period through the career of Robert Frost. Useful chapters on Emerson and Thoreau; composite chapters treating Bryant and Catharine Maria Sedgwick, "The Household Poets" (Longfellow, Whittier, Holmes, and Lowell), Dickinson and Tuckerman. Concise, clear overview of Puritan culture and the native origins of Transcendentalism. Gives special emphasis to women poets and to literary endeavor outside the Boston orbit.

Williams, Stanley T. *The Beginnings of American Poetry (1620- 1855)*. Reprint. New York: Cooper Square, 1970.
Originally published in 1951, this series of lectures surveys the pre- Whitman era in four chapters: "The Poet of Puritanism," "The Poet of the Enlightenment," "The Poet of Early Romanticism," "and "The Poet of Philosophic Thought." In the latter two chapters, Williams treats Bryant, Whittier, Poe, and Emerson. He draws careful parallels between the sophisticated strands of European Romanticism and the less esoteric and essentially nationalistic American brand. Fine handling of Bryant and Emerson as theorists and practitioners.

Wilson, Edmund. "Poetry of the War." In his *Patriotic Gore: Studies in the Literature of the American Civil War*. New York: Oxford University Press, 1962.
Although much verse was written about the Civil War, Wilson finds that the period and the subject were not fruitful for poetry. He comments on works by Whittier, Melville, Lowell, Whitman, and Tuckerman. Considers the highly praised "Commemoration Ode" by Lowell truly mediocre and Melville's *Battle-Pieces* hardly worth mentioning. Praises Whitman's "Drum-Taps" sequence as the finest poetic response to the war. Discusses a few other poets who are now obscure.

Ziff, Larzer. *Literary Democracy: The Declaration of Cultural Independence in American*. New York: Viking Press, 1981.
Ziff "narrates the life and times of those writers who established American literature as a distinct way of imagining the world." Focuses on the period from 1837 to the outbreak of Civil War, during which a changing society and a

"positive nationalism" brought a new literature into being. Emerson, Poe, Thoreau, Melville, and Whitman receive one or more chapters each. Considers whether democracy would mean the end of "high literature" as traditionally known and what would replace it. Includes an outline of important events and publications.

WILLIAM CULLEN BRYANT
(1794-1878)

General Studies

Allen, Gay Wilson. "William Cullen Bryant." In his *American Prosody*. New York: American Book, 1935.

"Bryant was . . . abreast of the times in his defense and use of trisyllabic substitution, in his breaking away from the tyranny of the heroic couplet, and in his deliberate attempt to work out a versification which fitted his needs rather than to shape his message to conform to inherited verse technique." Bryant did some interesting work with the alexandrine measure and in free verse. The gliding effect of the stanza of "To a Waterfowl" is considered a fine accommodation of form and content.

Arms, George. "Bryant." In his *The Fields Were Green*. Stanford, Calif.: Stanford University Press, 1953.

Argues that "the thought of Bryant is his least significant aspect," though this lack of intellectual rigor is usually masked by "brooding sympathy." Bryant's language has a justness and dignity about it, as well as a homespun simplicity that is purposeful rather than fortuitous. On occasion, Bryant's handling of image and symbol rises to a high order of accomplishment. He also has a fine sense of form. His most successful poems involve "dramatization of self or nature." Arms praises "Green River" and "Hymn to Death."

Bradley, William Aspenwall. *William Cullen Bryant*. New York: Macmillan, 1905.

Written a generation after Bryant's death, this study still depends on the facts amassed by Parke Godwin, the official biographer. Bradley is alert to Bryant's remarkable precocity and his long, influential career. Bradley discusses the Puritan influence on the poems, an influence neither orthodox nor gloomy. He also addresses the range of Bryant's poetic moods and his status as America's first poet of consequence.

Brodwin, Stanley, and Michael D'Innocenzo, eds. *William Cullen Bryant and His America*. New York: AMS Press, 1983.

These papers were given at the Bryant Centennial Conference sponsored by Hofstra College in 1978. They cover a wide range of topics, including Bryant's views on manifest destiny, his relationships with New York newspapers, and his role as a promoter of the arts. Several papers provide fresh insights into Bryant's poetic legacy, including Brodwin's on the "denial of death" in Bryant and Whitman.

Brown, Charles H. *William Cullen Bryant*. New York: Charles Scribner's Sons, 1971.
With as much detail as anyone could want, Brown describes how Bryant reflected the changing times of his long life. Bryant's career as poet was subordinated to other dimensions of his busy life, especially his role as a public figure. The locales of Bryant's work and travel are vividly portrayed, as are his political engagements. Though the poems are not evaluated, they are used to show how Bryant saw the world around him, particularly the natural world. Illustrated.

Glicksberg, C. I. "William Cullen Bryant and Nineteenth-Century Science." *New England Quarterly* 23 (March, 1950): 91-96.
Bryant's general enthusiasm for the discoveries of scientists is reflected in his newspaper work. "Bryant did not believe that poetry must suffer a decline in an age of science and reason." He believed that science could extend the influence of poetry. In later life, when he saw science promote skepticism in religious matters, his enthusiasm became qualified. He was never impressed by the mid-century pseudosciences that agitated Whitman and others.

Herrick, Marvin T. "Rhetoric and Poetry in Bryant." *American Literature* 7 (May, 1935): 188-194.
Attention to Bryant's work as an editor reveals an important issue regarding his poetry; that is, "the problem of the distinction between 'pure' poetry and poetry that is rhetorical." Bryant's own poetry "illustrates this leaning toward an eloquence which is often rhetorical." The revisions of "Thanatopsis" show Bryant writing to be heard rather than to be overheard. Bryant was aware of the distinction and often worked toward the end of "pure" poetry, but his success was intermittent and partial.

Krapf, Norbert, ed. *Under Open Sky: Poets on William Cullen Bryant*. Reprint. New York: Fordham University Press, 1986.
Contemporary poets respond in prose and verse to Bryant's legacy. The implicit argument here is that the founding father of American poetry has had a profound influence, even if an indirect one, on the current state of the craft. Contributors include Richard Wilbur, John Hollander, Richard Eberhart, and Paul Engle. These brief appreciations are well-focused and knowledgeable.

McDowell, Tremaine. *William Cullen Bryant*. New York: American Book, 1935.
This selection of Bryant's poems and prose pieces is accompanied by a useful introduction that places Bryant in the context of literary Romanticism. Shows affinities with pre-Romantics such as Blair, Cowper, and Thomson as well as with Lord Byron. McDowell discusses Bryant's reaction to *Lyrical Ballads*, his interest in language study, and his prosodic habits. "Bryant's concern with the elemental and the universal saved him from provincialism."

_____ . "In New England." In *Literary History of the United States*, edited by Robert E. Spiller et al. 3d ed., rev. New York: Macmillan, 1963.
Bryant expressed "the unity of past and present, of America and Europe." When Bryant was the foremost poet of his day, his *Poems* (1821) sold slowly and garnered only one favorable review in an important journal. His contemporary readers found him complex and difficult. He maintained a diversified literary career as an editor, journalist, critic, and writer as prose fiction. As a poet of America and an ardent nationalist, he nonetheless voiced a longer tradition—that of an Anglo-American. He is, moreover, "a poet of the eternal procession of mankind."

McLean, Albert F., Jr. *William Cullen Bryant*. New York: Twayne, 1964.
A brief biographical chapter precedes four sturdy thematic discussions of the poetry: poems of nature, death, progress, and the divided voice. The final chapter places Bryant in American literary history. Considers Bryant's concern with distinctly American landscapes and with the authority of nature's beauty while examining his unsentimental attitude toward death. Distinguishes the private from the public voice of Bryant while assessing his contributions to the development of free verse. Chronology and selected bibliography.

McMartin, Gaines. "Patterns of Enclosure: Unity in the Poems of William Cullen Bryant." In *William Cullen Bryant and His America*, edited by Stanley Michael Brodwin and Michael D'Innocenzo. New York: AMS Press, 1983.
Images of enclosure, especially enclosure in nature, create a feeling of unity in Bryant's work. Reeds bending over a nest of waterfowl or prairies hedged by forests are examples of such images. "An Indian Story" is set in a containing bower. Here and in poems such as "To a Waterfowl" and "A Forest Hymn," the images of enclosure seem to reflect an explicit moral. The circumscription of scene promotes clarity of ideas and feelings.

Moriarty, David J. "William Cullen Bryant and the Suggestive Image: Living Impact." In *William Cullen Bryant and His America*, edited by Stanley Michael Brodwin and Michael D'Innocenzo. New York: AMS Press, 1983.
Among critics, Bryant's historical importance has blunted full appreciation of his merit as an artist. He is not just the Americanizer of British Romanticism, but a distinctive voice. Bryant's modernism is in his use of the "suggestive, vital, epiphanic image." Distinction between image and metaphor are often blurred, but this feature does not create incoherence; rather, it clarifies a paradoxical view of nature at the heart of Bryant's vision.

Pearce, Roy Harvey. "Bryant." In his *The Continuity of American Poetry*. Princeton, N.J.: Princeton University Press, 1961.

Bryant saw poetry as a mediating force between the active and contemplative life. His poetry "surveyed human history, put it into natural, cosmic perspective, and concluded that Americans and their institutions were its heirs." He attends not to the intrinsic qualities in a scene or in his own response, but rather to a combination of the two. "His is a cautious, comforting orthodoxy, adapted to the capabilities of the least of his readers."

Peckham, Harry Houston. *Gotham Yankee: A Biography of William Cullen Bryant.* Reprint. New York: Russell & Russell, 1971.
First published in 1950, this biography followed a forty-year period of relative silence on Bryant's life. Peckham exploits documentary material not previously used in an attempt to correct the then-current view of Bryant as a "puritanical prig." This is less a critical biography than one in which Bryant's poetical career is given careful scrutiny. Peckham discusses the circumstances behind the poems and the reception of the principal works, and enthusiastically portrays Bryant as a cultural force.

Phelps, William Lyon. "Bryant." In his *Howells, James, Bryant and Other Essays.* Reprint. Port Washington, N.Y.: Kennikat Press, 1965.
First published in 1924, this useful introduction quickly summarizes key biographical facts and then assesses the best-known poems. Praises the revised rather than the original version of "Thanatopsis," which is viewed as a "purely pagan" poem by a devout Christian. Discusses the influence of Wordsworth and the similar position each writer held in his nation's literature. Bryant was especially able at portraying the autumnal scene and mood. His poems are more sculptural than painterly.

Ringe, Donald A. "Kindred Spirits: Bryant and Cole." *American Quarterly* 6 (Fall, 1954): 233-244.
Bryant's artistic interests are important to an understanding of his verse. He was in sympathy with the aesthetic views of the Hudson River painters, particularly with those of Thomas Cole with whom he had a close relationship. For both, "the importance of the natural landscape lay not solely in its order or beauty, but in the association that a perception of it could arouse in the receptive mind." Ringe compares journal entries of the two men and uses Bryant's poems to illustrate the shared philosophy.

——————. "Painting as Poem in the Hudson River Aesthetic." *American Quarterly* 12 (Spring, 1960): 71-83.
Ringe casts a wider net here than in the earlier Bryant/Cole article (above) as he discusses the theoretical and practical interactions between Bryant and the Hudson River painters. "Poetry is superior to painting because of the advan-

tage offered it by the highly suggestive nature of language." Yet Cole and others worked to capture this moral suggestiveness championed by Bryant, and thus their paintings were often likened to poems. Concepts of imitation and representation discussed.

_____ . "William Cullen Bryant and the Science of Geology." *American Literature* 26 (January, 1955): 507-514.
Not only is Bryant's interest in the physical sciences beyond dispute, but his "scientific knowledge bears a direct relation to his verse." Bryant's poems reveal an acquaintance with the most recent geological theory. The principle of change within order is illustrated by geological references in "The Fountain" and other poems. Bryant found what he needed in the new science to support and make vivid his traditional faith.

Sanford, Charles L. "The Concept of the Sublime in the Works of Thomas Cole and William Cullen Bryant." *American Literature* 28 (January, 1957): 434-447.
Both painters and poets of the American Renaissance strove to realize the sublime in their works. Bryant and Cole valued the ability to evoke strong emotions of exaltation. "The American deification of nature" through an art of the sublime was part of the American cultural project undertaken by Bryant, Cole, and others. Sanford discusses the role of river and stream imagery, allegory, and nature symbolism in the pursuit of the sublime.

Strong, Augustus Hopkins. "William Cullen Bryant." In his *American Poets and Their Theology*. Philadelphia: Griffith and Rowland, 1916.
Bryant's notion of God was not "mere impersonal spirit"; he found God more transcendent than immanent. He did not merge the finite with the infinite, as did other Romantic poets. His God was a personal God and a God of love; thus Bryant's optimism. Nature, in Bryant, reminds us of Eden, even though it shares with man the effects of sin. Bryant's poems pay little attention to the figure of Christ or to the theme of redemption through Christ's suffering.

Waggoner, Hyatt H. "William Cullen Bryant." In his *American Poetry from the Puritans to the Present*. Boston: Houghton Mifflin, 1968.
"Bryant wrote a dozen or so memorable poems, all of them very early in his life and most of them dark poems." He initiated a New England tradition brought to fruition in the work of Dickinson, E. A. Robinson, Frost, and Robert Lowell. "Hope deferred" is a theme Bryant treats convincingly. Bryant could not continue to be an effective poet after he turned forty because whatever he wished to say was cancelled out by something else he wished to say. His progressive opinions, revealed in speeches and editorial writing, never make their way into his successful poems.

"A Forest Hymn"

McLean, Albert F., Jr. *William Cullen Bryant*, 58-60. New York: Twayne, 1964.
Poems like this one are more confessions than credos. This is "a reasoned statement in verse about the appropriateness of worshiping God in natural surroundings." Bryant moves from rational abstractions and an argumentative mode to a far more personalized, subjective orientation. The accumulation of natural imagery and the re-creation of private communion overwhelm the conventional, rationalistic trappings. The poem is the process of discovery, not the argument about what is discovered.

"The Prairies"

McLean, Albert F., Jr. *William Cullen Bryant*, 41-44. New York: Twayne, 1964.
Bryant's strong impression of the Great Plains' vast expanses is captured "by the sweeping rhythms of the blank verse and by the sharp, plentiful imagery of the poem." Distinctly nationalistic, a "paean to the New World," it focuses on the unique flora, fauna, and archaeological features of the North American continent. The delight offered to man by these beauties must inspire him to great actions. Will the vision of plenitude speak through the individual, making him part of it, or will it only speak to him? This is Bryant's version of the unresolved question of Romantic sensibility.

Miller, Ralph N. "Nationalism and Bryant's 'The Prairies.' " *American Literature* 21 (May, 1949): 227-232.
Bryant's poem grows out of "the quarrel between the Old and New worlds." Not only is it an appealing Romantic document celebrating the inspirational value of the American Midwest, it is part of the defense against arguments that the American environment could not support a rich civilization. Bryant leans on arguments made by Buffon and others that considered America in an early stage of geological development. By implication, a great future lay ahead. Bryant's unusual imagery shows his awareness of the key documents in the controversy.

Newlin, Paul A. "*The Prairie* and 'The Prairies': Cooper's and Bryant's Views of Manifest Destiny." In *William Cullen Bryant and His America*, edited by Stanley Michael Brodwin and Michael D'Innocenzo.
Though these two works share a similar attitude toward the concept of manifest destiny, Bryant's poem "is more openly optimistic within its romantic poetic tradition" than Cooper's novel. Bryant's "sense of the past moves from Eden through an evolutionary process of cycles of destruction and savagery which destroy natural beauty and man; but Nature prevails and restores the

grandeur of the Garden with but the faintest trace of man's folly." No vision of America's destiny transcends Bryant's sense of its Edenic past and promise.

"Thanatopsis"

Arms, George. "Bryant." In his *The Fields Were Green*, 14-15. Stanford: Stanford University Press, 1953.
> Bryant had trouble deciding whether to have the poem dominated by "the voice of his better genius or the meditation of the author or the voice of nature." Arms believes that the poet's voice, not nature's, is the last one heard "in the didactic close." When nature speaks, "she offers at best cold comfort." Bryant's self-dramatization here is not a matter of biographical reference. The narrator is a persona—a man like Bryant who is presented to us independently in the poem.

Bryant, William Cullen II. "The Genesis of 'Thanatopsis.'" *New England Quarterly* 21 (June, 1948): 163-184.
> By misdating the composition of "Thanatopsis," critics have viewed the poem as an accidental masterpiece followed by a series of inferior imitative experiments. Actually, the poem was a culmination of these experiments. Bryant was guided by the mood of Robert Blair's "The Grave" and the meter of William Cowper's "The Task." The earlier poems on death are despondent. "Thanatopsis" reveals a Bryant who has moved to artistic and emotional maturity. Placed in the right order, the poems reveal his growth.

McLean, Albert F., Jr. *William Cullen Bryant*. New York: Twayne, 1964.
> Not "a refutation of the doctrine of immortality," this meditation "seeks other consolations for the inevitable coming of death"; it is largely a catalog of those consolations from a perspective "that speaks directly to the rationalist, empiricist mentality." Bryant revised and refined the poem's argument over many years, in its final version allowing Nature to voice the consolations. Death is the "fulfillment of the life of partial knowledge." Even man's projected ideas are aspects of a "monumental wholeness" to which death is subordinated. The poem borrows from Bishop Porteus' "Death" and Robert Blair's "The Grave." It is structured as a sermon in the plain style.

Rio-Jelliffe, R. "'Thanatopsis' and the Development of American Literature." In *William Cullen Bryant and His America*, edited by Stanley Michael Brodwin and Michael D'Innocenzo.
> The poem is "significant for adumbrating a concept of nature and art which generated over half a century a coherent poetic theory and practice denoting the character of the yet unborn American literature." This critic examines

opposition and paradox in the poem's dialectic while praising Bryant's functional use of poetic conventions and his "viable synthesis of tradition and innovation." Discusses Bryant's doctrine of analogies.

Waggoner, Hyatt H. "William Cullen Bryant." In his *American Poetry from the Puritans to the Present*, 38-40. Boston: Houghton Mifflin, 1968.
Bryant wrote the middle part, in which Nature speaks, first. He later added the introductory and concluding passages in another voice. The poem's unity is questionable. The original section is "stoical and naturalistic" while the added material attempts to remake the poem into a "religiously consoling one." Though memorable in parts, "Thanatopsis" is flawed by unresolved tensions and its concluding sentimentality. Still, the original section is as good as anything Bryant ever wrote.

"To a Waterfowl"

Arms, George. "Bryant." In his *The Fields Were Green*, 17-18. Stanford, Calif.: Stanford University Press, 1953.
This poem was considered one of Bryant's major achievements by his contemporaries, and it continues to be held in esteem. The poem has not only the didactic passage frequently noted, but a second one. The two taken together (appearing in the fourth and eighth stanzas) balance each other and help provide the poem's "pleasing framework." The thematic awareness "is bound to the scene as much emotionally as the poet is bound to the idea dramatically."

Clemente, Vince. "Bryant's 'To a Waterfowl' and the Painter W. S. Mount." In *Under Open Sky: Poets on William Cullen Bryant*, edited by Norbert Krapf. Reprint. New York: Fordham University Press, 1986.
Discusses the poem by noting its hold on the imagination of Bryant's Long Island contemporary, the genre painter Mount. Mount, though he never followed through, was inspired to do a painting based on the poem. His journals record his fascination with the poem's theme of moral courage and with the tension between "the self-imposed isolation of his artist's calling at odds with his deep-welling social nature, his huge-hearted communal self." Clemente considers the weariness of travel (the bird's flight) and the aspiring, affirmative stance of the poem.

Davie, Donald. "William Cullen Bryant: 'To a Waterfowl.'" In *American Poetry to 1914*, edited by Harold Bloom. New York: Chelsea House, 1987.
The subtle sequencing of images allows the poem to rise above a trivial didacticism. Without this complication of diction, the reducing of the effect of

supernatural guidance in human life to instinct in a bird would be a disappointment. Because the poem straddles the conventions of poetic diction of the
fading neoclassical age and the developing Romantic era, it has an evocative
precariousness. Its literary texture is "a makeshift convention compounded of
elements from both."

Waggoner, Hyatt H. "William Cullen Bryant." In his *American Poetry from the
Puritans to the Present*, 41. Boston: Houghton Mifflin, 1968.
The poem's meaning is explicit and is not compromised by the contradictions
that undermine much of Bryant's work: "The God who guides the waterfowl
in its migratory flight, keeping it safe from the hunter, will similarly guide us
through life to a final refuge." Bryant's images are appropriate throughout;
they deepen and personalize the felt truth that the poem is meant to share.
Because the trust of the poem is grounded in experience, the conclusion is
earned.

"The Yellow Violet"

McLean, Albert F. *William Cullen Bryant*, 47-48. New York: Twayne, 1964.
The blossom appears in April as a harbinger of spring. After the narrator
enters the poem, flower and narrator become contestants in a dramatic dialogue "which rises to a disclosure and eventual climax." The poem centers on
an awareness "of the degree of human pride involved in any observation of
natural forms." Bryant balances delight against reflection so that the poem can
be read both "as a statement about man's moral relationship to Nature and as a
comment upon one's social obligations."

RALPH WALDO EMERSON
(1803-1882)

General Studies

Alcott, A. Bronson. *Ralph Waldo Emerson: An Estimate of His Character and Genius*. Reprint. New York: Haskell House, 1968.
First printed privately and presented to Emerson on his birthday in 1865, this is the first of many attempts to mythologize Emerson. Alcott, a close friend, waxes enthusiastic about Emerson's role as an educator and a poet, calling him an inspiration to others. Alcott praises Emerson's optimism and his skills as a conversationalist. The same volume includes two elegies: Alcott's "Ion, A Monody" (1882) and another piece by F. B. Sanborn.

Allen, Gay Wilson. "Ralph Waldo Emerson." In his *American Prosody*. New York: American Book, 1935.
Emerson "purposely roughened" his verse in rebellion against the illusion of significance in what is merely technically polished. For Emerson, image and symbol were more essential aspects of poetry than rhythm because through those instruments poetry's spiritual nature as a link between the material and the ethereal worlds was manifest. Allen examines Emerson's handling of blank verse, four- and three-beat lincs, and ode structures. Connects the Transcendentalist fashion for short lines and poems to the fragmented or fragmentary quality of perceptions derived from inspiration.

——————— . *Waldo Emerson*. New York: Viking Press, 1981.
This biography traces the psychological changes in Emerson, including his preference for "Waldo" over "Ralph." Allen treats Emerson's gradual formation of an identity that would enable him to play his chosen role in the making of nineteenth century American literature. Adds social and intellectual background as well as intimate detail to the material found in earlier lives. Gives detailed attention to the poems and to Emerson's place as an innovator and advocate in the development of American poetry.

Anderson, John Q. *The Liberating Gods: Emerson on Poets and Poetry*. Coral Gables, Fla.: University of Miami Press, 1971.
A comprehensive treatment of Emerson's critical views on poetry including chapters on "The Nature of the Poet," "The Function of the Poet," and "The Poet's Use of Subject Matter and Form." The latter draws upon Emerson's own poems. Final chapters discuss Emerson's estimates of his English and American contemporaries and his contribution to poetic theory. Emerson played the role "of a new Plato in a New World."

Beach, Joseph Warren. "Emerson's Nature Poetry." In his *The Concept of Nature in Nineteenth-Century English Poetry*. New York: Pageant Books, 1956.
Within this sweeping survey of English language poets, Beach finds room for two Americans: Emerson and Whitman. "The constant theme of Emerson's nature-poetry is the identity of being which runs through all the diverse forms of nature, — which identity of being is the identity of spirit." Nothing is isolated or fixed; the eternal spirit infuses all as it passes through "a ceaseless cycle of change." Examines "Woodnotes" at length and compares Emerson's outlook to that of Wordsworth and Goethe.

Benton, Joel. *Emerson as a Poet*. New York: M. L. Holbrook, 1883.
Certainly the earliest volume to assess Emerson in this role, Benton's study considers Emerson's frequent opacity and difficulty as a necessary function of the "magnitude of his thought." Praises Emerson's portraiture and the evocativeness of nature description in "Woodnotes" and elsewhere. Observes the influence of his Persian studies and the lofty spiritual dimension of his poems. Many contemporary opinions cited.

Berry, Edmund G. *Emerson's Plutarch*. Cambridge, Mass.: Harvard University Press, 1961.
Shows the nature and extent of Plutarch's influence on Emerson. Not only did he draw anecdotes and expressions as examples, but his literary forms were in part derived from Plutarch. Emerson's journals and letters allow us to trace his ongoing study of Plutarch. Topics include Stoicism, the Plutarchan hero, and Plutarchan themes. Provides Emerson's own reasons for his borrowings.

Bishop, Jonathan. *Emerson on the Soul*. Cambridge, Mass.: Harvard University Press, 1964.
Asserting that Emerson's "master term" is not "Mind" but "Soul," Bishop explores Emerson's uses of that term and its relationship to the concept of "moral sentiment." Emerson divided the soul into separate faculties, a scheme best understood as a poetic device, not as a philosophical assumption. Part 2 of this three-part study involves literary uses and projections of the soul concept. Words, rhythm, metaphor, tone, and concern for audience are key issues. Literary activity is a process of the soul.

Blasing, Mutlu Konuk. "Essaying the Poet: Emerson's Poetic Theory and Practice." *Modern Language Studies* 15 (Spring, 1985): 9-23.
The law of correspondences posits a trinity of nature, language, and mind with language as the middle term. Blasing reviews Emerson's theories of language and poetry, especially his concept of poetic form, before turning to examples of theory in action. The functions of rhymes are to produce metaphors by coupling unlike senses, to embody fate, and "to descend below rhetoric." To

Emerson, poetry is "the language of law, perhaps even language as law."
Overlaps chapter in Blasing's book cited below.

—————— . "Ralph Waldo Emerson: Essaying the Poet." In her *American Poetry: The Rhetoric of Its Forms*. New Haven, Conn.: Yale University Press, 1987.
For Emerson, "the spiritual law of form and the natural law of death are identified in poetic form." In their "freedom, poets rediscover these forms." Poetic form is related to fate in its being an embodiment of pure intellect. Thus, it is absolute. The poet submits to language as if it were a law of nature, and this submission brings a paradoxical liberation. "The poems are formal constructs meant to parallel the correspondence of the orders of nature and Spirit."

Bloom, Harold, ed. *Ralph Waldo Emerson*. New York: Chelsea House, 1985.
Primarily excerpts from major book-length studies. Includes pieces by Whicher, Porter, Ellison, and Poirier. The thrust is a reevaluation of Emerson as part of the larger reconsideration of American Romanticism. Bloom's introduction is a spirited review of Emerson in critical history. As in all the books in this series, the selections represent the present generation of critics.

Bode, Carl, ed. *Ralph Waldo Emerson: A Profile*. New York: Hill & Wang, 1968.
Bode presents a sampling of recollections by Emerson's contemporaries. These include Edwin Percy Whipple, Annie Adams Fields, and Charles Eliot Norton; Holmes's biography is excerpted. Also, modern critics sketch Emerson's character and presence from a variety of documentary sources. Excellent recreations of Emerson as speaker and teacher.

Boswell, Jeanetta. *Ralph Waldo Emerson and the Critics: A Checklist of Criticism 1900-1977*. Metuchen, N.J.: Scarecrow Press, 1979.
Lists alphabetically by author books and articles about Emerson published during the period covered. The emphasis is on American publications. There is an index of coauthors, editors, and translators as well as a subject index where students can look up Emerson's works by titles. Scaled to the needs of college students in American literature courses.

Brooks, Van Wyck. *The Life of Emerson*. New York: E. P. Dutton, 1932.
A sensible, attractive biography that benefits from Brooks's curiosity about New England culture. Looks beneath the shifts in Emerson's professions to the essential nature of his vocation: his commitment to the world of ideas and to the search for expressive modes. Explores Emerson's role as an educator and as a theorist about education. Examines how Emerson's own personality is reflected in his concepts. Praises Emerson's personal courage.

Buell, Lawrence. "The Emerson Industry in the 1980's: A Survey of Trends and Achievement." *ESQ* 30 (2nd Quarter, 1984): 117-136.

An overview of the latest directions and accomplishments, in which the year 1982 is considered a high point. Buell addresses textual scholarship, biographical studies, the "de-Transcendentalization" of Emerson's image, gender criticism, and explorations of Emerson's habits as a writer. Provides fuller treatments of several works found in the present listing. Buell finds much of value, concluding that "we are living in an exciting and productive time for Emerson scholarship."

Burkholder, Robert E., and Joel Myerson. *Emerson: An Annotated Secondary Bibliography*. Pittsburgh: University of Pittsburgh Press, 1985.

Everything one needs to locate the printed commentary on Emerson. More than 5,600 entries on critical, biographical, and miscellaneous studies listed, abstracted, and indexed for convenient use. This is the ultimate research tool on our major poet-philosopher.

_____ , eds. *Critical Essays on Ralph Waldo Emerson*. Boston: G. K. Hall, 1983.

An unclassified but chronologically arranged series of responses to Emerson's writings. Avoids the standard anthology pieces and excerpts from readily available books on Emerson, choosing instead from uncollected periodical literature. Includes a discussion of "Nature" as a prose poem, a defense of "Brahma," and recent examinations of *Poems* (1847) and Emerson's response to English culture. A rich feast.

Cady, Edwin H., and Louis Budd, eds. *On Emerson: The Best from American Literature*. Durham, N.C.: Duke University Press, 1988.

Topics include Emerson's response to Quakerism, his relationship to William James, his understanding of Plato, antinomianism, and many other contemporaneous matters. Equally provocative are considerations of how Emerson's Transcendentalism relates to psychotherapy and the nature of Emerson's influence on and affinity with Henry Miller.

Carpenter, Frederick Ives. *Emerson and Asia*. Reprint. New York: Haskell House, 1968.

Considers the significance, symbolic and otherwise, of Oriental culture to Emerson's imagination. Demonstrates connections between Neoplatonic and Eastern thought. Reviews Emerson's readings, as noted in his journals and his essays, in Hindu, Persian, and Arabic literature. Applauds Emerson's role in opening up the East to American thinkers and writers.

Cary, Elisabeth Luther. *Emerson: Poet and Thinker*. New York: G. P. Putnam's Sons, 1904.

A presentation of Emerson to a new generation that gives plentiful attention to the role of *The Dial*. In a separate chapter on Emerson's poems, Cary doubts that they will have continued popularity. She worries over "a certain harshness in measure" and Emerson's tendency to give his vocabulary "an excess of substance." Observes Emerson's fondness for surprise endings. At his best, Emerson's poetry has "extreme beauty in metaphor, paradox, and symbol." Precise criticisms clearly illustrated.

Cheyfitz, Eric. *The Trans-Parent: Sexual Politics in the Language of Emerson*. Baltimore: Johns Hopkins University Press, 1981.
Emerson is understood as a "psychologist of power" who uses language as material for his experiments. Cheyfitz finds in Emerson's language an implicit conflict between the figure of "the beautiful mother" and the figure of the "FATHER." He explores the values these figures represent in Emerson's writings, particularly in the essay "Nature." This sometimes difficult book elucidates the battle between authority and democracy in nineteenth century thought and feeling.

Cowan, Michael H. *City of the West: Emerson, America, and Urban Metaphor*. New Haven, Conn.: Yale University Press, 1967.
An "attempt to capture the spirit as much as the letter of Emerson's dialectical approach to life and thought." Explores Emerson's use of urban material as an opening into the vision of the city that accompanied the American Renaissance. Emerson's complex attitude toward Boston is at the center of the study.

Donadio, Stephen, Stephen Railton, and Ormond Seavey, eds. *Emerson and His Legacy*. Carbondale: Southern Illinois University Press, 1986.
The editors and others present discussions that fashion "a dialogue between two periods in the history of American culture." The first is the response to Emerson in the quarter century before the Civil War; the second is the response to liberalism and Marxism beginning in the 1930's. Both periods are marked by attempts at comprehensive visions rather than specialist subdivisions of the human predicament.

Donoghue, Denis. "Emerson at First." In *Reading America: Essays on American Literature*. New York: Alfred A. Knopf, 1987.
Donoghue outlines the argument of the essay "Nature" to stress the primacy of will in Emerson's vision of the individual, the soul, and the mind. "Granted that Emerson is not a philosopher; it is enough that he is a poet and a sage." Emerson's essential thought concerns not knowledge and truth, but power and command. He is "the founding father of nearly everything we think of as American in the modern world."

Duncan, Jeffrey L. *The Power and Form of Emerson's Thought*. Charlottesville: University Press of Virginia, 1973.
Emerson is not a subtle strategist. His ideas are to be taken literally—at face value. His art is in the service of ideas; thus, one must "understand the ideas, their structure and relation, to appreciate his art." Emerson's concept of polarity is Duncan's controlling thread. The terms "power and form" are used for their inclusiveness. Nature, society, the individual, and consciousness are handled in separate chapters. A few poems are quoted.

Ellison, Julie. *Emerson's Romantic Style*. Princeton, N.J.: Princeton University Press, 1984.
This study of Emerson's prose style involves many issues of importance to the student of his poetry. These include figurative language, uses of narrative, devices of repetition, and methods of detachment and transition. In prose, as in poetry, Emerson experimented with and defied genre conventions. Like other Romantic writers, he sought "an art that because it absorbed all sorts of discourse, was beyond the bounds of any."

Firkins, O. W. *Ralph Waldo Emerson*. Reprint. New York: Russell & Russell, 1965.
First published in 1915, this was one of the first biographies to exploit the then-recently published ten-volume edition of Emerson's *Journals*. Firkins thus was able to follow Emerson's development as a thinker more carefully and critically than those writing just after Emerson's death. A chapter on "Emerson As Poet" questions the "structural laxity" of many poems. Emerson's method was not one of "conquest by installments" but rather one of "the immediate capture, and the continuous recapture, of the whole."

Frost, Robert. "On Emerson." In *Emerson: A Collection of Critical Essays*, edited by Milton R. Konvitz and Stephen E. Whicher. Englewood Cliffs, N.J. Prentice-Hall, 1962.
A brief appreciation by a true inheritor of Emerson's thought on language and poetry. Frost testifies to his indebtedness "for troubled thoughts about freedom" and for Emerson's successful coupling of poetry and philosophy. Praises the "Concord Hymn." Describes the relationship between Emerson's personality and his Unitarianism. Though mostly about Frost, the essay suggests Emerson's long reach. Emerson is the only non-president in Frost's list of the four greatest Americans.

Fussell, Edwin. "Emerson and the Meter-Making Argument." In his *Lucifer in Harness: American Meter, Metaphor, and Diction*. Princeton, N.J.: Princeton University Press, 1973.
"With Emerson's insight that verse techniques are for the most part the effects of poetic motives, and not, as Poe seems to have thought, their direct and

mechanical causes, together with his understanding (if only tentative and partial) that the relation between meter and culture could not possibly be quite the
same as in England, but must equally depend on a national literary situation,
American poetry was in a position to make its first major breakthrough."

Gelpi, Albert. "The Paradox of Organic Form." In his *The Tenth Muse: The Psyche
of the American Poet*. Cambridge, Mass.: Harvard University Press, 1975. Also
in *Emerson: Prophecy, Metamorphosis, and Influence*, edited by David Levin.
Argues that formalist criticism is based on assumptions that render it unable to
value Emerson's achievement as a poet. Formalist norms regarding structure
and diction "are largely irrelevant to what Emerson is doing, or at any rate
attempting." Gelpi advances the "underlying principles" of Emerson's poetics
in order to adjust our critical stance. Emerson believed in processes by which
structure emerged as "in the organic yet transcendent process of nature."
Technical virtuosity could be a dead end.

Gonnaud, Maurice. *An Uneasy Solitude: Individual and Society in the Work of
Ralph Waldo Emerson*. Translated by Lawrence Rosenwald. Princeton, N.J.:
Princeton University Press, 1987.
First published (in French) in 1964, this critical biography breaks with the
tradition of perceiving a removed, intellectual Emerson to whom experience
was closed. Gonnaud discovers a relatively open, sensuous man. This Emerson
is still an optimist, but one not immune to the range of human suffering.
Stresses Emerson's position on questions of class and community. Pays more
attention to the later years than is customary. This revised Emerson is neither
all revolutionary or all reactionary, but deeply middle-class.

Harding, Brian. "'Frolic Architecture': Music and Metamorphosis in Emerson's
Poetry." In *Nineteenth-Century American Poetry*, edited by A. Robert Lee.
Totowa, N.J.: Barnes & Noble Books, 1985.
Emerson's belief that man should find meaning in the flux of experience gave
rise to his attempt to imitate that flux in his poems. He fused two ideas about
poetry: that it was architectural and monumental and that it was also musical
and fluid. Harding surveys many poems to show how Emerson's yoking of
these apparently irreconcilable opposites creates his particular distinction.

Harding, Walter. *Emerson's Library*. Charlottesville: University Press of Virginia,
1967.
A listing of all the works in the Emerson library as donated to and housed in
the Concord Antiquarian Society. Additional works listed as discovered by
references in Emerson's writings and in holdings of other libraries. Through
this bibliography, we can discover possible sources of ideas, information, and

even language available and probably known to Emerson. Harding indicates
which volumes have marginal notations in Emerson's hand.

Holmes, Oliver Wendell. *Ralph Waldo Emerson.* Reprint. Detroit: Gale Research,
1967.
First published in 1885, this is a major assessment of one giant of American
letters by a contemporary of almost equal stature. Completed two years after
Emerson's death, Holmes's work is a mixture of fact and homage: a celebration. Based on conversations with Emerson's family and friends as well as
letters and other documents, this treatment is pleasantly familiar but not too
much so. Includes a chapter on the poetry that is useful even today. Often
excerpted in anthologies.

Hopkins, Vivian C. *Spires of Form: A Study of Emerson's Aesthetic Theory.* Reprint.
New York: Russell & Russell, 1965.
This study, first published in 1951, considers Emerson's theory in three phases:
the creative process, the work of art, and the aesthetic experience. The third
phase, how we respond to art, has been generally neglected by Emerson's
critics. Hopkins notes that Emerson stressed enjoyment rather than judgment.
Relates the concept of correspondence, the exercise of reason, and the mystical
ingredient in Emerson's thought to one another. Examines the principle of
organic form as it applies to meter.

Howe, Irving. *The American Newness: Culture and Politics in the Age of Emerson.*
Cambridge, Mass.: Harvard University Press, 1986.
Develops the subtle ways in which the contrasting outlooks of Emerson and
Hawthorne are linked. Both inherited a religious crisis, to which they re-
sponded differently, with Hawthorne more conscious of the weight of the past.
Both attempted to help the new nation find its way through its cultural adoles-
cence. Irving discusses the critics and disciples of Emerson as well as his long-
range literary legacy. Special attention to impact on Cooper and Melville.

Hubbell, George Shelton. *A Concordance to the Poems of Ralph Waldo Emerson.*
New York: H. W. Wilson, 1932.
Based on the Centenary Edition of Emerson's works, this word list gives usage
citations with line references. Like all such tools, Hubbell's concordance allows us to explore Emerson's habits of poetic diction, the shifting meanings of
works, the frequency with which certain words appear, and the ways in which
words are used in combination or in hyphenated compounds and coinages.

Keyes, Charlotte E. *The Experimenter: A Biography of Ralph Waldo Emerson.* New
Haven, Conn.: College and University Press, 1962.
This brief life can serve as a supplement to a course or unit on Emerson.

Basically a book for young readers, with colorful shaping and selecting of materials to emphasize the independent streak in Emerson—his special brand of heroism. Emerson viewed as teacher, husband, traveler, cultural statesman. Designed to attract the reader to Emerson's writings.

Konvitz, Milton R., ed. *The Recognition of Ralph Waldo Emerson*. Ann Arbor: University of Michigan Press, 1972.
A selection of contemporaneous criticism is followed by one that runs through the end of the nineteenth century. Two more groupings divide the twentieth century comment. Most selections are relatively self-contained, giving a satisfaction missing from anthologies that excerpt and divorce material from context. Konvitz's preface provides the thread that links these pieces together.

Konvitz, Milton R., and Stephen E. Whicher, eds. *Emerson: A Collection of Critical Essays*. Englewood Cliffs, N.J.: Prentice-Hall, 1962.
Claims to be "the first selection of Emerson criticism ever made." An astounding fact, considering Emerson's importance. The selections clarify Emerson's position as a philosophical thinker and shaper of America's cultural path. Includes comment by William James, George Santayana, Henry Nash Smith, and Sherman Paul. Most of the selections are from chapters of books. Konvitz's introduction stresses the scope of Emerson's interests and the inner consistency of his thought. Chronology and selected bibliography.

Leary, Lewis. *Ralph Waldo Emerson: An Interpretive Essay*. Boston: Twayne, 1980.
Neither a biography nor a critical evaluation, this book presents Emerson primarily as a moral philosopher and stresses the practical side of Emerson's thought. The discussion of Emerson's main concerns is arranged in three broad topics: "The Responsibility of Man," "Man Thinking," and "The Conduct of Life." A chapter called "Books Are for Idle Hours" reviews Emerson's ideas about poetry and refers to many poems. Leary believes, however, that Emerson's "best poetry was in his prose."

Levin, David, ed. *Emerson: Prophecy, Metamorphosis, and Influence*. New York: Columbia University Press, 1975.
These selected papers from the English Institute examine how Emerson's ideas and methods were formed and how they influenced his contemporaries and later writers. Some view Emerson as central to a basic change in American culture and to the way in which the country saw itself. Others consider his prophetic role and his relationship to European thinkers and writers.

Loving, Jerome. *Emerson, Whitman and the American Muse*. Chapel Hill: University of North Carolina Press, 1982.
Examines how the main lines of American poetry became established in the

complex relationship between these two men. Asserts that for all their differences in background and culture, the two were much alike in temperament
and talent. Assesses their major works as a figurative correspondence between
them: an imaginary conversation in which each fired the other's imagination.
A provocative exploration of how the two poets dealt with the conflict between
the law of the group and the freedom of the individual.

McAleer, John. *Ralph Waldo Emerson: Days of Encounter*. Boston: Little, Brown,
1984.
A huge yet graspable biography written to emphasize Emerson's relationships
with others and with history. Provides eighty brief chapters, vignettes, each
one a dramatic scene. The characters include Ellen Tucker (whom Emerson
married), Thomas Carlyle, Harriet Martineau, Jones Very, Margaret Fuller,
Nathanial Hawthorne, and Daniel Webster. Some of these are dramas of outlook, not of literal, personal conflict. A kaleidoscope. Illustrated.

Malloy, Charles. *A Study of Emerson's Major Poems*. Edited by Kenneth Walter
Cameron. Hartford, Conn.: Transcendental Books, 1973.
Facsimile reproductions of five printed lectures that Malloy prepared for
periodicals in the Boston area. Malloy, who organized the Boston Emerson
Society, was "the first extensive popularizer" of Emerson's poetry. Though his
essays have the peculiarities of late Victorian explication, they capture the spirit
in which Emerson was first read.

Marr, David. *American Worlds Since Emerson*. Amherst: University of Massachusetts Press, 1988.
Demonstrates the centrality of Emerson's thought to the main currents of
American intellectual history up to the present. "Emersonian privatism, mor-
alism, and anti-politicism are major elements in American social character."
Because certain aspects of Emerson have been codified in academic study,
other equally valuable ones are likely to be ignored. Examines, through Emerson, the role of social institutions and literary culture.

Matthiessen, F. O. "From Emerson to Thoreau." In his *American Renaissance: Art
and Expression in the Age of Emerson and Whitman*. New York: Oxford
University Press, 1941.
A detailed exposition on Emerson's thought and art, ranging from issues of
consciousness, eloquence, and expression to the achievement of Emerson as a
poet. A brief section, often reprinted, called "A Few Herbs and Apples"
explores Emerson's poetic style both in verse and prose. Matthiesen addresses
Emerson's metaphysical strain, his modification of Coleridge's organic principle, and the transmission of Emerson's concepts through Thoreau.

Metzger, Charles R. *Emerson and Greenbaugh: Transcendental Pioneers of an American Aesthetic*. Berkeley: University of California Press, 1954.

Argues that Emerson and Horatio Greenbaugh were "pioneers of an organic aesthetic in America itself—a branch aesthetic, actually, developed in America out of local conditions and running parallel with, rather than subordinate to, a similar organic aesthetic developing . . . in Europe." Metzger presents a synthesis of the religious and aesthetic aspects of New England Transcendentalism. He hopes to renew interest in the obscure Greenbaugh.

Miles, Josephine. *Ralph Waldo Emerson*. Minneapolis: University of Minnesota Press, 1964.

This excellent pamphlet-length study establishes the main lines of Emersonian thought by analysis of three major prose works. A brief life follows, and then a section of the poems. Miles is concerned with Emerson's "outreaching vocabulary" and his search for freer forms; she weighs the proportions of philosopher and poet in the man.

More, Paul Elmer. "Emerson." In *Paul Elmer More's Shelburne Essays on American Literature*, edited by Daniel Aaron. New York: Harcourt, Brace & World, 1963.

Emerson is "the outstanding figure of American letters." He gives the effect of often talking to himself, not arguing or analyzing, but pursuing illumination. His method is to throw "a direct light into the soul of the hearer." Emerson turned away from ritual by surrendering his pulpit, by valuing individuality and spontaneity over conformity and inherited patterns; his blindness to evil was a weakness. Moore's essay "The Influence of Emerson" is also included in this collection.

Myerson, Joel. *Ralph Waldo Emerson: A Descriptive Bibliography*. Pittsburgh: University of Pittsburgh Press, 1982.

Lists Emerson's own works. First come titles of separate publications, then collected editions and miscellaneous collections. First appearances of contributions to books and pamphlets are followed by first appearances in periodicals and newspapers. Titles of books edited by Emerson, reprints of editions, and works attributed to Emerson are the final categories. The appendix lists important book-length works about Emerson.

——————, ed. *Emerson Centenary Essays*. Carbondale: University of Southern Illinois Press, 1982.

These original essays by major Emerson scholars provide "new interpretations of important periods in Emerson's life and significant evaluations of his major works." Topics include Emerson's coping with illness, his shift in vocation and accompanying shift in outlook, his search for a persona, his attitudes toward

Shakespeare, and his role as a teacher. Ronald A. Sudal contributes "'The Adirondacs' and Technology," an analysis of one of Emerson's longer poems.

Neufeldt, Leonard. *The House of Emerson*. Lincoln: University of Nebraska Press, 1982.
A comprehensive critical analysis that uses Emerson's concept of metamorphosis as a springboard. Neufeldt's appreciation of Emerson rests more substantially on the poetry than do other studies. He gives attention to works, both in poetry and prose, not generally considered part of the essential corpus. Attempts to demystify and demythologize Emerson, while redefining his views. Chapters on "The Artist," "Emerson and Poetry," Thoreau, Daniel Webster, and science and technology. Analyses of "The Sphinx," "The Poet," and "Days."

Orth, Ralph H. et al., eds. *The Poetry Notebooks of Ralph Waldo Emerson*. Columbia: University of Missouri Press, 1986.
This is a primary source of infinite utility. The editors provide the manuscript material—jottings, early drafts, revisions—that lie behind Emerson's published poems. They also provide analyses of the relationships among these drafts and fragments to the end of tracing each poem's development. An exciting glimpse of the creative process that allows explorations into Emerson's habits of composition.

Paul, Sherman. *Emerson's Angle of Vision: Man and Nature in American Experience*. Cambridge, Mass.: Harvard University Press, 1965.
Describes Emerson's role in shaping our "way of thinking about the relatedness of man and the universe." Emerson's effort to find a bridge between nature and man led to the concept of "correspondence." Paul examines this concept, "how it entered [Emerson's] thought and permeated his vision." Though the idea was not new, Emerson's adaptation of it, his particular applications, and the force of his thought upon our culture make this a significant issue.

Perry, Bliss. *Emerson Today*. Reprint. New York: Archon Books, 1969.
Based on a series of lectures first published in 1931, these chapters consider "The Known and the Unknown in Emerson" (what criticism has uncovered so far), "The Daily Bread" (Emerson's career), "The Mystic and the Poet," and "Revaluations." Relates Emerson's thought to Plotinus and his poetry to Dante, Blake, and seventeenth century devotional writers. Considers Emerson's study of Hindu texts. Perry wonders why Emerson gave scant attention to certain major issues.

Porte, Joel, ed. *Emerson: Prospect and Retrospect*. Cambridge, Mass.: Harvard University Press, 1982.

This series of essays reconsiders Emerson's views on, or applies them to, a wide variety of topics, including the unconscious, social theory, history, and how nature is turned into commodity. Phyllis Cole treats the possible influence of Emerson's aunt, Mary Moody Emerson. Ronald Bush explores the meaning of T. S. Eliot's distaste for Emerson.

Porter, David. *Emerson and Literary Change*. Cambridge, Mass.: Harvard University Press, 1978.

Emerson was not only a culture hero but also "a revolutionary committed to the introduction of a radical esthetics." Porter aims to define Emerson's brilliance as an artist and poetic theorist. He finds in Emerson a conscious and successful effort to effect a shift in poetic form, to release a "new poetic consciousness and expressive idiom." Emerson's concern for art was so obsessive that it pervades almost everything he writes. He believed "that the material world rightly seen would yield its meaning."

Reaver, Russell J. *Emerson As Mythmaker*. Gainesville: University of Florida Press, 1954.

Examines "Emerson's evaluation of the human being in his role as creator." Contrasts Emerson's concern with how the intuitive mind creates with the modern emphasis on the creative powers of the rational mind. Sees Emerson as a forerunner of modern psychology. Chapters consider "The Personal Myth," "The Springs of Imagination," "The Organic Language of Poetry," and "The Shaping Intuition." Stresses Emerson's ideas about the process by which poetry is created.

Robinson, David. *Apostle of Culture: Emerson as Preacher and Lecturer*. Philadelphia: University of Pennsylvania Press, 1982.

Focuses on the public man, the orator whose personal force did so much to convey his ideas to his contemporary audience. Shows how Emerson's lectures take the form of sermons. His theological vision receives detailed attention here as Robinson explores the Unitarian assumptions that formed the early manhood of Emerson. Suggests that Emerson's sense of audience in written works derived from his experience as a speaker.

Rountree, Thomas J., ed. *Critics on Emerson*. Coral Gables: University of Miami Press, 1973.

A compact yet representative range of responses divided into chronological groupings. Focus is on the major essays, with some attention to the poetry. Rountree's introduction generalizes about the path of response to Emerson's achievement. Since Emerson's aesthetic and his poetry reflected his reading of nature, the attention given here to his prose writings on nature is useful for students of the poetry.

Rusk, Ralph L. *The Life of Ralph Waldo Emerson*. New York: Columbia University Press, 1949.
    For many years, this has been the standard biography, and for external detail it is still reliable. Re-creates the tone and texture of Emerson's time and the nature of his relationships with contemporaries, both personal and public. This impressive work of scholarship tries to find Emerson's sensibilities, but does not stray far from what the documents can support. Rusk helps us follow the growth of Emerson's ideas, his emotional set, and his situation in American cultural and literary history.

Sanborn, F. G. "Emerson Among the Poets." In *The Genius and Character of Emerson*, edited by Sanborn. Reprint. Port Washington, N.Y.: Kennikat Press, 1971.
    Praises the poetic qualities of Emerson's mind: his "clair voyance of the imagination." Establishes a "threefold unity of insight, expression, and will" that is met by Dante, Milton, and Shakespeare. In "recent times," Sanborn finds Emerson in the company of Wordsworth, Goethe, and Victor Hugo. He appeals to the precepts of Arnold and Symonds to validate his high claims for Emerson's achievement, arguing that the freshness of Emerson's verse was still strongly felt in the 1880's. Instructive comparison to Thomas Gray.

———————— , ed. *The Genius and Character of Emerson*. Reprint. Port Washington, N.Y.: Kennikat Press, 1971.
    Lectures given in 1884 at the Concord School of Philosophy (where Emerson taught) testify to Emerson's enormous influence by the late nineteenth century. Papers discuss "Emerson and Boston," "Emerson as a Preacher," "Emerson's Religion," "Emerson's Orientalism," and "Emerson's Relation to Goethe and Carlyle."

Scheick, William J. "Emerson the Poet: A Twenty-Year Retrospective." *American Poetry* 1 (Winter, 1984): 2-19.
    Scheick provides a concise overview of two decades' work on Emerson's poetry. He reacts to the various critics' assessments of Emerson's imagery, structure, and voice with observations of his own. These comments are brought together in an analysis of "Blight," taken as a representative Emerson poem. Emerson tends "to move away from concrete imagery and toward abstraction." His poems present themselves as "a freezing of the creative process."

Sealts, Merton M., Jr., "Mulberry Leaves and Satin: Emerson's Theory of the Creative Process." *Studies in the American Renaissance* (1985): 79-94.
    Traces the original formulations of Emerson's view of artistic creativity to his lectures on the philosophy of history that followed *Nature*. For Emerson,

literature is the conversion of action into thought and language. In the poem "The Problem" and elsewhere, Emerson affirms "that art, like mankind and like Nature itself, has its ultimate source in spirit, which employs the master artist's hand as its passive instrument."

Shucard, Alan. "Ralph Waldo Emerson and the Transcendental Poets." In his *American Poetry: The Puritans Through Walt Whitman*. Boston: Twayne, 1988.
Underscores the enormous influence of Emerson on the theory and practice of American poetry. Contrasts Emerson and Poe biographically, aesthetically, and in terms of the way each valued nature. Reviews Emerson's writings on poetry and briefly mentions a handful of key poems. Emerson "responsible for deemphasizing sound in favor of sense in American poetry." Chapter includes comments on Jones Very, Christopher Pearse Cranch, and Thoreau.

Spiller, Robert E. "Ralph Waldo Emerson," In *Literary History of the United States*, edited by Spiller et al. 3d ed., rev. New York: Macmillan, 1963.
Emerson emerged as the "delegated intellect" of a newly perceived American culture. His background and training prepared him for this role, as did the personal self-reliance that he promoted as an American virtue. Emerson's poetry alone assures him of a high place in American literature. His originality is as great as Poe's. Emerson's sense of inadequacy results from the high ideals he set for all poets. Less concerned with the music of poetry than with its way of seeing, he generated fresh uses of image and symbol.

Strauch, Carl F. "Emerson's Phi Beta Kappa Poem." *New England Quarterly* 23 (March, 1950): 65-90.
Gives the full text and argues that Emerson's first public literary effort deserves closer attention that it has received. While its subject was already hackneyed in 1837, "Emerson made the occasion and the address memorable with a distinctive philosophical doctrine and the unmistakable stamp of his apocalyptic style." Traces the tradition of Phi Beta Kappa poems to help sketch Emerson's situation, then examines the poem closely and explains contemporary references. Admires the mixture of moral idealism and practicality.

——————— . "The Mind's Voice" Emerson's Poetic Styles." *ESQ*, no. 60 (Summer, 1970): 43-59.
Explores Emerson's practice to illustrate the poet's complex awareness of the total integration of aesthetic elements required for effective poetic expression. Provides examples of Emerson's modulation of prosodic elements within poems, his interest in Miltonic catalog lines, his general movement toward freer verse forms, and his desire "to create an analogue to nature in an act of the imagination." Emerson experimented with accentual verse and with various distancing strategies.

_____ . "Emerson and the Doctrine of Sympathy." In *Critical Essays on Ralph Waldo Emerson*, edited by Robert E. Burkholder and Joel Myerson. Boston, G. K. Hall, 1983.
Considers "Emerson's treatment of sympathy in man's relations to nature" as revealed in his *Poems* (1847). Almost every poem in this volume "centers upon the problem of man's falling away from an inherent cosmic harmony." Aspects of this problem are examined by analyses of "The Rhodora," the "Ode to W. H. Channing," "Hamatreya," "Woodnotes," and other poems. In several poems, the figure of the poet invites the reader to join "in a universal sympathy of true feeling" that is opposed to materialism.

Summerlin, Timothy. "To Reconcile or to Submit: The Changing Face of Joy in Emerson's Poetry." *ATQ*, no. 49 (Winter, 1981): 5-20.
"Central to Emerson's poetry is the Romantic belief in poetic vision as an avenue to joyous affirmation of life. But his concept of the joyful visionary is not static. Some early poems, indeed, portray a divided, troubled psyche slowly moving to accept the voice within." The poetry of his major period is more fully ecstatic and celebratory. In the later poems, the quality of joy is more restrained and less passionate.

Sutcliffe, Emerson Grant. *Emerson's Theories of Literary Expression*. Reprint. New York: Phaeton Press, 1971.
Originally published in 1922, this study pays close attention to the value of fact and symbol as Emerson saw it. Examines Emerson's views on the relationship between word and thing, idiom, compression, understatement, and the superlative. Sutcliffe's far-reaching synthesis, which includes a chapter on "The Growth of Emerson's Theories of Style," has much to teach us even sixty years after it was written.

Thurin, Erik Ingvar. *Emerson As Priest of Pan: A Study in the Metaphysics of Sex*. Lawrence: Regents Press of Kansas, 1981.
Examines Emerson's ideas about love. Follows his quest for a reconciliation of the erotic and the Christian- Platonic. Important here is the poet's role as reconciler and redeemer. Discusses Emerson's position on the emancipation of women, the nature of sexual beauty, and the dynamic overlay of dialectical process and marriage. Other topics are androgyny, Europe and Asia, Heaven and Hell. Many references to Emerson's poems.

Van Leer, David. *Emerson's Epistemology: The Argument of the Essays*. Cambridge, England: Cambridge University Press, 1986.
A detailed consideration of Emerson as a philosopher within the context of nineteenth century idealism. Van Leer's purpose is to "show the individual works to be more carefully structured than many have assumed." Main con-

cerns are "the structure of nature," "the practice of divinity," "the revisions of self-reliance," and "the limits of experience." Uses four key essays to establish points considered applicable to the Emerson canon.

Von Frank, Albert J. "Emerson's Boyhood and Collegiate Verse: Unpublished and New Texts Edited from Manuscript." *Studies in the American Renaissance* (1983): 1-56.
The poems themselves take up most of these pages. Von Frank carefully places each poem in a biographical setting, measures its skill, and whenever possible records its reception. These poems, which include drinking songs, commemorative odes, and a valedictory poem, show the young Emerson freeing himself from the eighteenth century.

Wagenknecht, Edward. *Ralph Waldo Emerson: Portrait of a Balanced Soul*. New York: Oxford University Press, 1974.
Asks us not to think of Emerson so much as a philosopher and scholar or as a pill-sugaring sermonizer, but as a restless, dynamic experimenter with ideas, language, and genre. Suggests that Emerson is too easily buried under the headstone of Transcendentalism in spite of the fact that the Concord Transcendentalists were not in accord about very much. Wagenknecht is after the "disposition" of Emerson—a man risking much but able to find his equilibrium over and over again.

Waggoner, Hyatt H. *Emerson As Poet*. Cambridge, Mass.: Harvard University Press, 1974.
Taking his own advice from an earlier book (below), Waggoner provides a close study of Emerson's poetry. The first chapter surveys critical opinion and offers ideas toward a fresh consideration. Chapter 2 argues that Emerson's earliest poetry reveals his gifts and his abilities as a craftsman. The next chapter shows the variety of styles in Emerson's mature poems and how many of them follow an age-old "literary and philosophic tradition of paradoxy." The final chapters consider "The Poetry of the Prose" and "Vision and Voice."

_____ . "Ralph Waldo Emerson." In his *American Poets from the Puritans to the Present*. Boston: Houghton Mifflin, 1968.
Presents Emerson as the poet of the period "most in need of being rediscovered." His finest poems are rarely anthologized, and his work is largely dismissed as a result of the modernist era's distaste for any kind of idealism. Waggoner distinguishes lines of influence in which Whitman carried some aspects of Emerson's art forward, but submerged others that surface in the twentieth century. Our poetry cannot be understood without knowing Emerson, the prototype of the American poet.

Whicher, Stephen E. *Freedom and Fate: An Inner Life of Ralph Waldo Emerson.* Reprint. New York: A. S. Barnes, 1961.

In contrast to Ralph L. Rusk's compendious account "of the life Emerson's contemporaries witnessed," Whicher strives to present the inner man. Examines Emerson's complex and many- sided mind and his ability to struggle through contrary lines of exploration without settling for easy answers. There is always the drama of the mind at work, the process of discovery, in Emerson's writing. Whicher attempts to reproduce that drama.

Yanella, Donald. *Ralph Waldo Emerson.* Boston: Twayne, 1982.

Designed as an introduction for general readers or beginning students, this overview glides smoothly from the life to the ideas to the works. The poetry is treated in its own chapter, breaking away from the chronology needed elsewhere to show the development of Emerson's thought. Provides brief analyses of the major poems. Reliable, readable, and engaging, this study is framed by a chronology and a selected bibliography.

Yoder, R. A. *Emerson and the Orphic Poet in America.* Berkeley: University of California Press, 1978.

Emerson's theory and practice revived and modified the European concept of the prophetic or Orphic poet. Conceptually, Emerson's view of Orpheus was traditional. In his poems, he was an Orpheus descending into time and into the world. The Orphic figure in and behind the poems is "a man of common size or less" whose "poetry is a limited power." This version of the Orphic poet was Emerson's legacy to American poets who came after him.

"Brahma"

Leland, Charles Godfrey. "A Defense of 'Brahma.' " In *Critical Essays on Ralph Waldo Emerson*, edited by Robert E. Burkholder and Joel Myerson. Boston, G. K. Hall, 1983.

An early attempt to rescue Emerson from his detractors, this essay demonstrates the extent to which "Brahma" encapsulates the "character and leading points" of the "Bhagavat-Geeta," a portion of the great Eastern epic. Leland connects passages in Emerson's poem with corresponding passages in the Hindu masterpiece. Even the confusing resolution of the poem is in keeping with the spirit and wisdom of its source.

Waggoner, Hyatt H. *Emerson As Poet*, 156-160. Cambridge, Mass.: Harvard University Press, 1974.

An expression of Emerson's growing enthusiasm for Oriental wisdom, the poem maintains contact with Emerson's own religious heritage. May reflect worry over the divided nation or over Emerson's own conflict between "the impulse toward commitment and the impulse to withdraw into contemplation of the Real." The poem's paradoxes are subsumed in the final one, which argues that if find God makes us turn our backs on heaven, this might be a proper action—especially if heaven is fancied as a utopia for self-indulgence. Relates the philosophy of the poem to quietism, "a submerged minor strain in Western piety."

Yoder, R. A. *Emerson and the Orphic Poet in America*, 162-164. Berkeley: University of California Press, 1978.
Argues that the poem has the quality of a riddle: The answer the poem provides is no answer at all. "Brahma is the unfathomable reconciliation of all differences." The last line suggests that nature is sufficient in itself and doesn't need a theological construct to justify it. Poetry, however, needs to find a transforming language. If that is found, then the immediate subject or aspect of nature doesn't matter. The poem is concerned with the process of metamorphosis, and thus with the Orphic myth.

"Concord Hymn"

Porter, David. *Emerson and Literary Change*, 104-110. Cambridge, Mass.: Harvard University Press, 1978.
The poem celebrates "Emerson's first concern, freedom from stifling conventions." But it is also a "conversion poem," concerning itself with the broad philosophic question of "what is in motion and what holds fast." In the poem, "two Emersonian forces, one outward toward fluid dissipation and the other inward toward concentration and fixity, work simultaneously." The poem praises courage, and, like the "votive stone," transforms the moment into timelessness. For Emerson, the poetic imagination has "power and ability to convert the present moment into the ideal vision it contains."

"Days"

Gross, Seymour L. "Emerson and Poetry." In *Critics on Emerson*, edited by Thomas J. Rountree. Coral Gables: University of Miami Press, 1973.
The poem is successful because it deals with experience directly. It is rooted firmly in what Emerson understood, not in speculation or the "transcendental ether of intuitive feeling." The movement of emotion is persuasive in this reflection upon the problems of choice. The pain of choosing results from having to make moral distinctions. Often, choosing the lesser good brings the same feeling of guilt as choosing evil. Being only human, man will feel the scorn the follows from his inevitably flawed choices.

Matthiessen, F. O. "From Emerson to Thoreau." In his *American Renaissance*, 59-63. New York: Oxford University Press, 1941.

Agrees with Emerson that this is his best poem. Emerson expressed "here in a single sustained paragraph of blank verse . . . what he tried to say on literally dozens of other occasions." Here, as in no other poem, "Emerson's gift for swift and fragile images has for once been reinforced by the extension and enlargement of his metaphor into a parable." The parable's thought and feeling arose "from the central dilemma in his way of life." His ambiguous stances toward the value of experience and toward the inspired moment crystalize in "Days."

Neufeldt, Leonard. *The House of Emerson*, 164-167. Lincoln: University of Nebraska Press, 1982.

This is a poem "about the hazards with which the poet of metamorphosis must live." Examines the "negative dialectic" that runs through many of Emerson's works. Through this dialectic, "the necessary presence is defined in terms of its absence, desired success by failure, discipline through its lack, flying law through anarchic succession." Though the process leads to no "positive enactment," it does point to "exactly what is needed." Describes a crisis of "words without the word, spectral procession inducing failure of nerve."

Porter, David. *Emerson and Literary Change*, 128-130. Cambridge, Mass.: Harvard University Press, 1978.

The poem deals with failure of the imagination. The poet scorns himself for not being able to bring into being those essences, to make those conversions, necessary for the highest art. The female figure suggests "the analogy of impotence to convey a sense of passion missed, intimacy fumbled, and insight failed." Unable to attain a sense of the whole, the poet finds that the bits and pieces of his mundane world bring no sense of uplift or glory.

"Each and All"

Dameron, J. Lasley. "Emerson's 'Each and All' and Goethe's 'Eins and Alles.' " *English Studies* 67 (August, 1986): 327-330.

Goethe's "Eins and Alles" appeared in translation as "One and All" in the April, 1839 issue of *The North American Review*, a periodical of the type customarily read by Emerson. The poem deals with the reciprocal relationship between the particular and the universal, just as Emerson's second version of "Each and All" does. Dameron presents the translation and points out parallels in thought with Emerson's poem, remarking also on Emerson's revision of the title from the original "Each in All."

Gross, Seymour L. "Emerson and Poetry." In *Critics on Emerson*, edited by
Thomas J. Rountree. Coral Gables: University of Miami Press, 1973.
The poem lacks the organic form and consequent attention to transition that
Emerson values in theory. The generalized statement that follows the concrete
inventory startles the reader, who has not been prepared for it. The clipped
meter buries any suggestiveness the images might have. When the poet is
introduced, the poem seems to start all over again. Symbols whose values are
established in one section are jumbled and undermined in another. The closing
leap to the spiritual realm seems tacked on.

Miller, Norman. "Emerson's 'Each and All' Concept: A Reexamination." In *Critical Essays on Ralph Waldo Emerson*, edited by Robert E. Burkholder and Joel
Myerson. Boston, G. K. Hall, 1983.
Examines inconsistencies in a concept that concerned Emerson in his essays,
journals, and poems over decades. This doctrine explains "the essential relationship between the part and the whole, between the particular and the universal." The poem elaborates one side of Emerson's ambiguous position by stressing the "all" at the expense of the "each." In other writings, Emerson gives
higher value to the particular. Miller argues that man's role as the perceiving
intermediary is Emerson's fundamental concern. A useful context for examining the poem.

Yanella, Donald. *Ralph Waldo Emerson*, 76-77. Boston: Twayne, 1982.
This is a turning point in Emerson's development as a poet and in his understanding of man's relationship to nature. The conventional meter, structure,
and rhyming enclose commonplace yet evocative images through which the
theme of interdependence is expressed. Beyond the appeal to reason is the
appeal to direct sensory knowledge or intuition. One can feel the perfect whole
that overrides the varied array of sounds and sights. Emerson notes how the
beauty of natural objects is lost when they are removed from their proper
settings.

"Hamatreya"

Petry, Alice Hall. "The Meeting of the Twain: Emerson's 'Hamatreya.' " *English
Language Notes* 23 (March, 1986): 47- 51.
After reviewing the history of conjecture about the poem's title, Petry supports
the view offered by Richard Bridgman that Emerson's coinage derives from
Greek and means something like "Earth-Mother." She argues that the word
also alludes to "hamartia" as formulated by Aristotle in his discussion of
tragedy. The poem refers to the proud Yankee landlords, suggesting that they
will come to grief.

Waggoner, Hyatt H. *Emerson As Poet*, 146-155. Cambridge, Mass.: Harvard University Press, 1974.

While addressing Concord's history, Emerson insists on "the necessary humbling" that must "precede any valid affirmation." Waggoner elaborates Emerson's relationship to Concord as a basis for exploring the poem's mixed feelings toward the past that the town represents. Part of Emerson's achievement is to make vivid the lives of the founders—people whose strength was genuine, but whose vision became materialistic. Emerson both uses and breaks from traditional verse forms for thematic purposes.

"Ode Inscribed to W. H. Channing"

Gougeon, Len. "The Anti-Slavery Background of Emerson's 'Ode Inscribed to W. H. Channing.' " *Studies in the American Renaissance* (1985): 63-77.

Argues that the poem "was written in response to the funeral of the abolitionist Charles Turner Torrey, which Emerson attended." His interest in Torrey (who died in prison while serving a term for helping escaping slaves) "was a reflection of his growing interest in abolitionist activities in general and also his own desire to bring the populace to a higher degree of moral awareness." At the same time, Emerson feared the extreme abolitionist movement toward disunion. Virtuous men like Channing could further social improvement and cultural advance without disruption.

"The Rhodora"

Matthiessen, F. O. "From Emerson to Thoreau." In his *American Renaissance*, 48-50. New York: Oxford University Press, 1941.

This early success is, like Bryant's "To a Waterfowl," more indebted to an inherited eighteenth century formalism than Emerson knew. Emerson's genuine delight in beholding natural forms and his affection for native New England details is barely able to break through the stiff rhetorical manner. He worked to make the poem's sentiment pervade the whole rather than be preached on top of the descriptive material. "The beauty that is its own excuse is Puritan in its simplicity and bareness, Yankee in its insistence on fitness and utility."

Yoder, R. A. *Emerson and the Orphic Poet in America*, 79-86. Berkeley: University of California Press, 1978.

The first part "portrays the rhodora as a humble, self-sacrificing flower which, though equal to the celebrated rose, prefers obscure service to worldly fame." The second part identifies the speaker with the Christian values implicit in part 1. The sages, look for value in a narrow, self-seeking way, are shut out. This is one of Emerson's many poems in binary form: First a situation is presented with a real or implied question; then an answer is given—abruptly and without argument.

HENRY WADSWORTH LONGFELLOW
(1807-1882)

General Studies

Allen, Gay Wilson. "Henry Wadsworth Longfellow." In his *American Prosody*. New York: American Book, 1935.
Longfellow was less a theorist and analyst, more a skilled "adapter and appreciator." As a translator from twelve languages, Longfellow gained a practical knowledge of the versification of major world poets. He was a practitioner of the ballad stanza, a lavish employer of anapestic rhythms, and a competent sonneteer. He did major work in trochaic meters as well as in blank verse and hexameter lines. His poetry is more noteworthy for its remarkable range than for innovation. Much of his versification was influenced by German, Italian, and Norse models.

Arms, George. "Longfellow." In his *The Fields Were Green*. Stanford, Calif.: Stanford University Press, 1953.
Longfellow's work is "fully pledged . . . in the interest of morality." To recognize and praise the handful of nondidactic works is to miss what's central to this artist. Many of his poems follow a three-stage pattern that begins with a scene or image, develops through an analogy to the human condition, and concludes with an assertion. When his method is muted, his success is usually greatest. His sonnets often lack, to their advantage, the moralizing third stage. Arms does not treat the long narratives.

Arvin, Newton. *Longfellow: His Life and Work*. Boston: Little, Brown, 1963.
Sees Longfellow as a genial personality, a splendid indicator of the literary climate, but not a poet of the first rank. Arvin examines Longfellow's commitment to the study of languages and the impact of these studies on his work; he was a humane generalist, not a narrow specialist. Longfellow excels in expressing the softer emotions: Melancholy rather than terror dominates his poems of the night. His bloated reputation made him a severe casualty in the twentieth century, when his virtues of directness and simplicity were not valued highly.

Austin, George Lowell. *Henry Wadsworth Longfellow: His Life, His Works, His Friendships*. Boston: Lee and Shepard, 1888.
This early biography aims at "a clear but popular picture of the poet's literary life." Thus, there are few personal or family details and much that has to do with Longfellow's academic and literary careers. The second half of the book details the genesis, sources, and development of Longfellow's major works. Austin records contemporary reactions to these poems as he paints the poet's

growing commercial success and widespread fame. Treats Longfellow as a literary statesman.

Cameron, Kenneth Walter, ed. *Longfellow Among His Contemporaries*. Hartford, Conn.: Transcendental Books, 1978.
This collection supports Cameron's claim that in his own day Longfellow "received more estimable and valid criticism than any New England contemporary except Emerson." The response to his writings was international: "Europe recognized him as the first significant poet of the new world." There is no table of contents for the hundreds of pages of magazine and newspaper comment reproduced here, but an index helps students find authors and subjects.

Franklin, Phyllis. "The Importance of Time in Longfellow's Works." In *Henry Wadsworth Longfellow Reconsidered: A Symposium*, edited by J. Chesley Mathews. Hartford, Conn.: Transcendental Books, 1970.
Longfellow's concept of time is assumed rather than articulated in his poetry, giving his work a special flavor. He believed that history was progressive and that each individual could develop in time. He felt that the improved quality of religious belief furthered this progress. Longfellow sensed the continuity of human life, the ways in which the past lived in the present and the present in the future. His own work was a contribution to this progressive notion.

Gorman, Herbert S. *A Victorian American: Henry Wadsworth Longfellow*. Reprint. Port Washington, N.Y.: Kennikat Press, 1967.
First published in 1926, this study credits Longfellow with being "the first figure in American letters to discover Europe as a rich mine," prefiguring Henry James in some ways. Although Longfellow had something of the American common touch, he is best envisioned as "our great Victorian." Gorman demonstrates the need for and power of Longfellow's Victorian manner in American literary culture. Longfellow was much like Queen Victoria herself in his attitudes toward the proper conduct of life. Little critical comment. Illustrated.

Hatfield, James Taft. *New Light on Longfellow*. Boston: Houghton Mifflin, 1933.
One of the first scholarly studies to go beyond the materials made available in Samuel Longfellow's *Life of Henry Wadsworth Longfellow*. Hatfield's researches led him to a high estimate of Longfellow's intellectual and artistic achievement. He pays particular attention to the poet's relations to Germany, arguing that his translations and other efforts strengthened ties between the two countries. Stresses Longfellow's immense industry, sympathetic spirit, and intense patriotism.

Hawthorne, Hildegarde. *The Poet of Craigie House: The Story of Henry Wadsworth Longfellow*. New York: D. Appleton-Century, 1936.

A popular, novelistic treatment of Longfellow as an adventurous eminence. Hawthorne presents purported conversations at length. This practice and other scholarly lapses or liberties give flavor to this somewhat juvenile treatment. The theme is how fully Longfellow lived his long life and how successfully he managed his twin careers of literary artist and academic. The chapters are short, dramatic, and easily digestible. No documentation.

Helmick, Evelyn Thomas. "Longfellow's Lyric Poetry." In *Henry Wadsworth Longfellow Reconsidered: A Symposium*, edited by J. Chesley Mathews. Hartford, Conn.: Transcendental Books, 1970.
Longfellow's lyrics had a conscious social purpose. The symbolic relationship between poetry and the image of the bell clarifies Longfellow's concern. In his works, the bell functions as a tool of announcement—a rallying of the public. Poetry as bell performs the same social function. The bell-like clarity and simplicity of Longfellow's verse assures communication. The symbol of the ship has similar implications. Longfellow saw his poetry as having a public function, not an escapist one.

Higginson, Thomas Wentworth. *Henry Wadsworth Longfellow*. Boston: Houghton Mifflin, 1902.
Draws upon more sources than Samuel Longfellow's biography, especially those materials that reveal the poet's scholarly enterprises as catalysts and sources for his major creative works. A chapter on "Longfellow the Poet" admires the elevated tone and the common touch that made Longfellow beloved by the nation's readers. Longfellow's contribution "to a new and unformed literature was priceless." He can be read "for invigoration, for comfort, for content."

Hilen, Andrew. *Longfellow and Scandinavia*. New Haven, Conn.: Yale University Press, 1947.
Examines the poet's relationship with Scandinavian languages and literature both as a scholar and as a creative artist. Follows Longfellow's travels in Sweden and Denmark, his studies of those languages as well as Icelandic, and his relationship with the Swedish romantic writer, Esaias Tegner. After a while, Longfellow's romantic interest in the Scandinavian materials as a source for the remote and the unfamiliar replaced his original scholarly interest. Appendices of journals, letters, and books relating to the Scandinavian experience.

Hirsh, Edward L. *Henry Wadsworth Longfellow*. Minneapolis: University of Minnesota Press, 1964.
Longfellow's poetry was only indirectly responsive to the history of his own

time. Though exceptions exist, "events and causes served as catalysts rather than as subject matter or primary topics of the verse." Longfellow asserted over and over again the values of Western culture as he inherited them in his youth and early adulthood. He participated in the search for a usable past. Hirsh's pamphlet gives a reliable overview of the life, career, and literary merits of his subject.

Kreymborg, Alfred. "The Fallen Prince of Popularity." In his *Our Singing Strength: An Outline of American Poetry (1620-1930)*. New York: Coward-McCann, 1929.
An engaging discussion of how the ingredients of Longfellow's enormous popularity were the same ones that led to his fall. As a poet of the people, Longfellow left unexplored those areas of experience and art that later generations of critics would encourage and esteem. Kreymborg provides brief assessments of individual poems, including some not usually addressed. Longfellow remains a poet of utmost historical importance. His restraint, his sense of decorum, kept him from letting go in a way that would lead to greatness.

Long, Orie William. "Henry Wadsworth Longfellow." In his *Literary Pioneers: Early American Explorers of European Culture*. Reprint. New York: Russell & Russell, 1963.
First published in 1935, this is a detailed consideration of Longfellow's preparation for the role of interpreter and popularizer of European culture. Examines Longfellow's studies, travels, and university teaching as well as his labors as translator and adaptor. Stresses Longfellow's role in making American readers cognizant of German literature, particularly the work of Goethe. Discusses Longfellow's anthology, *Poets and Poetry of Europe* (1845).

Longfellow, Samuel. *Life of Henry Wadsworth Longfellow*. 3 vols. Reprint. New York: Greenwood Press, 1969.
First published shortly after Longfellow's death, this is an overly flattering portrait by the poet's younger brother based on extensive use of journals and correspondence. Indeed, this life is largely an assemblage of documents with connecting narrative links—but the documents themselves are important. Longfellow's travels are presented at length; the reader sees him absorbing the experiences that would be turned to use in his scholarship, translations, and poetry.

Mathews, J. Chesley, ed. *Henry Wadsworth Longfellow Reconsidered: A Symposium*. Hartford, Conn.: Transcendental Books, 1970.
A wide variety of approaches to Longfellow's life and work is represented here. Some of the concerns are "Longfellow and Music," "Longfellow's Studies in France," "Longfellow and Howells," "Longfellow's Houses," and "The

Influence of Vico Upon Longfellow." A few selections focus on the poetry. See
Franklin and Helmick, above.

More, Paul Elmer. *Paul Elmer More's Sherburne Essays on American Literature*.
Edited by Daniel Aaron. New York: Harcourt, Brace & World, 1963.
The poet's enormous popularity is in contrast to "the hesitation of his critics"
who find "dulled echoes of fine music" in his work. More presents samples of
such parallels between Longfellow and other poets. Longfellow works on a
less precise, less distinctive plane of imagery, seeming to present only smooth
commonplaces. Many of his poems transcend this level, gripping and holding
the reader's attention. Sentimental appeal and evocation of mood through
nature description are his strengths. His best work reveals "an artist of rare
tact and power."

Nemerov, Howard. "On Longfellow." In *American Poetry to 1914*, edited by Harold
Bloom. New York: Chelsea House, 1987.
Longfellow's fall from esteem followed the post-Victorian separation of popular poetry from good poetry. Longfellow was a good minor poet who aspired
to become a major one and thought he made it. He worked less on his craft
than on poetic projects that seemed to guarantee renown. He tried things he
had little talent for and too often settled for beautiful gestures and grandiose
sweep rather than "seeking patiently the truth of the matter at hand." A revised
canon can make Longfellow readable to the modern audience.

Pearce, Roy Harvey. "Longfellow." In his *The Continuity of American Poetry*.
Princeton, N.J.: Princeton University Press, 1961.
Longfellow failed to see that the universals he was after could only be reached
through rigorous attention to the particulars. The technical dexterity of his
verse invites readers to ignore his tendency to oversimplify experience. Because his poetry flatters his readers, it fails to challenge them. It is a poetry of
reassurance in which "the function of the teacher is overborne by the function
of the father." His role as a conduit of other literatures resulted in the dimin-
ishment of the originals.

Pritchard, John Paul. "The Horatian Influence Upon Longfellow." *American Literature* 4 (March, 1932): 22-38.
Pritchard is concerned less with formal issues than with ideas. References to
and quotations from Horace in Longfellow's work are not plentiful, but parallels in outlook are abundant. "Three of Horace's odes express ideas which
deeply impressed Longfellow." Most prominent is the "belief in the value of
the present, and lack of fretting about the future" that Longfellow expressed in
"Psalm of Life." Longfellow's attitudes toward the "choice of subject and
selection of material" also resemble those of Horace.

Shepherd, Odell. "The New England Triumvirate: Longfellow, Holmes, and Lowell." In *Literary History of the United States*, edited by Robert E. Spiller et al. 3d ed., rev. New York: Macmillan, 1963.
The Boston area had a fertile sense of community and culture in the 1830's. Each writer reconciled "the conflicting demands laid upon the scholar, the creative writer, and the gentleman." Each knew the audience well. Longfellow "was not a poet by compulsion," but still became our "first professional poet." Holmes was at once "the man of wit, the man of imagination, and the man of science." Lowell's life work shows less coherence; he was an intellectual and artistic vagabond.

Smeaton, Oliphant. *Longfellow and His Poetry*. Reprint. New York: AMS Press, 1971.
An introduction for younger students, this slim book, first published in 1913, puts the poems in the contexts that gave rise to them. This unabashed exercise in biographical criticism fits Longfellow into his times, examining his dual interest in the European literary heritage and in America's need for a sense of itself. Longfellow's life and personality are illustrated by long passages and sometimes entire poems. Smeaton considers Longfellow's translation of Dante as a key to the refined linguistic power of the later occasional poems.

Thompson, Lawrance. *Young Longfellow*. New York: Macmillan, 1938.
A detailed biography of the young man who would later become the white-bearded symbol of American poetry. Thompson argues against the tradition that Longfellow's path to prominence was smooth. He records false starts, hindrances, and delays. Longfellow's development grew out of an "inner struggle between his inherited Yankee opportunism and his dominantly romantic attitude." Only in his mid-thirties did Longfellow begin to find the direction that would bring him fulfillment and success. Examines the poet-scholar dichotomy.

Wagenknecht, Edward. *Henry Wadsworth Longfellow: His Poetry and Prose*. New York: Ungar, 1986.
One of the very few book-length critical studies of Longfellow, this accessible treatment gives a chapter each to his life, his poetic theory and practice, and his prose. The next six chapters explore individual poems in detail, while two more assess Longfellow's personality and his attempts as a dramatist. Longfellow's pursuit of the large audience led him to a conscious rejection of poetry that required a sophisticated response. He aimed to educate and inspire, yet he believed that poetry itself required inspiration and should not be prescriptive.

_____ . *Henry Wadsworth Longfellow: Portrait of an American Humanist*. New York: Oxford University Press, 1966.

A rewriting and expansion of Wagenknecht's earlier *Longfellow: A Full-Length Portrait* (1955), incorporating an additional decade of opinion and discoveries. Relates Longfellow's personality traits to the kind of poetry he wrote both in terms of subject matter and technique. "Essentially, Longfellow's was a devotional spirit, and it fed on what it looked upon." Longfellow searched for ways to formulate general rather than specific truths.

Waggoner, Hyatt. H. "Henry Wadsworth Longfellow." In his *American Poets from the Puritans to the Present*. Boston: Houghton Mifflin, 1968.
"Longfellow had just one thing to say, and he tried as best he could to deny it: that time is inherently and inevitably man's enemy, bringing only loss and nothingness." Longfellow's optimistic poems shout too insistently to cover his essential cheerlessness. His simplest, most personal lyrics are his best work. The long narratives lack suggestiveness: there is nothing beyond their literal meanings. His work suffers from a "lack of intelligence."

Williams, Cecil B. *Henry Wadsworth Longfellow*. New York: Twayne, 1964.
Gives considerable attention to Longfellow's academic career in order to trace the relationship between this occupation and the poetry. Williams distinguishes two major modes—the lyric and the narrative—within which Longfellow practiced a wide range of types. Longfellow's natural ease made him too little attentive to the fine points of technique. Provides plot summaries and assessments of the major poems. Longfellow's place in American literary culture was that of a transmitter.

"The Bells of San Blas"

Arvin, Newton. *Longfellow: His Life and Work*, 316-317. Boston: Little, Brown, 1963.
Longfellow based this poem on an article about a Mexican village by W. H. Bishop that appeared in *Harper's*. Bishop described the empty belfry and the crude wooden frame in which the bells had been relocated. A sketch accompanied the description. The reduced situation of the bells was used by Longfellow to represent "the whole grandeur of a proud and powerful past, both in the state and in the realm of faith—a past that one can only look back upon with reverence but that it is folly to attempt to revive." The poem may carry a premonition of Longfellow's own death.

Williams, Cecil B. *Henry Wadsworth Longfellow*, 137-138. New York: Twayne, 1964.
This poem, written only two weeks before Longfellow's death, is one of his finest lyrics. It is in the Victorian tradition of such works as Matthew Arnold's "Dover Beach" in lamenting the passing of an age of religious faith. However,

while Arnold's spokesman seems personally overwhelmed by these changes, Longfellow's speaker maintains "an unshaken and confident personal faith." If Longfellow had written only the short lyrics of which this is an example, he would still be considered a significant nineteenth century American poet.

The Courtship of Miles Standish

Arvin, Newton. *Longfellow: His Life and Work*, 173-180. Boston: Little, Brown, 1963.
Here, Longfellow sees the Indians through the eyes of the Puritans, "with a certain harshness of realism." There is less idealization than in his other long narratives. Nevertheless, the focus in on simplicity of manners and youthful innocence. This "pastoral" is a "quiet domestic comedy" into which a few grim moments intrude. The relaxed versification still has an edge. The Puritan spirit is supplied in the characterizations, the austere landscape, and the scriptural language and imagery.

Tucker, Edward L. "Longfellow's *The Courtship of Miles Standish*: Some Notes and Two Early Versions." *Studies in the American Renaissance* (1985): 285-321.
Tucker first reviews the history that lies behind this narrative and its companion piece, a play called *John Endicott*. Lying behind the poem are two earlier versions. The first is a play with the same name; the second is a poem entitled *Priscilla*. Students can see the creative process in action by studying the relationship between these earlier versions, printed here for the first time, and the final poem. Tucker provides a summary and sampling of contemporary reaction.

Williams, Cecil B. *Henry Wadsworth Longfellow*, 164-168. New York: Twayne, 1964.
Longfellow's notes show him developing materials for this "Puritan pastoral" based on a love story of his own ancestors. Longfellow's treatment of a romantic triangle in the early day's of Plymouth's pilgrim colony is "one of his most perfectly realized poems." His version of this story has lodged it permanently in the cultural heritage of America. This was Longfellow's goal and his achievement. Williams summarizes the plot and remarks on the characterizations of Standish, John Alden, and Priscilla Mullins.

Evangeline

Hawthorne, Manning, and Henry Wadsworth Longfellow Dana. *The Origin and Development of Longfellow's "Evangeline."* Portland, Maine: The Anthoensen Press, 1947. Reprinted from *The Papers of the Bibliographical Society of America* 41 (1947).
Reviews the contemporary accounts of the expulsion of the Acadians from

Nova Scotia as well as the historical treatments of this event published up until the time Longfellow began working on the subject. Discusses Nathaniel Hawthorne's role in encouraging Longfellow in this project. Briefly examines the various manuscript stages of the work, touches upon the theme of exile, and notes where Longfellow drew place descriptions from his own travels. Assesses influence of the poem.

Seelye, John. " 'Attic Shape': Dusting Off *Evangeline.*" *Virginia Quarterly Review* 60 (Winter, 1984): 21-44.
Explores Longfellow's mood at the time of writing as well as the catalysts and sources for the work. "Longfellow's West is a wilderness sanctuary and preserve sacred to the national memory, a territory of the mind through which a great river flows, an American Alph emblematic of the national imagination and darkly prophetic of the national fate." Longfellow's conventional narrative is rendered as a series of disconnected segments.

Wagenknecht, Edward. "*Evangeline.*" In his *Henry Wadsworth Longfellow: His Poetry and Prose*. New York: Ungar, 1986.
The first long poem in American literature to live beyond its own time. The plot is skeletal in terms of significant event, but Longfellow builds up his material by expansions in time and space. By widening the scope of Evangeline's travels, he prolongs her search and thus increases the test of her faith. He also gives himself additional descriptive possibilities. The idealization of the characters is their charm, a charm broken by any of the tests of realism.

Williams, Cecil B. *Henry Wadsworth Longfellow*, 148-156. New York: Twayne, 1964.
Longfellow drew materials from a number of printed sources and from the diorama of the Mississippi River painted by John Banvard. His descriptions of Nova Scotia may derive from boyhood memories of Maine and from places he visited in the Swedish countryside. Longfellow's success lies in his delicate portrayal of the central character's "embodiment of steadfast human love," his description of scenery, and "the sheer musical charm" of the dactylic hexameter line. His dramatization of events in the Acadian settlement in Louisiana is particularly effective.

"The Jewish Cemetery at Newport"

Arvin, Newton. *Longfellow: His Life and Work*, 187-188. Boston: Little, Brown, 1963.
Longfellow meditates upon the disused synagogue, using it as "a focusing symbol for the long tragedy of the Jewish people, summoning up a whole

cluster of grave, stately, and mournful associations—of ancient greatness, of exile, of persecution—and evoking an emotion of controlled and impersonal sadness." He plays on the nature of Hebraic writing by observing how "human history is now spelled backwards by the Jews." This poem is in Longfellow's Coleridgian manner, in which he proceeds by building associations around a particular image.

Wagenknecht, Edward. *Henry Wadsworth Longfellow: His Poetry and Prose*, 131-132. New York: Ungar, 1986.

The poem denounces anti-Semitism, showing Longfellow in agreement with the view that the Christian world owes a large debt of gratitude to the Jewish people. Emma Lazarus objected to what she felt was an unfortunate assumption in the poem: that Judaism had no future. This implication grew from the fact that in Longfellow's time the synagogue that adjoined the cemetery was inactive. Longfellow's churchyard poems have no connection with the "graveyard school" of poetry which was then still popular.

"A Psalm of Life"

Hovey, Kenneth. " 'A Psalm of Life' Reconsidered: The Dialogue of Western Literature and Monologue of Young American." *ATQ*, n.s., 1 (March, 1987): 3-19.

This seemingly simple and universally known poem is not so simple or clear to anyone who reads it carefully. "It is at once both monologue and dialogue, for the sole speaker . . . is clearly engaged in an argument with someone else. The speaker is trying to restore the vital spark that Western civilization has lost. In preaching the active spirit, Longfellow confected a conflict "between the morbid mind and the young heart" that runs through all his work. Longfellow's poem reveals America's youth, but implies that it is time to grow up.

Wagenknecht, Edward. *Henry Wadsworth Longfellow: His Poetry and Prose*, 62-63. New York: Ungar, 1986.

Judges this to be one of Longfellow's poorest poems; "nothing has harmed his reputation more than its inclusion in every selection from his work." Figures of speech are illogically wrought: "cattle do not participate in battles, nor are battles fought in bivouacs." One cannot leave footprints in the sands of time unless one lives in an hourglass or stops the waves from lapping the shore. Nevertheless, this is a poem of incomparable popularity and influence—a celebration of heroic striving through life's unending difficulties.

Williams, Cecil B. *Henry Wadsworth Longfellow*, 132-133. New York: Twayne, 1964.

Suggests that this early poem, enormously popular in its own day but cruelly parodied by later critics, "reflects a harassed and lovelorn young professor's reaction to Goethe." Intended as the first in a series of psalms, it was not followed by any that bear similar titles—though others are clearly related in spirit. Problems of sentimentality and clashing imagery are at odds with the poem's obvious hold over naive readers. Are the poem's expressions commonplace, or has the power of the poem made them seem so?

The Song of Hiawatha

Arvin, Newton. *Longfellow: His Life and Work*, 154-173. Boston: Little, Brown, 1963.
One of the earliest works to represent the American Indians' own mythology rather than to change them into mythical figures. Influenced by the Finnish epic *Kalevala*, Longfellow linked a series of folktales, unifying them through association with a single hero. In the character of Hiawatha, Longfellow invented the "Gentle Savage," a valuable corrective to existing literary portraits. The poem succeeds in conveying primitive man's sense of intimacy with his surroundings. The poem's symbolism is immediately transparent and without resonance. The pronounced meter never really drowns the poem and often energizes it.

Keiser, Albert D. "Hiawatha—The Dawn of Culture." In his *The Indian in American Literature*. New York: Oxford University Press, 1933.
A detailed study of the sources out of which Longfellow fashioned "whatever is poetic and appealing in the primitive man of America." Presents the mixed opinions upon the poem's publication and since. For his positive version of the Indian hero, Longfellow eliminated such elements found in his sources as the "trickster." In spite of many historical inaccuracies, the poem's inspiring vision has appealed to countless readers. The poem is more palatable to a child's taste than to an adult's. Keiser reviews Indian references in Longfellow's other poems.

Osborn, Charles S., and Stellanova Osborn. *Schoolcraft, Longfellow, Hiawatha*. Lancaster, Pa.: Jacques Cattell Press, 1942.
Employs the controversies over Longfellow's use of his sources to bring renewed interest to Henry Rowe Schoolcraft and his contribution to American Indian studies. The authors review and resolve the plagiarism issue, along the way providing an enormous amount of opinion and background material for the study of Longfellow's poem. Longfellow's sources are reproduced. A biographical sketch of Schoolcraft included.

Wagenknecht, Edward. "*The Song of Hiawatha*." In his *Henry Wadsworth Longfellow: His Poetry and Prose*. New York: Ungar, 1986.
Shows how Longfellow borrowed certain epic conventions, including the supernatural origin of the hero's forebears and the devices of enumeration and

repetition. However, Hiawatha is not the founder of a new nation, but the last great representative of one soon to be replaced. Longfellow's heroic Indian is subject to domestic emotions and is otherwise representative more of European Romantic notions than of Indian values and experience. Such observations, however, are not the true tests of art: Shakespeare's Romans are really Renaissance Englishmen.

JOHN GREENLEAF WHITTIER
(1807-1892)

General Studies

Arms, George. "Whittier." In his *The Fields Were Green*. Stanford, Calif.: Stanford University Press, 1953.
   The traditional division of Whittier's poems into the legendary, antislavery, personal, and religious is somewhat misleading. All of the poems are personal, and many "transform into personal reminiscence even matter that is remote." Whittier is not confessional or intimately personal, yet in his best work he makes "his material relevant to himself." He has a workmanlike control of technique that is most admirable in poems that have the least emotional impact.

Bennett, Whitman. *Whittier: Bard of Freedom*. Reprint. Port Washington, N.Y.: Kennikat Press, 1972.
   Considers Whittier to be "the most effective literary man in direct personal influence on our political and social system" that the United States ever produced. Bennett describes how Whittier made himself into a poet and pays particular attention to the antislavery poems. He also gives detailed discussions of the poems of legend, of "Snow-Bound," and of the late devotional verses. Suggests that Whittier's burst of creativity while in his sixties is unparalleled among American poets. Appendices present new source materials. First published in 1941.

Kribbs, Jayne K., ed. *Critical Essays on John Greenleaf Whittier*. Boston: G. K. Hall, 1970.
   A balanced survey of the early reviews as well as later estimates of Whittier's work. Kribbs's introduction provides a succinct, engaging overview of the problems presented in Whittier studies. Whittier's stock, she argues, is slowly rising, but he will undoubtedly continue to be seen as a "major minor" poet, a representative figure rather than a great one. The essays consider Whittier's station as a historical personage as much as they explore his writing. There are only a few explications among these discussions.

Leary, Lewis. *John Greenleaf Whittier*. New York: Twayne, 1961.
   Reviewing the details of Whittier's literary career in a direct, accessible manner, Leary relates Whittier's expression of his own limitations as a poet and also of his aspirations. Whittier wrote for an unsophisticated audience. He did not aim at immortality. Self-taught, he often found himself stirred by emotional promptings that he had no means to express. He aimed at a vivid but

uncomplicated rendering of the commonplace. His love of nature's beauty rubbed against his ascetic Quaker upbringing. Whittier often used verse for moral and political persuasion, focusing on immediate issues instead of abstract ideals.

Lewis, Georgina King. *John Greenleaf Whittier: His Life and Work*. London: Headley Brothers, 1913.
A short life of Whittier based on existing publications rather than new research. Written for an English audience, Lewis' book introduces the man, his poetic accomplishments, and especially his manner of handling difficulties, with enthusiastic admiration. The poems are used extensively as biographical tools and as indicators of Whittier's principles. The wholeness of Whittier, the integration of his various careers, is described convincingly.

Mordell, Albert. *Quaker Militant: John Greenleaf Whittier*. Reprint. Port Washington, N.Y.: Kennikat Press, 1969.
Rejecting the traditional image of Whittier as a "modest, mild, and passionless saint," Mordell argues that the poet was in fact a "militant and radical agitator." "The legend of his utter innocuousness" masks the true zeal of the man and much of his writing: He is closer to being our Milton than our Burns. Whittier is here viewed primarily as a poet, but also from sociological and psychological perspectives. Mordell explores at length Whittier's role as a "male coquet," attracting women but remaining celibate. Detailed chronology and bibliography. Separate chapter on "The Poet." First published in 1933.

More, Paul Elmer. "Whittier the Poet." In *Paul Elmer More's Shelburne Essays on American Literature*, edited by Daniel Aaron. New York: Harcourt, Brace & World, 1963.
An enthusiastic overview of Whittier's exemplary life and his poetic focus on the ideal of the home. Whittier's middle-class outlook, his veneration of the family and its dwelling place, single him out in our literature. Whittier's lack of pretension is his virtue. Even his religious verse has a domestic flavor, as if heaven was a memory of home. He creates "domiciles of the spirit." "The Pennsylvania Pilgrim" is offered as Whittier's best work, as the poet himself believed.

Murray, Augustus T. "The Religious Faith of Whittier: An Interpretation." In his *Religious Poems of John Greenleaf Whittier*. Philadelphia: Friends's Book Store, 1934.
One of a number of publications sponsored by the Quakers to help immortalize their foremost poet, this selection of his poems is introduced by an essay on his religious thought. Whittier's blend of orthodoxy and common sense, moral outrage and serene faith, makes him an appealing figure. His religious

views stress deeds above articles of faith. Whittier's attitudes toward the doctrines of incarnation, atonement, and revelation are explored. He sees the Bible as only one of the ways through which God speaks to man.

Oster, Harry. "Whittier's Use of the 'Sage' in His Ballads." In *Studies in American Literature*, edited by Waldo McNeir and Leo B. Lévy. Baton Rouge: Louisiana State University Press, 1960.
Most of Whittier's poems based on folklore incorporate the story type folklorists call the *sage*, a type characterized by marvelous encounters or happenings. Some versions of this genre come from Whittier's favorite source: Cotton Mather's *Magnalia Christi Americana*. Oster reviews instances of such storytelling in a number of poems and connects it to the figure of the prophetic witch. References to "Skipper Ireson's Ride" and "Barbara Frietchie."

Pickard, John B. *John Greenleaf Whittier: An Introduction and Interpretation*. New York: Holt, Rinehart and Winston, 1966.
A compact appreciation of Whittier's life and works that treats the poems in four overlapping categories: the ballads, genre poetry, nature poems, and religious lyrics. Examines Whittier's attempt to capture and extend the range of native American folklore and legend. A local colorist, Whittier worked best with the setting and beliefs of his Essex region of New England. In his own day, his religious lyrics were more widely read than his other poems. Whittier is unique in his ability to re-create and preserve the patterns and texture of the past.

_____ . "Whittier's Abolitionist Poetry." In *Critical Essays on John Greenleaf Whittier*, edited by Jayne K. Kribbs. Boston: G. K. Hall, 1970.
Reviews the limitations and successes of the least critically acclaimed portion of Whittier's work. For more than thirty years, Whittier fired off poem after poem, disseminating his crusading message as widely as possible. The emotional appeal of these poems reached people who would not be moved by editorials or sermons. The religious tone and force of the most successful "help purge their topical and journalistic nature." Whittier's allusions to biblical prophecy are examined, particularly the title allusion in "Ichabod."

Pollard, John A. *John Greenleaf Whittier: Friend of Man*. Boston: Houghton Mifflin, 1949.
This enthusiastic biography views Whittier primarily as a historical figure and a moral force. The poetry is one means to Whittier's broad humanitarian ends. Poems are examined as keys to Whittier's positions and as proofs of the intensity of his beliefs and his compassion. A chapter called "A Poet's Revisions" describes habits of composition. In many cases, the production of a poem was a "long agony" covering years or even decades. Whittier's doubts

made him scrupulous; his questionable ear made those scruples, in certain instances, ineffective.

Pray, Frances Mary. *A Study of Whittier's Apprenticeship As a Poet*. State College: Pennsylvania State College Press, 1930.
Focuses on poems written between 1825 and 1835 that were not selected for the first collected edition of Whittier's writings, issued in 1888-1889. Pray discusses these early poems under the headings "Poems Inspired by Reading," "Poems on Social and Political Questions," "Reflective Poems," "Love Poems," "Dialect and Humorous Poems," and poems of New England history or background. She emphasizes Whittier's lack of good literary models and his sensitive attempt to learn from the few examples available to him.

Schlaeder, Louis C. "Whittier's Attitude Toward Colonial Puritanism." *New England Quarterly* 21 (September, 1948): 350-367.
Traces the development of Whittier's outlook on the Puritans as it is illustrated in his poems and other writings. Whittier's first interest was in Puritan history and lore as literary matter. In the 1830's, his attitude became clearly critical, with Puritan bigotry becoming one of his targets. In "The Familist's Hymn," Whittier "turned all his hatred on the Puritans," especially the clergy. This harsh treatment is connected to local circumstances regarding Whittier's antislavery advocacy. In later years, his outrage softened.

Stevens, James Stacy. *Whittier's Use of the Bible*. Reprint. Folcroft, Pa.: Folcroft Library Editions, 1974.
Finds 816 passages that come from the King James version of the Bible. Whittier supports his concerns for abolishing slavery, for religions freedom, and for nature's beauty and grandeur through biblical allusion and quotation. Occasional comments accompany the listings, which follow the order of poems in the Houghton Mifflin edition. Originally published in 1930.

Wagenknecht, Edward. *John Greenleaf Whittier: A Portrait in Paradox*. New York: Oxford University Press, 1967.
Not a formal biography, but rather a personality study in which the poems and the available facts are allowed to interact. Seeks to explore the tensions in Whittier: the split between the artist and the social activist, the desire for personal fame and the sense of obligation to others, the strong attraction to women and the life of celibacy. Whittier's reading and his attitudes toward literature are examined closely, especially his admiration for Robert Burns. Wagenknecht makes constant reference to the poems, but provides no extended analyses.

Warren, Robert Penn. *John Greenleaf Whittier's Poetry*. Minneapolis: University of Minnesota Press, 1971.

This selection of Whittier's poems is introduced by Warren's "John Greenleaf Whittier: Poetry As Experience." Warren stresses Whittier's literary beginnings and the remarkable sophistication of a man usually thought of, patronizingly, as a peasant poet. Whittier's slow artistic growth was the result of conflicting demands he placed upon himself. "Ichabod," written when Whittier was forty-two, is called "his first really fine poem." Whittier's success came, in part, through repudiating the superficial 'poetical' notions of poetry and through writing from experience rather than from theories or models.

"Barbara Frietchie"

Bennett, Whitman. *Whittier: Bard of Freedom*, 270-272. Reprint. Port Washington, N.Y.: Kennikat Press, 1972.
    Whittier received the story in a letter from Mrs. Southworth, a popular sentimental novelist, who probably confused two stories she had heard. Whittier's rendering in thirty couplets is notable for its "extraordinary combination of brevity and completeness." The poem's dramatic structure heightens its effect. Comparing it to Tennyson's "Charge of the Light Brigade," Bennett feels Whittier's poem is "less artificial, more moving, and more completely rounded." Barbara Frietche's Union flag-waving in the midst of Confederate advances has entered the nation's mythology.

"Ichabod"

Warren, Robert Penn. *John Greenleaf Whittier's Poetry*, 25-29. Minneapolis: University of Minnesota Press, 1971.
    The poem's strength comes from subtlety of feeling and dramatization. The "tension between old trust and new disappointment, old admiration and new rejection, the past and the present" gives the poem a rich complexity. Rather than receiving outright condemnation, the target (Daniel Webster) is made an object of pity—an attitude even more humiliating to a prideful man. The title's allusion to I Samuel 4:21 is matched by a concluding reference to Genesis 9:20-25, in which Noah's sons cover their father's drunken nakedness while averting their eyes. Technically, this is among Whittier's most effectively controlled pieces. Also in Kribbs.

"Laus Deo"

Pickard, John B. *John Greenleaf Whittier: An Introduction and Interpretation*, 114-115. New York: Holt, Rinehart and Winston, 1966.

The poem is a response to the ringing of Amesbury's town bells announcing the passage of the amendment that abolished slavery. Whittier's meter and rhyme scheme reproduce the long, heavy peals of the bells along with the slight pauses between strokes. Whittier must remind himself to credit God, not man, with putting slavery to an end. The bells are likened to the thundering voice of God in the Old Testament, and the final stanzas paraphrase Miriam's song of triumph over the Egyptians.

"Skipper Ireson's Ride"

Arms, George. "Whittier." In his *The Fields Were Green*, 40-41. Stanford, Calif.: Stanford University Press, 1953.
This poem is characteristic of Whittier's structural control, blending details from his own boyhood with thematic materials addressing evil into a cohesive whole. The mob action against Ireson does not receive Whittier's approval. The poet mediates "between two forces of evil," allowing the action to control the poem in its early stages. At the end, Ireson's repentant confession and accompanying sense of self-punishment seem to beg for his liberation. Yet the refrain still speaks of his hard heart, leaving it difficult to render a simple judgment.

Pickard, John B. *John Greenleaf Whittier: An Introduction and Interpretation*, 69-73. New York: Holt, Rinehart and Winston, 1966.
Based on a well-known folk song, this poem was written over a thirty-year period. Whittier draws upon classical patterns and allusions to ridicule Ireson. By presenting the punishment before the reasons for it are given, Whittier creates suspense. The mixed mood of the poem reflects the genuine losses of the townspeople and their failure to balance those losses by punishing Ireson. Ireson's hate changes to remorse. The punishment he brings himself is greater than his humiliation by others. This poem succeeds in its structure, tone, and evocation of New England locale and psychology.

"Snowbound"

Arms, George. "Whittier." In his *The Fields Were Green*, 44-46. Stanford, Calif.: Stanford University Press, 1953.
Whittier here "reached for once on a large scale that harmony in art which he seems to have achieved during the greater part of his life only in spirit." The poem's appeal lies in its pastoralism during an age of rapid urbanization, but it also is an artistic success. "Beyond the realistic details but arising from them is a symbolic richness" that is centered on the hearth. Whittier's two family

guests and his antislavery passages are smoothly integrated into the whole. "The central intent of the poem is not to memorialize a way of life, but rather to memorialize life that is always lost to death."

Budick, E. Miller. "The Immortalizing Power of the Imagination: A Reading of Whittier's 'Snowbound.' " *ESQ* 31 (2nd Quarter, 1985): 89-99.
Examines how the poem works to reconcile Whittier's belief in immortality with the inevitability of death. Budick believes that "the poem identifies the imaginative faculty—the dreaming, remembering part of human consciousness—as a force that can counter the deimagizing threats of time and change." This lucid and persuasive analysis shows how continuity is expressed by "a circling succession of triumphs and failures" while the imagination moves from earthly engagements to spiritual ones.

Leary, Lewis. *John Greenleaf Whittier*, 157-165. New York: Twayne, 1961.
The poem sets the constants of the family household against the flux of time and the elements. It expresses mood and meaning through contrasts that include fire and snow, past and present, people and nature, inside and outside. The poem's effectiveness comes from Whittier's perfect integration of his materials into a firm three-part structure with further subdivisions and connecting interludes. The poem moves from a "mood of isolation" to a celebration of love and companionship to a portrait of the world's impingement on the solitude and stillness of the rural New England winter.

Pickard, John B. *John Greenleaf Whittier: An Introduction and Interpretation*, 90-99. New York: Holt, Rinehart and Winston, 1966.
"The crumbling of the once great logs hints of nature's eventual triumph over the family unit, while the ominous black watch, like a living spirit of darkness, also specifies that time has run out." The ashes that the uncle knocks from his pipe extend this pattern, and the versification that describes the uncle rhythmically captures his careful but awkward manner. Whittier uses the family unit to suggest the larger social union, the sense of community, that is threatened by but survives the elemental forces. Firewood is the poem's dominant symbol.

"Telling the Bees"

Leary, Lewis. *John Greenleaf Whittier*, 154-157. New York: Twayne, 1961.
One of Whittier's few successful poems written in the first person, it has "the simple directness characteristic of his best prose." The conversational quality and impressionistic description combine to place it among his highest achievements. The poem's carefully controlled tone, seemingly artless representation

of local custom, and lack of a forced moral all contribute to its powerful effect. The draping of the beehives in black signals a death in the family. The bees need to be told in this special way so that they won't swarm away from their hives to seek a new home.

EDGAR ALLAN POE
(1809-1849)

General Studies

Alexander, Jean, ed. and trans. *Affidavits of Genius: Edgar Allan Poe and the French Critics, 1847-1924*. Port Washington, N.Y.: Kennikat Press, 1971.
Traces, by presenting representative selections, the history of Poe's critical fortunes in France. Includes not only the expected Baudelaire, but also comments by E. D. Forgues, Armand de Pontmartin, Stephane Mallarmé, Paul Valery, and others. Alexander's three introductory essays synthesize the issues that lie behind Poe's enthusiastic reception among French poets and critics. He is viewed in his roles as "The Outlaw," "The American," and "The Poet."

Allen, Gay Wilson. "Edgar Allan Poe." In his *American Prosody*. New York: American Book, 1935.
Poe wrote nearly three times as many poems in four-stress couplets as he did in any other form. The range of his works in octosyllabic lines includes poems in which the stresses are regular and underscored by frequent alliteration and poems such as "To Helen" and "Israfel" in which no foot clearly prevails. The apparent eight- stress lines of "The Raven," so heavily divided by caesuras and internal rhymes, may be simply doubled versions of the characteristic four-stress couplet. Poe's sonic lavishness is discussed in detail.

Allen, Hervey. *Israfel: The Life and Times of Edgar Allan Poe*. Rev. one-volume ed. New York: Farrar & Rinehart, 1934.
Based on then-recently released primary materials, this biography, originally published in 1926 in two volumes, illuminated many mysteries of Poe's life for the first time. An early attempt to demythologize Poe without denying his extraordinary character. Sees Poe against the swirl of social change in the environments he moved through. Provides occasional interpretive comments on individual poems, more on process of composition and reception. Explores Poe's physical and mental condition. Illustrated. Appendices on ancestry and legal documents.

Asselineau, Roger. *Edgar Allan Poe*. Minneapolis: University of Minnesota Press, 1970.
An introductory pamphlet that examines the reasons for Poe being a controversial figure. Considers the "panic fear of death" as the primary spur to Poe's writing and the key to interpretation. The poems and stories reflect the fear of being engulfed by nothingness, of losing identity and control. The mixed forces of inspiration and rigorous application show the two sides of Poe: the

dreamer and the realist. Too often, signs of the intellect at work break the mood Poe tries to create.

Blasing, Mutlu Konuk. "Edgar Allan Poe, the Poet to a *T*." In her *American Poetry: The Rhetoric of Its Forms*. New Haven, Conn.: Yale University Press, 1987.
According to Blasing, Poe's "estrangement from both his English and American backgrounds . . . shapes his work." His "self-defeating formalism" is a consequence of recognizing the distance between vision and natural or poetic forms. Because Poe's paranoia is so great, everything he writes is reflexive— an allegory of its own making. Poe's figurative habits demonstrate "the triumph of the deadly letter over the life-giving spirit."

Bloom, Clive. *Reading Poe Reading Freud: The Romantic Imagination in Crisis*. London: Macmillan Press, 1988.
A meditation on the relationship between the texts of the master psychoanalyst and those of a poet who invites psychoanalytic examination. Poe's *Eureka* is explored as a source of parallels for many ideas found in Freud's writings. "While the central issue of Poe's reason has for many commentators become the essential way of reading Poe, the issue of Poe's 'sanity' becomes in my work the problem of reading itself." Filled with references to structuralist and post-structuralist theory, this study does not focus on the poems, but on the mind that created them.

Bonaparte, Marie. *The Life and Works of Edgar Allan Poe: A Psycho-Analytic Interpretation*. Translated by John Rodker. Reprint. New York: Humanities Press, 1971.
First published in 1949, this is a landmark work in psychoanalytic criticism, graced with a brief foreword by Sigmund Freud. Book 1 treats Poe's life and the poems; books 2 and 3 develop interpretive themes around "Tales of the Mother" and "Tales of the Father"; book 4 presents "Poe and the Human Soul." There is little extended analysis of individual poems, but general patterns are argued in which "the poet, disappointed in external love-objects and women, turned his libido narcissistically inwards" to "put himself and his creative faculty first." Stresses wish-fulfillment and the death wish in Poe's writings.

Booth, Bradford A., and Claude E. Jones. *A Concordance of the Poetical Works of Edgar Allan Poe*. Reprint. Gloucester, Mass.: Peter Smith, 1967.
This word inventory, the basis for any analysis of Poe's poetic diction, was compiled from Killis Campbell's edition of *The Poems of Edgar Allan Poe*. Each entry is followed by a contextual phrase (usage instance) and the work in which that phrase appears. Method of entries allows for making distinctions among variant texts. Indispensable for studies in style and imagery.

Braddy, Haldeen. *Three Dimensional Poe*. El Paso: Texas Western Press, 1973.
This introductory survey of Poe's life and career provides separate chapters on Poe's stories, poems, and essays. "Poems Carnal and Platonic" argues that physical love is only occasionally recognized in Poe's verse. Even the mention of anatomical detail is usually in the service of some transcendent vision. Poe developed a religion of love that connects him to the feminine vogue of his time. Argues that the "American Civilization" approach to Poe does little to enlighten us about him.

Broussard, Louis. *The Measure of Poe*. Norman: University of Oklahoma Press, 1969.
The first half of the book is a review of Poe criticism from 1845 to the mid-1960's. The second half is called " 'Eureka' and 'The Raven': A Study in Unity." This piece uses Poe's late theoretical essay to resolve the apparent meaninglessness of one of his best-known poems. The raven is a symbol of memory, and as such can only offer the message that what has been lost cannot be restored. Destruction is the theme of experience. All life is "matter destined for disintegration." This theme of reality's decay dominates Poe's later works. Often anthologized.

Buranelli, Vincent. *Edgar Allan Poe*. 2d ed. Boston: Twayne, 1977.
An introductory examination of the "complex personality" as it responds to the Romantic movement. Chapters called "Retreat for Reality" and "Return to Reality" convey the pathological and logical elements in Poe's writing. Poe's fiction and poetry are treated thematically and as extensions of theory. "Lyric Strains" has concise discussions of how Poe handles symbols and auditory devices. Argues that even Poe's "jingles" have depth.

Campbell, Killis. *The Mind of Poe and Other Studies*. Reprint. New York: Russell & Russell, 1962.
Seven essays that deal with early reactions to Poe's work, his controversy with Rufus Griswold, "The Poe Canon," Poe's education, his habitual reading, and his use of sources. A most useful essay explores the ways in which Poe draws upon his own experience and reveals himself in the poems and tales. First published in 1933.

Caputi, Anthony. "The Refrain in Poe's Poetry." *American Literature* 25 (May, 1953): 169-178.
Poe considered that the refrain had been used unimaginatively and monotonously by earlier poets. By varying the context in which the refrain appeared, Poe hoped to create an effect of varied emotional content. Poe used refrains more extensively in his later work. Caputi explores the kinds of variation, including ironic tonal shifts, that Poe achieves in "Eldorado," "The Raven,"

"The Bells," and other poems. He also discusses the related issue of incremental variation.

Carlson, Eric W., ed. *Critical Essays on Edgar Allan Poe*. Boston: G. K. Hall, 1987.
Selections are grouped into three categories: "Poe's Contemporaries," "Creative Writers on Poe," and "Modern Criticism." Carlson's introduction provides a succinct overview of Poe criticism, with especially useful comments on Poe's value to various critical schools. A small number of essays were specially prepared for this volume. More attention to the poetry and to the techniques Poe uses than is found in other essay collections.

Charvat, William. "Poe: Journalism and the Theory of Poetry." In *Aspects of American Poetry*, edited by Richard M. Ludwig. Columbus: Ohio State University Press, 1962.
Tries to answer the question of how Poe could have called his essay *Eureka* a prose poem. What conception of poetry could unite his lyrics and this work of exposition? Suggests that both present a private vision of the universe. The discussion involves the kind of unity that books have. *Eureka* is an assemblage, less like individual poems than a collection of poems. Also, Poe aspired to an elevated journalism unlike the ephemeral works that died after periodical publication.

Chase, Lewis. *Poe and His Poetry*. Reprint. New York: AMS Press, 1971.
First published in 1913, this study argues that the essential Poe is found in his poetry. Scans the outer and inner life of Poe by reference to the major poems, presenting them in full. There is little analytical comment here, but a juxtapositioning of the skeletal facts of Poe's life with poems that Chase claims have autobiographical value. The assumption is dubious.

Cody, Sherwin. *Poe—Man, Poet, and Creative Thinker*. Reprint. Port Washington, N.Y.: Kennicat Press, 1973.
A sympathetic treatment of Poe's life and work frames a generous selection of what Cody thinks are Poe's best efforts. Though this volume is essentially a collection of Poe's writings, Cody's "Biographical Study" and his introductions to various sections make many valuable points. Cody is most concerned with making a case for Poe as an original and disciplined thinker on literary and aesthetic issues. First published in 1924.

Dameron, J. Lasley, and Irby B. Cauthen, Jr. *Edgar Allan Poe: A Bibliography of Criticism, 1827-1967*. Charlottesville: University Press of Virginia, 1974.
A guide to scholarly and critical work organized alphabetically by author. One section lists English language commentary; the other lists materials in foreign languages. The index allows students to find listings for particular Poe titles

and subjects. Names of coauthors, editors, translators, and compilers are also indexed. The entries are briefly annotated. Especially good for locating articles in periodicals.

Davidson, Edward H. *Poe: A Critical Study*. Cambridge, Mass.: Harvard University Press, 1966.
A "philosophic inquiry" into Poe's mind and art that cuts across the poetry and the stories. Poe's works are grouped to reveal distinct stages both in Poe's development and in Davidson's theory. The problem of Poe turns on his appearance late in the Romantic period, when the force of that spirit was fading. Poe's work was not fashioned to reveal meanings in traditional ways. Both for Davidson and Poe, "Poetry is a form of philosophy," though not a discursive or direct form. "Poe's art was the spectrum of symbolic ir-resolution."

Ensley, Helen. "Metrical Ambiguity in the Poetry of Edgar Allan Poe." In *No Fairer Land: Studies in Southern Literature Before 1900*, edited by J. Lasley Dameron and James W. Matthews. Troy, N.Y.: Whitston, 1986.
Employs a method of scansion that distinguishes four degrees of stress and four degrees of juncture or separation to analyze three of Poe's lyrics. "Spirits of the Dead," "The Valley of Unrest," and "A Dream Within a Dream" are more characteristic of Poe's verse than the steady beat of "The Raven." In the chosen poems, Poe's metrical variety and ambiguity complement mood and theme by enacting indefiniteness, hesitancy, or otherwise correlating rhythm with other expressive concerns. Shifts in metrical patterns often correspond to changes described in the poems.

Fagin, N. Bryllion. *The Histrionic Mr. Poe*. Baltimore: Johns Hopkins University Press, 1949.
The theatrical quality of Poe's behavior is viewed as a key to his personality and art. Even Poe's suffering is in part a role through which "he achieves self-importance and exultation." Poe's words and gestures in life and in his poetry are understood as performances. Poe's dramatic skills are reviewed to support this thesis. The scenic elements, especially the lighting of scenes, have special dramatic effect in Poe's stories and poems.

Fletcher, Richard M. *The Stylistic Development of Edgar Allan Poe*. The Hague, Netherlands: Mouton, 1973.
Argues that Poe's manipulation of a stock vocabulary "acted like magic incantation in providing him with inspiration." Distinguishes a "mechanical vocabulary" that is a special version of the Gothic, an "inspiratory" vocabulary of mood- setting and unifying terms, and a "vocabulary of literary and classical allusions." Poe's juggling of this "stock" in seemingly endless variations hides, while it creates, the very narrow range of themes in his work.

Forrest, William Mentzel. *Biblical Allusions in Poe*. New York: Macmillan, 1928.
Forrest identifies quotations, allusions, scriptural proper names, and references to Christ in Poe's poetry. He also tries to assess Poe's knowledge of Hebrew. Issues such as spirituality, pantheism, mysticism, death and what lies beyond death, and Judgment Day receive attention. Forrest finds resemblances between Poe's poetic techniques and those found in the Bible. He is an admirer of Poe's technical skill.

Gale, Robert L. *Plots and Characters in the Fiction and Poetry of Edgar Allan Poe*. Hamden, Conn.: Archon Books, 1970.
A study guide comprising two alphabetical listings. The list of works includes brief summaries, some interpretive comment, and a list of characters. Poems and stories are listed together. The second list alphabetizes the names of the characters, locates each in the appropriate work, and provides a quick sketch. This guide is a good memory-jogger; also a basis for finding patterns in Poe's work.

Gelpi, Albert. "Edgar Allan Poe: The Hand of the Maker." In his *The Tenth Muse: The Psyche of the American Poet*. Cambridge, Mass.: Harvard University Press, 1975.
Poe's theory and poetry raise the question "at what point does self-expression become self-indulgence and 'soul-passion' become narcissism?" Poe's ideas "could only be perceived in perverse and neurotic terms." His genius was not able to soar into the empyrean; rather, his overreaching led him to plummet "into the maelstrom of the psyche, terrified and fascinated at his decent into the underworld." Poe is the true Apollonian in contrast to Dionysian Emerson.

Halliburton, David. *Edgar Allan Poe: A Phenomenological View*. Princeton, N.J.: Princeton University Press, 1973.
Connects Poe's thought to the philosophies of Leibniz, Pascal, and Schopenhauer as well as Sartre and Heidegger. Looks for the intention of the "text," not of the author. The finished works are phenomena in themselves, not just the successful results of the author's ambition. Useful antidote to Poe criticism based on biographical and psychological speculation. Phenomenology strives to dissolve the boundary between subject and object. Halliburton finds an overlooked affirmative strain in Poe.

Hammond, J. R. *An Edgar Allan Poe Companion*. Totowa, N.J.: Barnes & Noble, 1981.
The first part surveys Poe's life and literary reputation. Then comes "An Edgar Allan Poe Dictionary," really an alphabetical listing of all stories, essays, and poems that Poe collected into books along with the earlier periodical ap-

pearances. Separate chapters on stories, romances, essays, and poetry. Stresses Poe's quest for technical perfection, his early awareness of his strengths and weaknesses, and the autobiographical thread in his poems. "His was an original and disturbing voice."

Hoffman, Daniel. *Poe Poe Poe Poe Poe Poe Poe*. Garden City, N.Y.: Doubleday, 1972.
A highly personal series of responses to Poe's power over the reader's imagination and the sources of that power. Hoffman considers the different qualities of Poe's art that we respond to at different ages. Partly the autobiography of Hoffman reading Poe, the book explores Poe's "marriage group," his concern with the unearthly dimensions of existence, and the voyage motif. Delightfully urbane and conversational: "Poe's poems were efforts to crack the Ultimate Secret Code."

Humphries, Jefferson. *Metamorphosis of the Raven*. Baton Rouge: Louisiana State University Press, 1985.
A provocative, imaginative, abstruse study that employs the phenomenon of Poe and particularly "The Raven" to explain the "symbiosis between French and southern writers." Humphries traces historical affinities between France and the American South: humiliating military defeat and the consequent ethos of loss are significant factors. Poe's southernness and his own obsession with loss is a starting point for examining affinities in the twentieth century.

Hyslop, Lois, and Francis E. Hyslop, Jr., trans. and eds. *Baudelaire on Poe*. State College, Pa.: Bald Eagle Press, 1952.
Collects Baudelaire's writings on Poe. These essays, prefaces, and notes stress Poe's aims and methods, his neglect of Romantic subjects, his careful and utilitarian craft. Baudelaire "acts as Poe's apologist" and attacks the American society and institutions that brought Poe pain and rejection. The impact of Poe on French Symbolist poetry is clearly felt in the enthusiasm and careful elucidations of this major French voice.

Jacobs, Robert D. "Edgar Allan Poe." In *The History of Southern Literature*, edited by Louis D. Rubin et al. Baton Rouge: Louisiana State University Press, 1985.
Discusses the anomaly of this famous southerner being exposed to international influences almost from birth. By the time Poe was in private schools in Richmond, he seemed like an outsider or foreigner. Jacobs follows Poe's brief careers as college student and military man, noting his preoccupation with succeeding as a writer. While Poe "was for his time the best writer of poems and short stories claiming the south as his home," he was never really at home there. His work shows little connection with Southern literary traditions.

Kennedy, J. Gerald. *Poe, Death, and the Life of Writing*. New Haven, Conn.: Yale University Press, 1987.

Addresses the theme of death as it informs Poe's preoccupation with writing and with the power of words. Places Poe's concerns within "a contextual study of death in the nineteenth century." The act of writing explores death and psychologically holds death at bay, yet all writing carries with it an element of death. The stories and poems given balanced attention, especially as they concern themselves with the figure of the dead or dying woman.

Kesterson, David. B., ed. *Critics on Poe*. Coral Gables, Fla.: University of Miami Press, 1973.

Four sections provided: critical comments up to 1940, after 1940, general critical evaluations, and criticism on specific works. Most of the material reprinted here is easily available elsewhere, but this is still a handy mingling of opinions on all aspects of Poe's work. The poetry is slighted somewhat. Brief introduction along with table of important dates and selected bibliography.

Ketterer, David. *The Rationale of Deception in Poe*. Baton Rouge: Louisiana State University Press, 1979.

Considers deception a central theme and technique in Poe's work. Against "a sensed visionary reality" the reality of daily life is "one gross deception." In his later poems, "Poe goes furthest in his efforts to disperse the fabric of deception and thus justify his conception of the artist's role." Poe saw his poetry as an organic whole, like Whitman's *Leaves of Grass*. He defied conventional boundaries, always trying to close or transcend the gap between deceptive reality and "real" ideality.

Knapp, Bettina L. *Edgar Allan Poe*. New York: Ungar, 1984.

An introduction for general readers, this book moves through the life, poems, and tales in a straightforward, reliable manner. The chapter on the poetry notes the influence of the British Romantics as well as Poe's emphasis on discipline and control. Connects Poe's vision to the Platonic and Apollonian traditions: "the contemplation of the beautiful." Major individual poems are analyzed and the importance of music in Poe's aesthetic is discussed. Jungian orientation.

Krutch, Joseph Wood. *Edgar Allan Poe: A Study in Genius*. Reprint. New York: Russell & Russell, 1965.

A classic psychological portrait of Poe, first published in 1926, Krutch's study traces "Poe's art to an abnormal condition of the nerves and his critical ideas to a rationalized defense of the limitations of his own taste." Probes the causes of Poe's obsessive return to "gruesome subjects," idealized women, and his struggle "against a realization of the psychic impotence of his sexual nature." Explores Poe's tendency to mythologize himself and those in his life.

Lawrence, D. H. "Edgar Allan Poe." In his *Studies in Classic American Literature*.
Reprint. New York: Viking Press, 1964.
Though the evidence is drawn from Poe's stories, this discussion of Poe's
"disintegrative vibration" is applicable to the poems as well. Poe studies
himself, with an almost scientific scrutiny, but the analysis is entirely destructive. Soul and consciousness are reduced to their basic elements, as are sensual
and spiritual love. The scientific nature of Poe's mind is accompanied by a
"mechanical quality" in his poetry that turns life into force and matter. Poe's
facility masks the absence of real passion. First published in 1923. Often
anthologized.

Lee, A. Robert, ed. *Edgar Allan Poe: The Design of Order*. Totowa, N.J.: Barnes &
Noble Books, 1987.
Lee's introduction records the process by which critics have tried to separate
fact from myth in Poe studies. The selections deal primarily with Poe's fiction,
but some of the thematic or general discussions touch upon the poetry as well.
John Weightman's "Poe in France" argues that French interest in Poe ironically
led to the decline of his reputation. Prepared in England, this collection has
mostly British contributors.

Ljungquist, Kent. *The Grand and the Fair: Poe's Landscape Aesthetics and Pictorial Techniques*. Potomac, Md.: Scripta Humanistica, 1984.
Primarily a study of Poe's fiction, placing it within the context of American
landscape literature, this work includes a chapter on the poetry as well. Connects many of the poems to the "picturesque consciousness" of nineteenth
century American art. Traces a shift from the sublime to the picturesque that
parallels shift in the fiction. Praises "Poe's ability to inject a degree of psychological interest into a poetic landscape."

Mabbott, Thomas Ollive. "Introduction to the Poems." *Poems*. Vol. 1 of *Collected
Works of Edgar Allan Poe*. Cambridge, Mass.: Harvard University Press, 1969.
Brief comments on Poe's poetic style, scansion, rhyme, and influences. Each
poem receives its own short introduction, some actually short articles, that
considers allusions and sources. On occasion, Mabbott speculates on the
poem's composition, and he always provides a textual history. Elaborate notes,
often interpretive, follow each poem. As he states, "the annotation will be as
nearly exhaustive as possible." This is a "modified variorum" edition.

Mankowitz, Wolf. *The Extraordinary Mr. Poe*. New York: Summit Books, 1978.
A generously and attractively illustrated biography in which references to the
stories and poems are used to illuminate places and situations in Poe's life.
This is probably the most readable, engaging life now available, though it is far
from being a thorough scholarly endeavor and breaks no new ground. A lovely
coffee-table book of real substance.

Matthiessen. F. O. "Edgar Allan Poe." In *Literary History of the United States*, edited by Robert E. Spiller, et al. 3d ed., rev. New York: Macmillan, 1963.
Poe is still the most controversial of the major nineteenth century authors, and the range of evaluations of his work runs to extremes. No succeeding American poet has pointed to Poe as an inspiration or model. Poe is important more as an innovator than for his absolute achievement. Reactions to "Ulalume" represent the "paradoxes that have so divided Poe's critics." Some praise its perfect music, others call it too musical, and yet others find it unmusical. For some its theme is put forth too programmatically, for others it is too vaguely indefinite.

Moss, Sidney P. *Poe's Literary Battles: The Critic in the Context of His Literary Milieu*. Durham, N.C.: Duke University Press, 1963.
Poe's attacks were neither sporadic nor spiteful, but carefully unified campaigns aimed at smashing the power of the Boston and New York literary cliques and establishing conditions favorable for authorship. The battles sharpen our understanding of Poe's critical views by properly contextualizing them. Poe's grotesque reputation was shaped by literary enemies who attacked him as a man in order to discredit him as a critic.

Murray, David. "'A Strange Sound, as of a Harp-string Broken': The Poetry of Edgar Allan Poe." In *Edgar Allan Poe: The Design of Order*, edited by A. Robert Lee. Totowa, N.J.: Barnes & Noble, 1987.
Argues that Poe was closer to his Romantic predecessors than is generally acknowledged. His use of symbol is close to Paul de Man's understanding of its place in Romantic art. Poe's use of synesthesia and handling of time get special attention. The allegorical impulse and the role of melancholy in Poe's work firmly connect him to the major Romantic poets.

Ober, Warren U., Paul S. Burtness, and William R. Seat, Jr., eds. *The Enigma of Poe*. Boston: D.C. Heath, 1960.
This casebook provides a selection of Poe's poems and stories, a series of letters which document the Griswold controversy and other matters of reputation, and some early critical responses. Variant versions of five poems show Poe's revising strategies. The collection is designed to introduce the key issues in Poe studies and to encourage informed, independent judgment. Comment by Lowell, Baudelaire, Whitman, and Huxley.

Pettigrew, Richard C. "Poe's Rhyme." *American Literature* 4 (May, 1932): 151-159.
Argues "that Poe, like few poets of his importance, indulges freely in the 'licence' to which, as a critic, he so unreservedly objects." Poe does not admire light rhyme, but he uses it fifty-three times. "Imperfect vowel identity occurs

in 80 rhymes." Poe often invents proper names to complete rhymes, and these
are usually ostentatious disyllabic rhymes. Pettigrew catalogs other problems
and stresses how repetitive Poe's rhyming is. Poe's practice falls far below his
stated standards.

Phillips, Elizabeth. *Edgar Allan Poe: An American Imagination*. Port Washington,
N.Y.: Kennikat Press, 1979.
Three essays consider the interplay of Poe's respect for fact and his faith in the
imagination. The first views aspects of Poe's career as a response to Tocqueville's *Democracy in America*. The second looks at Poe's handling of imaginary landscapes, drawing quotations primarily from the poems. The third is
called "Mere Household Events: The Metaphysics of Mania"; it treats the
fiction only.

Phillips, Mary E. *Edgar Allan Poe—the Man*. 2 vols. Chicago: John C. Winston,
1926.
An enormously detailed, straightforward biography making full use of documentary evidence and the written reminiscences of those who knew Poe. The
intrusion of documents fractures the narrative at times, but the welter of facts
is digested into a vision of the man that plays down the notion of eccentricity.
Not concerned with literary analysis. Illustrated throughout.

Pollin, Burton R. "Poe and the Dance." *Studies in the American Renaissance*
(1980): 169-182.
Surveys the "dance elements in Poe's life and social surroundings, the instances of dance in his creative works and in his criticisms, and the varied
ways in which those works have been shown on the dance stage." Poe's interest
in dance is made clear by "a stream of allusions to ballet terms and works in
his creative writing." Pollin briefly notes dance references in eight poems
before turning to the richer fields of the stories. Dance works based on Poe's
writings offer interpretive insights.

——————— . "Poe and the River." In his *Discoveries in Poe*. Notre Dame, Ind.:
Notre Dame University Press, 1970.
Finds that Poe "attaches a distinctive complex of associations to each of three
aspects of nature: the sea, the river, and the lake." The sea is dangerous,
fathomless, sinister in scale and mystery, sometimes monotonous. The lake is
associated with darkness and fatal fascinations. The river's power is energizing
and purifying. Evidence drawn largely from the poems, but also from the tales.

——————— . *Poe, Creator of Words*. Rev. ed. Bronxville, N.Y.: Nicholas T.
Smith, 1980.

Pollin has compiled a list of more than one thousand words "either coined by Edgar Allan Poe or rightfully to be ascribed to him as first instances in print." Poe's career, more than that of other writers, was focused on language-making. His coinages, in both prose and verse, testify to his habits of mind, his striving for distinction, and his need to overcome the limits of conventional diction. In many cases, he may have simply been the first to put into print expressions current in the spoken language. Each entry includes usage citation.

Quinn, Arthur Hobson. *Edgar Allan Poe: A Critical Biography*. New York: Appleton-Century-Crofts, 1941.
This monumental study attempts to reveal "Poe the American, not the exotic" of countless other treatments. Shows Poe's relationships to the other writers who produced a major literature in the period before the Civil War. Views Poe as more of an insider than generally considered. Short analyses of many poems embedded in the narration. Illustrated, with copious appendices.

Quinn, Patrick F. *The French Face of Edgar Allan Poe*. Carbondale: Southern Illinois University Press, 1957.
An attempt to explain the extent and nature of Poe's impact on French literature. The appeal involved the mixture of psychological probing and rational thought in Poe's work. Observes that translations of Poe's writings might improve them. Quinn studies those writers who most admired Poe to find clues in their own lives, outer and inner, accounting for their fascination. Suggests that the visionary element in Poe's work was probably the most important feature occasioning the French response.

Rans, Geoffrey. *Edgar Allan Poe*. Edinburgh, Scotland: Oliver and Boyd, 1965.
A compact handling of Poe's critical views and his creative work, with separate treatments of the poetry and fiction. Poe's poetry aims at a kind of literal indefiniteness that reproduces within the reader the desired feeling or experience. Poe works by the power of suggestion, refusing within the poem to account for or explain his vision. Poe has submerged his meanings so that the reader's own imagination is challenged, but by so doing he has made the success of his technique difficult to measure.

Ransome, Arthur. *Edgar Allan Poe: A Critical Study*. Reprint. Folcroft, Pa.: Folcroft Press, 1970.
Considers "Poe's brain . . . more stimulating than his art." Regards the stories and poems as mere by-products of Poe's search for "a philosophy of beauty that should also be a philosophy of life." Chapter on the poetry views it as overshadowed by Poe's achievement in critical theory. Asserts that Poe's best-known poems are his weakest: well-shaped technical marvels without

soul or inspiration. Praises "The Sleeper" and "The City in the Sea." First published in 1910.

Regan, Robert, ed. *Poe: A Collection of Critical Essays*. Englewood Cliffs, N.J.: Prentice-Hall, 1967.
A gathering of responses to Poe's achievement as poet, short story writer, and critical thinker. This sweep across Poe's areas of concern allows us to discover some of the common denominators of his unique sensibility. Selections include Aldous Huxley's argument that Poe is not a major poet, Allen Tate on the Southern element, and an excerpt from Patrick F. Quinn's "The French Response to Poe." Includes a chronology of important dates and selected bibliography.

Richard, Claude. "The Heart of Poe and the Rhythmics of the Poems." In *Critical Essays on Edgar Allan Poe*, edited by Eric W. Carlson. Boston: G. K. Hall, 1987.
"The ultimate aim of Poe's poetry is to try to make the reader overhear the *echo* of something else—an unrefracted ray, an unheard rhythm, a pregnant silence, an unperceived harmony." Poe works toward hypnotic effects by manipulation of rhythms. The heartbeat is the essential mortal sign translatable into art. He aspires to the soundless rhythms beyond the cadences of life, the rhythms of the spirit usually masked by the "palpitating body" whose vibrations bring the imagination down to earth.

Shanks, Edward. *Edgar Allan Poe*. New York: Macmillan, 1937.
In his preface, Shanks complains that few commentators have paid serious attention to the writings of the man whose life so fascinates them. He hopes to remedy this situation. After presenting biographical chapters, Shanks provides separate discussions of the poems, the stories, and the criticism. Poe's development as a poet involved deepening his skill at expressing the mysterious and the inexplicable. Poe's vision was odd, but it was entirely his, and he found the means to entice others to share it.

Shucard, Alan. "Edgar Allan Poe: The Hyper-Romantic." In his *American Poetry: The Puritans Through Whitman*. Boston: Twayne: 1988.
Discusses Poe's life as the psychic source of his work; the themes of anguish and despair, given Poe's fortunes, were unavoidable. In the many poems on women, Poe transforms "the physical into some ineffable condition." Though Poe has clear ties to his period, "Poe's voice has remained eerily disembodied from the preponderance of American poetry." Poe's "necromancer ways are transparent, yet his readers are hoodwinked while they watch themselves being hoodwinked."

Sinclair, David. *Edgar Allan Poe*. Totowa, N.J.: Rowman and Littlefield, 1977.
Sinclair explores "Poe's particular hell—how he came to it, how he tried to escape from it, how it swallowed him up, and how he managed to triumph over it through his work." Poe clung to an image of himself as a genteel, scholarly man of letters. It was an image that never had a chance of being realized. Ill health, escapist tendencies, and pride combined to defeat Poe's limited genius. In his work, and through his work, Poe studied and made a private arrangement with death.

Smith, C. Alphonso. *Edgar Allan Poe: How to Know Him*. Indianapolis: Bobbs-Merrill, 1921.
Separate sections on Poe as world author, as individual, as critic, poet, fiction writer, and fabulist. The various sections are largely selections of Poe's writings imbedded in a running critical commentary which often points out relationships among works and notes publication circumstances. Each section has a sturdy introduction laying out the essentials of Poe's methods.

Spiller, Robert E. "The American Literary Dilemma and Edgar Allan Poe." In *The Great Experiment in American Literature*, edited by Carl Bode. New York: Frederick A. Praeger, 1961.
Examines the cultural background that produced the need for radical experiment in Poe and others. Considers Poe to be the first American writer to recognize the need for "deriving satisfactory literary forms" from the new experience of the American nation. Poe's relative success came from turning inward rather than dealing with the "physical, outward aspects of the life of the United States."

Stovall, Floyd. "The Conscious Art of Edgar Allan Poe." In *Poe: A Collection of Critical Essays*, edited by Robert Egan. Englewood Cliffs, N.J. Prentice-Hall, 1967.
Against the traditional view that Poe was a careless, intuitive, or unconscious artist, Stovall argues for the conscious element in Poe's craft. The manuscripts of Poe's poems show him to be a "frequent and meticulous" reviser, and many of his long poems, like "The Raven," seem to have been carefully planned before they were drafted. A "healthy and alert intelligence" was required to construct such poems, though they are calculated to express distorted, disordered sensibilities.

——————. *Edgar Poe the Poet*. Charlottesville: University Press of Virginia, 1969.
A cycle of essays developed over a period of forty years that may be read independently of one another. One piece treats Poe's satire, "The Musiad," while another examines Poe's debt to Coleridge. There is a lengthy analysis of

"Al Aaraaf" and a comprehensive discussion of "Mood, Meaning, and Form in Poe's Poetry" that demonstrates the shifting dominance of these elements through three stages of Poe's career. Poe's quest for the poet's career is also examined.

_____ . Introduction to *The Poems of Edgar Allan Poe*, edited by Stovall. Charlottesville: University Press of Virginia, 1965.
This most authoritative general essay on Poe's poetry considers Poe's struggle to get his works published, the dominant themes, and Poe's various ways of grouping poems in collections. Stovall comments on Poe's habits of revision, noting that he kept the spirit of early poems rather than recast them in a later style. The section on Poe's achievement, often reprinted, considers the ways in which Poe was a poet of his age and yet a true original. Sees Poe's originality as his greatest literary virtue.

Strong, Augustus Hopkins. "Poe." In his *American Poets and Their Theology*. Philadelphia: Griffith and Rowland, 1916.
Charges that Poe ignored the moral issues of his day; he was "a soured and self-willed unbeliever" as well as "an absolute materialist." Strong, who easily praises men of faith, struggles to give Poe his due as a poet. He praises Poe's powerful imagination and technical skills. Strong argues that Poe's references to God and to the Bible are merely "conventional and rhetorical" accommodations to his readers' taste. "Poe's atheism was an atheism of the heart, rather than an atheism of the head. He lacked the will to believe."

Symons, Julian. *The Tell-Tale Heart: The Life and Works of Edgar Allan Poe*. New York: Harper & Row, 1978.
In an approach intended to avoid blurring the boundary between life and work, Symons isolates his critical concerns so as to avoid using the poems as sources for biography. The brief section on the poems sees them as the extensions of Poe's theories, which are treated more fully. Agrees that Poe's poems are noteworthy for their release of sensations, not profundities. Considers Poe's achievement as a poet modest. Even in his best poems he borders on the ridiculous. The stories hold Poe's real genius.

Tate, Allen. "The Angelic Imagination: Poe As God." In his *Essays of Four Decades*. Chicago: Swallow Press, 1968.
A detailed discussion of three philosophical prose works by Poe that illuminate his poetic stance. Tate discovers what he calls "the angelism of the intellect" as a prominent aspect of Poe's vision. Poe's failure to harmonize himself "resulted in hypertrophy of the three classical faculties: feeling, will, and intellect." The theme of disintegration in Poe is both an outgrowth of a morbid psychology and a conscious philosophical stance. Poetry, uncontaminated by the dissolving material world, can save us by re-ordering our minds.

_____ . "Our Cousin, Mr. Poe." In his *Essays of Four Decades*. Chicago: Swallow Press, 1968.
Tate explores the mood and vision of Poe, drawing more upon the prose works than the poetry. Poe remade and spiritualized "the standard cult of Female Purity in the Old South." Strange fires in Poe's semi-erotic landscapes are his leading visual symbol. Poe exploits two aspects of fire: "it lights and it burns." In itself it is pure, but it is also destructive. As action, "it becomes the consuming fire of the abstract intellect, without moral significance, which invades the being of the beloved." (This and the preceding entry were gathered earlier in Tate's *Selected Essays*, 1959).

_____ . "The Poetry of Edgar Allan Poe." In his *Memoirs and Opinions, 1926-1974*. Chicago: Swallow Press, 1975.
An introductory essay with an autobiographical slant. Tate examines the "theme of annihilation" and the existentialist motif in Poe's work. In Poe's world, man is "trapped in a consciousness which cannot be conscious of anything outside itself." Tate argues that Poe's poetry does not develop significantly over time: there is "no acquisition of range and depth" between "Tamerlane" and "Ulalume." More than any other Romantic poet, Poe "became the *type* of the alienated poet." He wrote few poems because he exhausted the number of ways, within Romanticism, of presenting "his message of spiritual solipsism and physical decay."

Thomas, Dwight, and David K. Jackson. *The Poe Log: A Documentary Life of Edgar Allan Poe, 1809-1849*. Boston: G. K. Hall, 1987.
Presents all "the verifiable facts of Poe's life as revealed in excerpts from contemporary documents." These include letters, newspaper reports, periodical articles, legal records, and reminiscences. Includes biographical notes on person's mentioned, the log itself, a list of sources, and a comprehensive index. No interpretation, just the available data.

Thompson, G. Richard. *Circumscribed Eden of Dreams: Dreamvision and Nightmare in Poe's Early Poetry*. Baltimore: Baltimore Poe Society and Enoch Pratt Library, 1984.
Explores the ways in which Poe refined the preexisting genre of the apocalyptic landscape. After showing how Poe used framing devices and Byronic distancing in "Tamerlane," Thompson examines the theme of the visionary dream overwhelmed by evil forces of the imagination in other poems from the *Tamerlane* volume. Less biographical emphasis than most Poe criticism.

Wagenknecht, Edward. *Edward Allan Poe: The Man Behind the Legend*. New York: Oxford University Press, 1963.

A careful yet colorful examination of Poe's character and personality as revealed by documentary sources as well as by Poe's imaginative writings. Though only marginally concerned with Poe's achievement, Wagenknecht has constructed a levelheaded treatment that avoids the excesses of psychoanalytic criticism while taking advantage of any solid clue to Poe's inner nature. Includes an excellent section on Poe's formal and informal education that discusses Poe's curiosity, his areas of genuine knowledge, and his weakness for posing as more knowledgeable than he was.

Walker, I. M., ed. *Edgar Allan Poe: The Critical Heritage*. London: Routledge & Kegan Paul, 1986.
A large collection of responses to Poe's work by his contemporaries and near-contemporaries. Organized by grouping reviews of Poe's published volumes. Includes a brief cluster of "General Estimates" by Lowell, Thomas Dunn English, and William Gilmore Simms. Also, a gathering of obituaries and "Views from Abroad." Introduction traces the progress of Poe's critical reception. Poe's personal reputation may have interfered with the reception given his work.

Werner, W. L. "Poe's Theories and Practice of Poetic Technique." *American Literature* 2 (May, 1930): 157-165.
Poe's particular musical signature employs a higher proportion of *n*-sounds than *r*-, *l*-, or sharp *s*-sounds. This is the reverse of his contemporaries. Poe's care in the succession of sounds and rhythms creates the desired smoothness in his work. "Careless in his rhymes, conservative in his use of meter, modern in his choice and order of words, Poe is most noteworthy for his unusual stanza forms." These various features are illustrated.

Wilbur, Richard. "The House of Poe." In *Poe: A Collection of Essays*, edited by Robert Regan. Englewood Cliffs, N.J.: Prentice-Hall, 1967.
Because Poe thought of God as a poet, he considered the universe to be "a poem composed by God." Thus, he felt an aesthetic response to the universe to be an appropriate one. To be unappreciative of this beauty and divine harmony is to be blasphemous. Poe found the rationalism and materialism of his time a sign of human frailty. The earth, corrupted by man, had become a fallen planet, unfit for the poetic spirit. The fundamental subject of Poe's work is the war between the poetic spirit and the "mundane physical world."

Williams, Michael J. S. *A World of Words: Language and Displacement in the Fiction of Edgar Allan Poe*. Durham, N.C.: Duke University Press, 1988.
Despite its title, this study has value to the student of Poe's poetry. It explores the degree to which language itself is a topic of Poe's texts. Williams shows

how Poe characterizes the relationship between the author and reader as a struggle for authority, how the self that writes is in conflict with the self created by writing, and how Poe debunks the redemptive properties of the Romantic symbol.

Winters, Yvor. "Edgar Allan Poe: A Crisis in the History of American Obscurantism." In his *In Defense of Reason*. Reprint. Denver: Alan Swallow, 1961.
Asserts that Poe is a poor theorist and a poor poet. Finds Poe an exclusionist not willing to admit intellectual content into poetry. Poe confuses the source of beauty, finding it in subject matter instead of style. Poe's theory and practice distance poetry from moral issues of ordinary life. Calls Poe "an excited sentimentalist" with "a formula for the production of a kind of emotional delusion." Considers "The City in the Sea" Poe's best poem; that is, his "most startling and arresting failure." Poe's techniques of repetition outlandishly excessive, and his themes barely existent. Often reprinted.

Winwar, Frances. *The Haunted Palace: A Life of Edgar Allan Poe*. New York: Harper & Brothers, 1959.
A sweeping, novelistic treatment that tries to elaborate Poe's emotional ties to his parents, other relatives, and the women in his life. Throughout this narrative, Poe's poems are employed as emotional markers. Winwar works toward creating a suspenseful plot out of the available facts. This method makes the story engaging, but not fully convincing. Little, if any, new evidence.

Zayed, George. *The Genius of Edgar Allan Poe*. Cambridge, Mass.: Schenkman, 1985.
The first part summarizes Poe's critical reputation at home and abroad, attempting to explain the divergent views. The second part divides Poe's genius into component parts, addressing each briefly. Zayed praises Poe both as thinker and artist. Two brief chapters explore "The Symbolism of the Poems" and Poe's notions of melody and incantation. The symbolism is divided into three categories: aesthetic, emotional, and philosophical. An enthusiastic, but sketchy presentation.

"Annabel Lee"

Bonaparte, Marie. *The Life and Works of Edgar Allan Poe: A Psycho-Analytic Interpretation*, 124-132. Reprint. New York: Humanities Press, 1971.
Poe mourns for his wife, Virginia, even before her death. The character's name may be a condensation of Elizabeth, the name of Poe's mother and Virginia's middle name; Rosalie, Poe's sister's name and the title character of Philip Pendleton Cooke's "Rosalie Lee," which Poe admired; and Annie Richmond,

another important woman in Poe's life. Poe invents a myth of "high-born kinsmen" symbolically standing for the royal we, "the awe-inspiring father who, in the Oedipus situation, disputes the child's possession of his mother and takes her from him." Both the moon and the sea are universal mother symbols.

Fletcher, Richard M. *The Stylistic Development of Edgar Allan Poe*, 155-168. The Hague, Netherlands: Mouton, 1973.
This late poem exemplifies the style and control developed over a lifetime of experimentation. Fletcher pays particular attention to the modulations of sounds, juxtapositions that are "almost cold-bloodedly mathematical." The feeling that manner prevails over matter may be one Poe hoped to produce. The subtext of these excesses is the admission that attempts "at depicting true feeling within a poetic context are vain and ludicrous." At bottom, Poe is satirizing the too obvious sentimentalizing of his own poem. He may be writing for two audiences.

Halliburton, David. *Edgar Allan Poe: A Phenomenological View*, 172-174. Princeton, N.J.: Princeton University Press, 1973.
For the speaker, Annabel Lee is most fully alive in her death. She is at once lost and recovered to him. As do the other poems to women, this one "ends in a present tense suggestive of a timeless realm. The past having been outlived, nothing remains but an eternal now in which [the speaker's] continuing salvation depends upon a guardianship that protects [him] from the threat of victimization to which every man is prey."

Jones, Buford, and Kent Ljungquist. "Poe, Mrs. Osgood, and 'Annabel Lee.'" *Studies in the American Renaissance* (1983): 275-280.
Frances Sargent Osgood's poem "The Life-Voyage" has many internal parallels and is a possible source. The relationship between Poe and Osgood was one of (at least) mutual appreciation and admiration. He praised her poems, she his. It is possible that this woman was the model for the title character, though she denied it. A reciprocal influence is also possible.

"The Bells"

Knapp, Bettina L. *Edgar Allan Poe*, 95-96. New York: Ungar, 1984.
Bells not only mark the hours of the day—of life itself—but they specifically mark the four ages of man. Silver bells announce youth; gold bells ring the harmonies of love and marriage; brazen bells bring awareness of the polarities and dichotomies of existence. The iron bells signal old age and foreshadow death. Poe's technical artistry in onomatopoeia and vowel gradations is aimed

at creating emotional response. Ideas in "The Bells" are of less importance than the auditory experience.

Stovall, Floyd. *Edgar Poe the Poet*, 231-232. Charlottesville: University Press of Virginia, 1969.
The rhythm of the poem is predominantly trochaic, though irregular, with the primary stress falling near the middle or at the end of the line. As the intensity of the material increases, so does the length of each succeeding stanza. The third, which has the largest number of end rhymes, also presents the greatest number of separate ideas. Liquid and nasal consonants dominate the poem, especially the final stanza, and contribute to the mellifluous flavor of the whole. Stovall considers these and other prosodic observations in evaluating the expressiveness of Poe's craft.

"The City in the Sea"

Clough, Wilson O. "Poe's 'The City in the Sea' Revisited." In *Essays on American Literature in Honor of Jay B. Hubbell*, edited by Clarence Gohdes. Durham, N.C.: Duke University Press, 1967.
Clough's careful, detailed appraisal of the criticism on this poem pays particular attention to the views of Allen Tate, Edward Davidson, and Richard Wilbur—all of whom examine Poe's critical prose as a clue to his poetic vision. The poem carries its meaning literally: The city has no moral import; it simply disintegrates, along with the human pomp that it contains. Death sinks with it, "for there is no more death where nothing ever lives." Poe envisions an eternal void more terrifying than the populated hells of conventional imaginings. Death is "without palliatives."

Knapp, Bettina L. *Edgar Allan Poe*, 75-78. New York: Ungar, 1984.
The sunken city is "ancient and outworn, its atmosphere stale and arid." So too is the fate of any individual who has reached a creative impasse and who can only "repeat and refurbish past themes and phrases." The sea into which the city settles is like the eternal unconscious: It links heaven and hell, good and evil, and it provides the raw materials for renewal. This fate of the city is neither punishment nor reward. It is simply the necessary stage for possible replenishment of the artistic imagination.

Ljungquist, Kent. *The Grand and the Fair: Poe's Landscape Aesthetics and Pictorial Techniques*, 172-177. Potomac, Md.: Scripta Humanistica, 1984.
An analysis of Poe's revisions of the early poem "The Doomed City" through the intermediate "The City of Sin" to the final version shows a pattern of removing expansive images. Gone are looming towers, a star-filled heaven,

and an emphasis on the sea's depth. Such sublime images are replaced by ones of less spatial emphasis and greater psychological implication. The absence of action makes the poem into a "pictorial symbol of paralysis."

Pound, Louise. "On Poe's 'The City in the Sea.' " *American Literature* 6 (March, 1934): 22-27.
    Pound refers us to a number of biblical passages—in Isaiah and Revelation in particular—as possible sources for Poe's descriptions and meanings. Yet she notes that there are many differences between Poe's city and the legendary Babylon and Gomorrah. For example, Poe's city is already below the sea when the poem opens; it is not sunken or razed. She also finds echoes of Poe's earlier poem "Al Aaraaf." Still, these and the even more prominent European conventions seem remote. The poem stands out as particularly original and imaginative.

"Eldorado"

Hammond, J. R. *An Edgar Allan Poe Companion*, 161-164. Totowa, N.J.: Barnes & Noble, 1981.
    Written during the California gold rush, the poem reflects Poe's longing for "emotional and intellectual fulfillment." The opening images suggest Poe's "fluctuating moods of hope and disillusionment." Biblical connotations of "shadow" are evoked, as well as suggestions of Poe's lifelong preoccupation with the concept of the double—the shadow who accompanies one and threatens to steal one's identity. This short, late poem recapitulates several of Poe's key themes. It may be read as his final testament.

"Israfel"

Knapp, Bettina L. *Edgar Allan Poe*, 67-69. New York: Ungar, 1984.
    The eight stanzas may reflect the Pythagorian understanding of eight: two concentric circles representing an unlimited circular round of motion and cosmic equilibrium. Sideways, the eight is the infinity sign. The dialogue between Israfel, a wise and beautiful angel who sings the music of absolute poetry, and the mortal poet who approaches him represents the earthbound soul's longing for the pure, everlasting beauty beyond sensation and illusion. Israfel's song is depersonalized, its fire serene.

St. Armand, Barton Levi. "Poe's Unnecessary Angel: 'Israfel' Reconsidered." In *Ruined Eden of the Present: Hawthorne, Melville, Poe*, edited by G. R.

Thompson and Virgil Lokke. West Lafayette, Ind.: Purdue University Press, 1981.

Poe is generally identified with his title character, an idealized artistic figure. Unlike Emerson in "Uriel," Poe "does not so much want to regain the paradise he pictures as to undermine it, displace it, or annihilate it." Israfel's performance has a deadening effect; it produces stasis. Poe's praise of Israfel is always equivocal and ironic. He does not fully admire the pure emotional power that Israfel represents. Poe's aesthetic, articulated in many places, requires a balance of mind and emotion.

"Lenore"

Halliburton, David. *Edgar Allan Poe: A Phenomenological View*, 157-161. Princeton, N.J.: Princeton University Press, 1973.

Though there is no literal or demonstrable exchange of opinions, the poem may be thought of as a debate over "the proper mode of remembrance for the dead Lenore." Does one mourn or celebrate her passing? A conflict between emotion and will runs parallel to the debate, conveyed in part by the counterpointing of exclamations and imperatives. The poem is less an elegy than a prefatory dialectic that looks forward to an elegy.

"The Raven"

Blasing, Mutlu Konuk. "Edgar Allan Poe, the Poet to a I." In her *American Poetry: The Rhetoric of Its Forms*, 27-35. New Haven, Conn.: Yale University Press, 1987.

Demonstrates Poe's nonorganic form as the mechanical, clock-time devices of metrical and stanzaic regularity destroy any illusion of fictive or narrative time. "The word 'Lenore' names the poetic possibilities of language" while the echoing "Nevermore" drowns out these possibilities. The poem mocks "the human desire for transcendence of mortal limits" by slavishly chaining the highest aspirations to the limiting factors of poetry's formal features—features culturally and historically determined.

Davidson, Edward H. *Poe: A Critical Study*, 84-92. Cambridge, Mass.: Harvard University Press, 1966.

The fulfillment of a dozen years of Poe's work since his 1831 collection, the poem records stages in the process of self-knowledge, a process that includes awareness both of being and nonbeing. "The poem is a symbolic destruction of the mind by the impact of reality upon it." The imagination falls victim to bird and bust, each suggesting its complete finitude and the "reality" that there is nothing beyond reality. The poem enacts the limits of the power of symbols to mediate between reality and imagination. (Also in Rupp.)

"Romance"

Fletcher, Richard M. *The Stylistic Development of Edgar Allan Poe*, 29-31. The Hague, Netherlands: Mouton, 1973.

"In this, as in the bulk of Poe's early poems, we are made uncomfortably aware of the poet as a suffering presence." The poet poses before his audience, making himself too ridiculous to take seriously. Yet there is no trace of humor here; at this time in his career Poe expected readers to take this posturing seriously. Examination of revisions shows an immature reluctance to do more than fiddle with minor details. Some of the changes underscore Poe's "perpetual uncertainties about sound values."

Richard, Claude. "The Heart of Poe and the Rhythmics of the Poems." In *Critical Essays on Edgar Allan Poe*, edited by Eric W. Carlson, 199-201. Boston: G. K. Hall, 1987.

The poem is a celebration of the myth of a poet's education. The poet as child receives a lesson from the spirit of romance that gives him an essential language. In adulthood, moments of access to the poetic soul are intermittent. "They are the rare moments when the heart and the primary poetic rhythm vibrate coincidentally in a harmony generated by the vibration . . . of stringed instruments." These sympathetic vibrations are the basis of all truly valuable artistic activity.

Stovall, Floyd. *Edgar Poe the Poet*, 207-208. Charlottesville: University Press of Virginia, 1969.

"Romance" is an accomplished poem that clarifies Poe's theory of poetry. It defines the effect of poetry as indefinitive: Poetry presents "not truth itself but truth reflected in forms of beauty." The poem suggests that in his youth Poe's expressed sentiments were imitative and insincere. In his maturity, only his own voice is released, and that voice "expresses its genuine nature and feelings." The 1831 version of the poem records three phases of development.

"Sonnet—To Science"

Davidson, Edward H. *Poe: A Critical Study*, 13-14. Cambridge, Mass.: Harvard University Press, 1966.

Though it reads like just another Romantic lament about how science destroys the myths on which poetry depends, this poem is aimed at the eighteenth century "view of an inanimate, mechanistic nature and a presumed animate, thinking man living in it." Poe feels that modern man's belief in his ability to "reduce the phenomenal universe to his own convenient measurable detail" is a delusion.

"To Helen"

Claudel, Alice Moser. "Poe As Voyager in 'To Helen." *ESQ*, no. 60 (Fall, 1970): 33-37.
On its obvious level, "To Helen" is "a love poem directed to a beautiful woman who is a source of comfort to an anguished soul, leading him by means of her idealized loveliness to his intellectual and spiritual home." Helen's beauty is itself a vehicle or vessel—it "transports" the speaker. Many of Poe's images and allusions have Christian rather than Greek overtones. The poem is a precursor of Yeats's "Sailing to Byzantium"; its speaker is a pilgrim sailing to his ideal home.

Davidson, Edward H. *Poe: A Critical Study*, 32-34. Cambridge, Mass.: Harvard University Press, 1966.
Less important than discovering the original for Poe's title character is the clear allusion to Helen of Troy. "As the Grecian Helen she represents all the urgent longing with which medieval and romantic poets sought to resolve as mystery, pure beauty, and the agony of never realizing in fact what the imagination continually sought as myth or fiction." The poem is, finally, an exploration of how the poetic imagination works.

"Ulalume"

Bonaparte, Marie. *The Life and Works of Edgar Allan Poe: A Psycho-Analytic Interpretation*, 143-152. Reprint. New York: Humanities Press, 1971.
Poe attempts to cure himself of his "necrophilist fixation." Various approaches to female figures represent not only his urges toward women but also his psychic attempt to unite with his dead mother. These attempts are thwarted by guilt, which manifests itself as impotence (Psyche's trailing wings). The mother fixation bars the way to normal sexuality. Problems of memory and infantile amnesia complicate the poem. "Psyche is . . . Poe's mother, to whom he unconsciously remained faithful through life and . . . [also] the educative mother who, by moral injunctions, protects her developing child from incest and sexual indulgence."

Buranelli, Vincent. *Edgar Allan Poe*, 103. 2d ed. Boston: Twayne, 1977.
Explication can not explain the power of this poem, in which shapes made out of sounds move the reader. Poe can "imply those vague fancies and half-dreams that escape direct description." Logic cannot decipher what a "most immemorial year" is, but the sound is just right, as are the place names "Auber" and "Weir." These create in readers "a mood resonant with dim memories and hoary times and uncanny places." Appreciation precedes understanding, sometimes replaces it, with Poe.

Carlson, Eric W. "Symbol and Sense in Poe's 'Ulalume.'" *American Literature* 35 (March, 1963): 22-37.

After placing this poem at the center of controversy about Poe's status as a poet, Carlson examines its dramatic structure, its conflict and theme, and its symbolism. His approach is psychoanalytic, but Carlson finds Poe relying on the combined effect of his symbols (which he often invented) and sound impressionism. "The protagonist is driven to despair in an effort to recapture his ideal integrity." Even after being reunited with his soul, the speaker remains isolated in his "stoic acceptance of reality."

Fletcher, Richard M. *The Stylistic Development of Edgar Allan Poe*, 177-184. The Hague, Netherlands: Mouton, 1973.

The poem is "an exercise in onomatopoeia, in synonymous usage, in employment of seemingly foreign terms." The feeling, suffering narrator is familiar from Poe's earlier work, as is the somewhat spurious moral stance. Perhaps best read as a late satire in which Poe mocks himself and his readers. Every aspect of manner and methodology is exaggerated to the point of parody. The virtuosity that plays upon the speaker's grief creates a satiric distance, gleefully yet painfully poking fun at itself.

Ketterer, David. *The Rationale of Deception in Poe*, 177-179. Baton Rouge: Louisiana State University Press, 1979.

The action of the poem instructs the narrator that the fulfillment of his love comes only with death. This principle is emphasized by the poem's dualism. The narrator is doubled as Psyche (soul) and heart. Two five-stanza groupings are ruled in turn by heart and soul. The word "duplicate" reverberates with echoes not only of doubleness but also of duplicity and deception. Key images are expressed as dualist pairs, reinforcing this motif. "In the last stanza, Psyche and the narrator speak as one."

Shucard, Alan. "Edgar Allan Poe: The Hyper-Romantic." In his *American Poetry The Puritans Through Whitman*, 116-118. Boston: Twayne, 1988.

Describes the "great seductive power" that grows out of placing natural images "in the mesmerizing context of the repetitive cadence and diction." The self receives a message in his dreamland ramble with Psyche, his soul: "real amorous entanglements lead to the tomb and sorrow. Better 'the spectre of the planet,' an antiworld created by the creative imagination." The poem doesn't operate on the rational level, but through the conjuring of emotions in "the sanctum of mists and shadows and phantom stars."

OLIVER WENDELL HOLMES
(1809-1894)

General Studies

Allen, Gay Wilson. "Oliver Wendell Holmes." In his *American Prosody*. New
York: American Book, 1935.
Holmes's prosodic thinking and practice is generally conservative. As an occasional poet, his attention was more on what he had to say than on technique. In
his earlier period, he often wrote in the ballad stanza, as exemplified by "Old
Ironsides." Many of his effective poems are in four-stress iambics or heroic
couplets, the latter underscoring his fondness for eighteenth century forms.
"The Chambered Nautilus" is Holmes's most successful poem and his most
ambitious formal experiment.

Arms, George. "Holmes." In his *The Fields Were Green*. Stanford, Calif.: Stanford
University Press, 1953.
Although Holmes has some affinities with the metaphysical poets, especially in
technique, he lacks the subtlety of the masters. He often achieves a "perverse
complexity" that is more an exercise of wit than imagination. Holmes worked
against the sentimental excesses of his age, and in his own work "holds pathos
in check with humor." Comfortable with science and fact, Holmes consciously
embraced a neoclassical attitude toward art and language in resistance to the
Romantic current.

Brooks, Van Wyck. "Dr. Holmes." In his *The Flowering of New England,
1815-1865*. Rev. ed. New York: E. P. Dutton, 1937.
As a young law student, Holmes wrote "Old Ironsides" and was immediately
famous. After Paris and medical school, Holmes began a secondary career on
the speaker's platform where he became "poet laureate by avocation, always
prepared to present his bouquet at a banquet or an ode at a county fair." From
his "nimble tongue, as from no other American tongue or pen, tripped the
phrase, the epithet, on each occasion, that fired in every mind the appropriate
strain." His few solemn lyrics are the exception to the stream of rhymes by
which he revealed himself to be the wittiest man in America.

Carter, Everett. "The Typicality of Oliver Wendell Holmes." In *Themes and Directions in American Literature*, edited by Ray B. Browne and Donald Pizer.
Lafayette, Ind.: Purdue University Studies, 1969.
"Faith in nature and man, and faith in the possibility of progress as a basis for
faith in experience, these together comprised the structure of feeling of most
sentient Americans, to which Oliver Wendell Holmes gave significant imagina-

tive form." Holmes rejected the myth of the noble savage as both unnecessary and unrealistic. His poems celebrate the superiority of life over art. Self-mockery usually tempers his satires, yet in his light verse Holmes takes on his century's major issues.

Connor, Frederick William. "Holmes: Evolution Without Transformation?" In his *Cosmic Optimism: A Study of the Interpretation of Evolution by American Poets from Emerson to Robinson.* Gainesville: University of Florida Press, 1941.

Holmes was an evolutionist before Darwin's writings appeared, and he was not totally enthusiastic about Darwin's brand of evolutionism. Holmes drew most of his arguments from organic chemistry. Connor reviews Holmes's position as revealed in specialized and general essays as well as in his novel, *Elsie Venner.* Holmes's optimism and his faith in progress had both theological and scientific sources.

Crothers, Samuel McChord. *Oliver Wendell Holmes: The Autocrat and His Fellow Boarders.* Boston: Houghton Mifflin, 1910.

A cheerful biographical sketch that describes the "Autocrat" persona as well as other characters developed by Holmes. Reviews the poet's reflection of "the intelligent and right- minded, but somewhat self-conscious Boston of the Transcendental period." Holmes preserved that society for posterity. He fought for the union of science and poetry "in a new and higher type of culture." Followed by "Selected Poems."

Howe, M. A. DeWolfe. *Holmes of the Breakfast-Table.* London: Oxford University Press, 1939.

A reassessment of Holmes some fifty years after the high point of his eminence. Stresses the impact of Holmes throughout the English-speaking world, not just in his native New England. This sympathetic biography considers the background forces that shaped Holmes, the influence of the "Wednesday Evening Club," the occasions that prompted his verse, and the merits of that verse. Holmes's generous and penetrating insight into human nature, manifest in his various roles and writings, is what makes him exceptional. Illustrated.

Hoyt, Edwin P. *The Improper Bostonian: Dr. Oliver Wendell Holmes.* New York: William Morrow, 1979.

Holmes was a somewhat rebellious Renaissance man whose work survived the cutting off of literary ties formed in his hometown of Cambridge, Massachusetts. Hoyt attends to Holmes's careers as physician, lecturer, and tastemaker. Discusses Holmes's major poems, his novels, and his periodical essays. This is a breezy, upbeat, yet respectful treatment.

Kennedy, William Sloane. *Oliver Wendell Holmes: Poet, Litterateur, Scientist*. Reprint. Folcroft, Pa.: Folcroft Library Editions, 1974.

An amiable mixture of biography and criticism, this early appreciation (first published in 1883) considers Holmes's areas of activity in separate chapters. The chapter on poetry praises Holmes's humorous verse, while granting him passages of beauty in his other work. Kennedy recovers the circumstances of Holmes's occasional poems, unraveling references. Kennedy admires Holmes's technique of placing "familiar and homely objects . . . in the most incongruous relations." Sees Holmes in the tradition of Pope, Goldsmith, and Thomas Hood.

Pearce, Roy Harvey. "Oliver Wendell Holmes." In his *The Continuity of American Poetry*. Princeton, N.J.: Princeton University Press, 1961.

Holmes determined early "that authentic poetry, high poetry, demanded absorption and dedication of which he himself was not capable." His characteristic poems show Holmes's remarkable wit "daring to be almost but not quite sentimental." His poems forestall deep meditation and shun profundity. He chose to be a poet "of the least common denominator." Holmes believed in the experimental or scientific method of thought governed by common sense. His attitude toward nature was that of a scientist: He could not lose himself in it.

Small, Miriam Rossiter. *Oliver Wendell Holmes*. New York: Twayne, 1962.

This straightforward account of Holmes's life and work breaks the general chronology only for the convenience of discussing related works. Holmes's career as a poet is treated in a chapter that also embraces his work as a physician and lecturer. There is a separate chapter on *The Autocrat of the Breakfast Table* and another on his three novels. Many "Autocrat" essays contained poems. Holmes's later years of celebrity are handled appreciatively. Chronology and selected bibliography.

Strong, Augustus Hopkins. "Oliver Wendell Holmes." In his *American Poets and Their Theology*. Philadelphia: Griffith and Rowland, 1916.

Acknowledging that humor was Holmes's chief gift, Strong explores the poet's argument with the hardened "hyper-Calvinism" of his time. "Holmes hated Calvinism because it held God to be the ordainer of all things. He accepted a materialistic idealism which subjected all things to an irrational and fatal necessity." Extensive demonstration of Holmes's views through reference to the poems.

Tilton, Eleanor M. *Amiable Autocrat: A Biography of Dr. Oliver Wendell Holmes*. New York: Henry Schuman, 1947.

A comprehensive, lively biography that concerns itself with the "Autocrat" persona and the Holmes personality. Holmes's upbringing, including the books on his father's shelves, receives sensitive attention. Tilton finds that the poems written during Holmes's student days at Harvard are justly considered to be some of his best work. He discovered his distinctive voice early. This study provides separate chapters on "Occasional Poet" and "Poet at the Breakfast Table" while following the upward curve of Holmes's reputation and influence.

_____ . Introduction to *The Poetical Works of Oliver Wendell Holmes*, edited by Tilton. Boston: Houghton Mifflin, 1975.
A biographical introduction traces Holmes's pursuit of his several careers. Tilton summarizes Holmes's attitude toward poetry, his reasons for writing it, and his own estimate of his achievement. She observes the wide range of Holmes's poetic voices: the romantic sublime, the colloquial, the professorial, the man of wit. Holmes was comfortable in the post-Darwinian world for which his scientific training prepared him.

Waggoner, Hyatt H. "Oliver Wendell Holmes." In his *American Poets from the Puritans to the Present*. Boston: Houghton Mifflin, 1968.
Holmes became America's most famous after-dinner speaker and an occasional poet of some note. He was always able to "turn out a graceful and fitting poem" to mark a public event. His effective verse is not poetry of feeling but a play of wit that "came from the top of his mind." Only "The Chambered Nautilus" runs at a deeper, more complex level. Most typical of his genius are poems such as "The Deacon's Masterpiece," in which narrowly logical systems of thought are attacked in the name of common sense.

Wentersdorf, Karl P. "The Underground Workshop of Oliver Wendell Holmes." *American Literature* 35 (March, 1963): 1-12.
References to the nature of the creative process are scattered through Holmes's writings. The early "Poetry: A Metrical Essay" emphasizes the transfiguring power of the poetic imagination. In the preparatory phase of art, there is some element of conscious activity. However, Holmes believed "that the words, phrases, and images which gather in the poet's underground workshop undergo varying degrees of transformation while there." The personality of the writer determines the nature of the changes. Holmes can be considered a pioneer in the psychology of creativity.

"The Chambered Nautilus"

Arms, George. "Holmes." In his *The Fields Were Green*, 108-110. Stanford, Calif.: Stanford University Press, 1953.
Arms praises Holmes's "delicate handling of language in a poem that in many other respects shows a remarkable coordination of poetic abilities." The first

stanza introduces poetic fancy; the second sounds a scientific note and also a pessimistic one; the third presents an antithetical optimism. The fourth stanza prepares for the message made specific in the fifth. Holmes effectively contrasts his images in a poem that asserts a philosophy of personal growth complicated by an awareness of "a triumph ultimate in death."

Small, Miriam Rossiter. *Oliver Wendell Holmes*, 95-96. New York: Twayne, 1962.
The poem's success comes from "a close following of one idea . . . and using as concrete image an object [Holmes] had long known and studied." The poem's other strengths include its suggestive diction, its effective melody, and the concentrated power of its individual stanzas. The balance of attention between exposition of idea and elaboration of image is not satisfying to many twentieth century readers.

JONES VERY
(1813-1880)

General Studies

Boswell, Jeanetta. "Jones Very." In her *Spokesmen for the Minority*.
This is a bibliography of secondary materials with selected annotations. See full entry in "General Treatments of the Period."

Buell, Lawrence. "Transcendental Egoism in Very and Whitman." In his *Literary Transcendentalism*. Ithaca, N.Y.: Cornell University Press, 1973. Also in Bloom, *American Poetry to 1914*.
Very was a poet before he was a mystic. His speaker is not the old Adam but the new man in Christ. This prophetic speaker "does not ventriloquize through the mask of deity or biblical figure . . . He has an identity of his own." Buell examines the nature of the persona in a series of Very's poems, noting the alternation and mingling of divine, prophetic, and human voices and their "disorienting effect on the reader." Very's poems rise or fall on the self-righteous stance justified by his sense of spiritual authority.

Deese, Helen R. "A Calendar of the Poems of Jones Very." *Studies in the American Renaissance* (1986): 305-372.
Deese provides "a comprehensive and reliable index" to Very's poems in order to further the understanding of his development as an artist, to trace his career as a published poet, and to promote the possibility of a complete edition of his work. The calendar has two alphabetical indexes: by first lines and by titles. The first line index gives location of manuscript, first appearance in a newspaper or periodical, first appearance in an anthology, and location in each edition of Very's poems.

_____ . "Unpublished and Uncollected Poems of Jones Very." *ESQ* 30 (3rd Quarter, 1984): 154-162.
Deese reviews the shortcomings of existing editions of Very's poems and surveys the manuscript collections. These hold a large number of uncollected and unpublished poems that span the length of Very's career. There are hymns, occasional verse, and some tediously didactic verse sermons. Many of the poems have biographical importance, while some few of them match the quality that has earned Very his reputation. The best are nature poems. Deese brings some of these into print and comments on them.

Dennis, Carl. "Correspondence in Very's Nature Poetry." *New England Quarterly* 43 (June, 1970): 250-273.

Although he is often figured in opposition to Emerson, "Very sees nature as a source of analogues for the highest laws of the mind." In this way at least, he is a disciple of Emerson's doctrine of correspondence—a theory in contrast to the attitudes of the British Romantics. Though Very stresses man's dependence on God, he is not submissive before nature. Inspiration for both poets comes from within or from above. Nature may embody the laws of self and serve as a standard, but correspondences are such that both nature and man are submissive to their maker.

Gittleman, Edwin. *Jones Very: The Effective Years, 1833-1840*. New York: Columbia University Press, 1967.
Attempts to show what about Very impressed "those idealistic intellectuals, those liberal ministers and egocentric writers" known collectively as Transcendentalists. This biography looks closely at Very's Harvard years and at the evidence of Very's commitment to poetry as a vehicle for mastery and release of ideas and feelings growing within him. Very's focused, solitary habits are described and understood as producing the symbolic world of his "epic-dramatic sonnets." He achieved something near greatness by the age of twenty-seven; little thereafter.

Robinson, David. "The Exemplary Self and the Transcendent Self in the Poetry of Jones Very." *ESQ* 24 (4th Quarter, 1978): 207-214.
Very's sonnets confront the reader with questions regarding the inspiration and identity of the speaker. In some poems, the speaker seems to relate the words of an overheard Christ. Elsewhere, Christ seems to speak through the poet. It may even be that the persona identifies himself as a new Christ. Very's art makes a conclusion about the speaker difficult. His poems are most effective when the speaker occupies a position of yearning after God without severing himself from the human condition.

Seed, David. "Alone with God and Nature: The Poetry of Jones Very and Frederick Goddard Tuckerman." In *Nineteenth-Century American Poetry*, edited by A. Robert Lee. Totowa, N.J.: Barnes & Noble, 1985.
In Very's poems, "isolation defines man's relationship to God"; in Tuckerman, "it becomes a liability since his poems are all the more secular." The essay places these recently rediscovered poets into the traditional categories of belief and poetic manner, though neither fits very well. "Very's sonnets show the egotism latent in Transcendentalism turning itself inside out." Tuckerman's self-analysis is strikingly modern in its refusal of religious props.

Waggoner, Hyatt H. "Jones Very." In his *American Poets from the Puritans to the Present Day*. Boston: Houghton Mifflin, 1968.
Traces the superficial ties and fundamental contrasts between Emerson and

Very. Stresses Very's religious conservatism and his affinity with Hawthorne as Puritan descendant and with Thoreau as natural philosopher. Very's best work has a "depth and complexity of meaning" rare in American poetry of his time. Thematically, his work is close to that of Gerard Manley Hopkins; stylistically, it is close to contemporary objectivist poetry. Many poems have an immediacy of impact that gives them "value beyond their use as devotional aids."

Winters, Yvor. "Jones Very and R. W. Emerson: Aspects of New England Mysticism." In his *In Defense of Reason*. Reprint. Denver: Alan Swallow, 1961.
This first modern appraisal, originally published in 1947, explains why Very should claim our attention. Winters gives biographical material and discusses Very's association with Emerson. Very's mysticism was Christian, not Transcendental. He managed a "haunting precision" in rendering both feeling and dogma. Very was the last representative of the mystical Puritanism found in Anne Hutchinson, Jonathan Edwards, and in Hawthorne's *The Scarlet Letter*. "The Created" is his best poem, perfect in structure and phrase with great moral scope and "sublimity of conception."

HENRY DAVID THOREAU
(1817-1862)

General Studies

Bloom, Harold, ed. *Henry David Thoreau*. New York: Chelsea House, 1987.
Reprinted articles and excerpts from recent book-length studies represent the range of interests in and approaches to Thoreau's work. Much here on Thoreau's esthetics as manifest both in his theories and practice. The notion of the poet in the broadest sense informs many of the contributions, though only Richard Bridgman addresses particular poems.

Bode, Carl. "The Hidden Thoreau." In his *The Half-World of American Culture*. Carbondale: Southern Illinois University Press, 1964.
This brief Freudian approach to Thoreau's life observes that Thoreau, with one exception, took no interest in young women. He was more responsive to older women, and his behavior toward them suggests a displaced mother- fixation. The concept of Mother Nature in Thoreau's writings extends beyond the conventional personification. Thoreau's aggressive independence substituted for his inability to form normal friendships. Emerson was his father-substitute, Mrs. Emerson the unacknowledged love object in this Oedipal drama.

——————— . "Thoreau and the Borrowed Reeds." In his *Themes and Directions in American Literature*, edited by Ray B. Browne and Donald Pizer. Lafayette, Ind.: Purdue University Studies, 1969.
Early in his career, Thoreau found models in the work of the metaphysical poets. George Herbert influenced him most, and Thoreau's poems often echo Herbert's stanza forms and patterns. Odd metaphors, too, were staples of Thoreau's early verse. His worksheets, over time, show a tendency to engage in simpler forms. Even while reflecting the manner of other poets, Thoreau sounded an individual note, an awkward strength of his own. His eclectic practice contradicted what he preached—an organic poetry that grew from within.

——————— . "Thoreau's Young Ideas." In *The Half-World of American Culture*. Carbondale: Southern Illinois University Press, 1964.
For about ten years, from 1837 to 1847, Thoreau expressed his most significant ideas in poetry. Bode provides a brief summary of the leading ideas manifest there. In "Inspiration," Thoreau writes of knowledge beyond sense. The idea of God-in-nature occurs occasionally. Thoreau's philosophy of male friendship, which requires restraint and sincerity, is an important feature of his thought in

verse. Ideas on love and politics are also found in the poems. "The essence—though not the sum—of Thoreau's philosophy is to be discovered in his verse."

Borst, Raymond R. *Henry David Thoreau: A Descriptive Bibliography*. Pittsburgh: University of Pittsburgh Press, 1982.
First lists all books, pamphlets, folios, and broadsides wholly or substantially by Thoreau, including printings to 1880 and selected reprintings to 1980. Next lists editions of collected works, first appearances of contributions to books, first appearances of contributions to periodicals, and finally single-volume selections of Thoreau's works. Establishes the shape of Thoreau's literary career and reputation.

—————— . *Henry David Thoreau: A Reference Guide, 1835-1899*. Boston: G. K. Hall, 1987.
This bibliography of secondary materials "carries the writings about Henry David Thoreau from the first discovered notice of his name in public print through to the last day of the nineteenth century." The chronological arrangement helps readers discover the shape of Thoreau's critical fortunes. By using the index, readers can look up the commentary on specific Thoreau titles. Within each year, periodical materials are given by the month and book references alphabetically by author.

Boswell, Jeanetta, and Sarah Crouch. *Henry David Thoreau and the Critics: A Checklist of Criticism, 1900-1978*. Metuchen, N.J.: Scarecrow, 1981.
This checklist is arranged alphabetically by author and is followed by two indexes. The first lists coauthors and editors; the second is an index of subjects. Individual works by Thoreau are referenced here. Especially useful for articles in periodicals.

Bridgman, Richard. *Dark Thoreau*. Lincoln: University of Nebraska Press, 1982.
Only selective readings have allowed us to see Thoreau as a celebrant of individuality and of nature's benign glory. Other evidence shows "that he was a deeply pessimistic man who could barely bring himself to admit it; that he had a hostile, punishing streak in him, manifested most vividly in his imagery." Bridgman explores the reasons for and consequences of "psychological strains" in Thoreau.

Channing, William Ellery. *Thoreau: The Poet-Naturalist*, edited by F. G. Sanborn. New ed., enl. Boston: Charles E. Good, 1902.
An early life by a friend and admirer originally published in 1873. Sanford's introduction discusses additions made from Channing's manuscripts for this edition. Provides firsthand glimpses of Thoreau with too much enthusiasm and

too little critical perspective. Reconstructs extended conversations, allowing us to enjoy Thoreau as a walking companion. Some attention to the poetry.

Christie, John Aldrich. *Thoreau As World Traveler*. New York: Columbia University Press, 1965.
Juxtaposes the limited geographical range of Thoreau's travels with the wide range of insight and experience gathered there. Much of this experience was the result of patient, curious observation, yet just as much was the result of reading. Christie shows how Thoreau's reading of travel books informed his own writing. The microcosm of Concord was imagined as holding the same truths available anywhere else. Thoreau made his travels more monumental than those of most other writers.

Dennis, Carl. "Correspondence in Thoreau's Nature Poetry." *ESQ*, no. 58 (1st Quarter, 1970): 101-108.
Demonstrates that the notion of correspondence as developed in Wordsworth, Coleridge, and Emerson is a controlling idea in Thoreau's nature poems. Thoreau's position is explicit in his early journals and in such poems as "The Inward Morning" and "All Things Are Current Found." Dennis groups Thoreau's nature poetry into "poems of fancy, deliberate readings, and poems of mystery." Thoreau keeps the worlds of mind and nature autonomous in order to "perceive the correspondences that unite them."

Derleth, August. *Concord Rebel: A Life of Thoreau*. Philadelphia: Chilton, 1962.
The hand of an accomplished fiction writer animates this story of Thoreau's development into a practitioner of quiet rebellion. Derleth gives only ten pages to Thoreau's youth, somewhat more attention to his apprenticeship in poetry and his relationship with Emerson. Thoreau's journeys and experiments in living occupy most of the book. Little assessment of Thoreau's art, much on his outlook and courage.

Dombrowski, Daniel A. *Thoreau the Platonist*. New York: Peter Lang, 1986.
Divides the topic into sections on Thoreau's Platonic sources, the Platonic structure of Thoreau's universe, "Thoreau's Dipolar Theism," "Thoreau, Sainthood, and Vegetarianism," "Thoreau and the Platonic Functions of Language." Invokes the notion of meontic mimesis as addressed in Plato's *Ion* as a key to Thoreau's aesthetic. Thoreau's views on the afterlife are more non- and pre- Christian than Christian. Relates Plato's treatment of Socrates to Thoreau's doctrine of civil disobedience.

Edel, Leon. *Henry D. Thoreau*. Minneapolis: University of Minnesota Press, 1970.
A vivid treatment of Thoreau's life and art in pamphlet form. Edel, a master biographer, considers the environment surrounding Thoreau and its influence upon his decisions, his topics, and his methods. The myth of Thoreau at

Walden was, in its own time, a rural comedy. Edel examines briefly the major essays and the enormous journal—"one of the more impersonal journals of literary history." No assessment of the poems.

Friesen, Victor Carl. *The Spirit of the Huckleberry: Sensuousness in Henry Thoreau.* Edmonton, Canada: University of Alberta Press, 1984.
Thoreau's sensuousness has been noted but not explored in previous criticism, which usually views Thoreau as stoic and ascetic. For Friesen, the essential Thoreau is "attuned to each sight, sound, flavor, taste, and touch of nature individually." Connects Thoreau's sensuousness to his ideas about health and wildness. Thoreau's stance is an oscillation between civilization and the wild.

Garber, Frederick. *Thoreau's Redemptive Imagination.* New York: New York University Press, 1977.
A tentative exploration of Thoreau's idiosyncratic place in the Romantic movement. Focuses on Thoreau's "modes of organizing his experience of the world," though Garber draws analogies to other Romantic figures, particularly Jean-Jacques Rousseau. *The Maine Woods* and "Walking" are the primary texts examined. For Thoreau, "though nature is satisfying in itself, it is not satisfying enough."

Glazier, Lyle. "Thoreau's Rebellious Lyric." *ESQ*, no. 54 (1st Quarter, 1969): 27-30.
The rhythmical pattern of "Smoke" is purposely ambiguous, no doubt in pointed rebellion against formal absolutism. It approximates a seven-syllable tetrameter, but there is no way to be certain if the rhythm is rising or falling. Glazier's meticulous scansion and discussion concludes: "the lyric has the energetic power of rhythm that is forming itself." In this way, the metrical texture is like the smoke. Lack of rhyme contributes functionally in this poem whose images and allusions point to "the focal mythic symbols of rebellion."

Glick, Wendell, ed. *The Recognition of Henry David Thoreau.* Ann Arbor: University of Michigan Press, 1969.
An excellent sampling of responses to Thoreau's writing divided into four chronological sections. In the period 1848-1890, critics harped on Thoreau's eccentricities and praised him as a naturalist. A period of revaluation extended through 1916, followed by the years of his rise to fame (to 1941). The final section presents mid-century insights. Glick's preface summarizes the history of Thoreau's reputation.

Harding, Walter. *The Days of Henry Thoreau.* Reprint. New York: Dover, 1982.
First published in 1966, this standard biography, superseding earlier ones by Henry S. Salt (1890) and Henry Seidel Canby (1939), is a meticulous yet flowing piece of scholarship. Harding has no thesis to offer, letting the para-

doxes that make Thoreau so fascinating stand unresolved. The chapters, relatively short, are further divided into passages of two to six pages each holding a tiny drama. Makes use of the poems.

——————— . ed. *Thoreau: Man of Concord*. New York: Holt, Rinehart and Winston, 1960.
A selection of reactions to Thoreau by his contemporaries. "Thoreau the man" is in focus is this collection of biographical materials by Thoreau's foremost biographer. Comment by Emerson, Lowell, Ellery Channing, Louisa May Alcott, and many others. Materials include letters, newspaper columns, memoirs, and poems. Appendices include a chronology, some brief selections from Thoreau, and notes on the eyewitnesses.

Harding, Walter, and Michael Meyer. *A New Thoreau Handbook*. New York: New York University Press, 1980.
A reliable, conveniently arranged presentation of the salient facts and issues in Thoreau studies. The five chapters deal in turn with Thoreau's life, his works, his sources, his ideas, and his reputation. Considers most of Thoreau's poetry to be poor, with only a few pieces of true significance. Thoreau made no innovations and was for the most part backward-looking in technique. This handbook reviews critical materials on each of the five subjects. Includes a Thoreau chronology.

Hicks, John H., ed. *Thoreau in Our Season*. Amherst: University of Massachusetts Press, 1966.
This volume took shape as a special "Centenary Gathering" issue of *The Massachusetts Review*. The essays tend to seek for the essentials in Thoreau's character and to measure the continuing relevance of Thoreau's thought and example. The ethical issues are presented concretely, as are the ways in which Thoreau writings point toward fruitful relationships between the individual and the community. Not concerned with his artistic merit.

Hough, Henry Beetle. *Thoreau of Walden: The Man and His Eventful Life*. New York: Simon & Schuster, 1956.
A readable popular biography lacking in documentation. Chapters divided into brief sections, each a self-contained narrative, so the reader can easily find places to rest. Thoreau's major relationships are presented, and his ties to his region are captured well. An idealized treatment in a familiar tone for bedside reading.

Krutch, Joseph Wood. *Henry David Thoreau*. New York: William Sloane, 1948.
A spirited biography that honors Thoreau's dictum about the dangers of complication. The range of Thoreau's interests are in sharp contrast to the unen-

cumbered business of his life. Krutch warns against overstating Emerson's influence. Thoreau took what he needed and made it his own. An attractive mix of biographical and critical materials with a Freudian slant. The poems are not treated.

Lane, Lauriat, Jr. "Finding a Voice: Thoreau's Pentameters." *ESQ*, no. 60 (Summer, 1970): 67-72.
Thoreau's few experiments in the iambic pentameter tradition reached a high degree of accomplishment with two poems written in 1850. The untitled poem employed irregular rhyme and a loose handling of the iambic norm. "Tall Ambrosia" is in blank verse with two closing couplets. Lane traces Thoreau's stylistic development up through these poems, arguing that "Thoreau may be said to have found his poetic voice at the moment he lost it." His mastery of and restlessness with poetic vehicles led him to abandon poetry for prose. The poems discussed represent predicative and adjectival modes.

Lebeaux, Richard. *Young Man Thoreau*. Amherst: University of Massachusetts Press, 1977.
Most earlier biographies pass over Thoreau's youth and young adulthood in a rush to get him to Walden Pond. Lebeaux re-creates those early years in an attempt to trace the development of Thoreau's identity. This search involves gathering and interpreting details on family background, emerging ideology, stances on cultural issues, and the search for models. Largely a psychological study on the making of a self. Ends with the impact of the death of Thoreau's brother.

_____ . *Thoreau's Seasons*. Amherst: University of Massachusetts Press, 1984.
A continuation of *Young Man Thoreau* from the beginning of the Walden experiment until Thoreau's death. Like the earlier work, an application of Eriksonian psychology. Uses theories of the life cycle and adult development to examine Thoreau's coming to terms with the aging process and the approach of death. Discusses the seasonal motif in Thoreau's images and metaphors for their conscious and unconscious meanings.

McIntosh, James. *Thoreau As Romantic Naturalist*. Ithaca, N.Y.: Cornell University Press, 1974.
Sees Thoreau as a more serious naturalist than other Romantic writers. McIntosh treats Thoreau's nature descriptions as direct expressions of experience rather than as literary material or metaphor. Examines the conflict between Thoreau's wish for involvement with nature and his sense of separation from it. Comparisons to Wordsworth and Goethe help explore the shifts in Thoreau's attitudes toward nature. Many poems treated.

Matthiessen, F. O. "The Organic Principle." In his *American Renaissance: Art and Expression in the Age of Emerson and Whitman*. New York: Oxford University Press, 1941.

This magnificent chapter on the American development of a central aesthetic concept pays close attention to Thoreau's contribution. A section on "New England Landscapes" examines passages from the prose and poetry of Emerson and Thoreau. Thoreau's "Smoke" receives particular attention as an example of Coleridge's theory of imitation. Thoreau's language gained the capacity to express "acute sensation" from his intimate contact with nature.

Metzger, Charles R. *Thoreau and Whitman: A Study of Their Esthetics*. Seattle: University of Washington Press, 1961.

These writers subscribed to "related versions of the same transcendentalist tradition." Their religious views influenced their aesthetic positions. They are more practical, less theoretical, than Emerson. Like Emerson, they favor architectural examples in discussing aesthetic issues. Both were conscious of the role of art in personal salvation as well as the salvation of others. Differences are more superficial than essential.

Meyer, Michael. *Several More Lives to Live*. Westport, Conn.: Greenwood Press, 1977.

Traces Thoreau's reputation as a political and social thinker among American critics and readers. The thought of the nation more or less caught up with Thoreau's visionary insights. His appeal to those coming of age in the 1960's is emphasized, particularly the doctrine of civil disobedience, the abhorrence of violence, and the back-to-nature fashion of antiestablishment voices. Thoreau was oversimplified by those who appealed to him as an authority on American principles.

Miller, Perry. *Consciousness in Concord*. Boston: Houghton Mifflin, 1958.

An edition of Thoreau's "lost journal" is preceded by a long commentary on that text as it relates to the journals in their entirety. Miller considers the themes and the conscious artistry of Thoreau's work in this form, with key sections on method, quality of awareness, attitudes toward death, attitudes toward men and women, and the strategy of anticipation.

Moller, Mary Elkins. *Thoreau in the Human Community*. Amherst: University of Massachusetts Press, 1980.

Looks closely at Thoreau as a citizen and as a friend. Distinguishes among spheres of community and theories of interaction with each: local, national, intellectual. Examines seven friendships in detail, including those with Harrison Blake and Daniel Ricketson. Thoreau's "need for mystical experience is closely related to the complex patterns of attraction and repulsion in human relationships." Though often expressing bitterness and disillusionment, Thoreau was not a misanthrope.

Murray, James G. *Henry David Thoreau*. New York: Twayne, 1968.
Thoreau is presented here as a "great thinker" rather than as a personality or literary artist. Murray presents a "biography of the mind" covering such topics as "Sense of the Self," "Society as Burden," "Confrontation with Evil," and "Freedom and Simplicity." A sensible, straightforward representation of Thoreau's ideas. Murray's afterword stresses the continuing relevance of Thoreau's positions.

Oehlschlaeger, Fritz, and George Hendrik, eds. *Toward the Making of Thoreau's Modern Reputation*. Urbana: University of Illinois Press, 1979.
Brings together the correspondence of five men who were active Thoreau scholars in the 1890's and the early years of the twentieth century. Through their exchanges, we can discover how Thoreau's early reputation underwent significant revision during this period. The men are Dr. Samuel A. Jones, A. W. Hosmer, Henry S. Salt (who wrote the first comprehensive biography), Harrison G. O. Blake, and Daniel Ricketson.

Paul, Sherman. *The Shores of America: Thoreau's Inward Exploration*. Reprint. New York: Russell & Russell, 1971.
Thoreau's development as a thinker and artist is anatomized. Paul searches for crises that may be "buried deep in the ambiguities of expression, whether in deed or word." Less an interpretation of the works than a reading that looks for clues to the "inner life" of Thoreau. Novel views of the relationship with Emerson and of Thoreau's way of dealing with tragedy. Many references to the poems, though only excerpts are quoted.

———, ed. *Thoreau: A Collection of Critical Essays*. Englewood Cliffs, N.J.: Prentice-Hall, 1962.
A wide variety of approaches to Thoreau's life and art, some on particular works and others on recurrent themes. These essays represent the developments in Thoreau criticism during the twentieth century. Leo Stoller's essay "Thoreau's Doctrine of Simplicity" and Edwin Fussell's on the Indian in Thoreau's work are particularly useful.

Richardson, Robert D., Jr. *Henry Thoreau: A Life of the Mind*. Berkeley: University of California Press, 1986.
This intellectual biography focuses on the private Thoreau—the man at his desk. Richardson's "main purpose has been to give an account of the development of Thoreau as a writer, a naturalist, and a reader." The study begins with Thoreau's return from Harvard to Concord, steps back to trace his Harvard

education, and then forward to detail the responses of Thoreau's mind to the intellectual currents of his time. We witness Thoreau's developing concepts of nature, America, and art as well as his intellectual affinities and friendships.

Sattelmeyer, Robert. *Thoreau's Reading: A Study in Intellectual History*. Princeton, N.J.: Princeton University Press, 1988.
This biography of Thoreau as reader examines the immediate and long-range impact of his reading on his thought and art. Traces shifts in Thoreau's interests as reflected in his reading. For Thoreau, the works of other writers were his own professional tools. Sattelmeyer comments on Thoreau's eclecticism and on his way of taking notes. Through reading, Thoreau extended his participation in the life of his times. A bibliographical catalog follows Sattelmeyer's interpretive essay.

Sayre, Robert F. *Thoreau and the American Indians*. Princeton, N.J.: Princeton University Press, 1977.
Explores the identity in outlook between Thoreau and prominent leaders in the Indian communities. Like them, he finds a spiritual dimension in ecological issues. Thoreau was fascinated by Indian life and spent a good part of his time learning about it and attempting to imitate it. Sayre examines the metaphor of "savagism" along with Thoreau's attacks on civilization.

Schneider, Richard J. *Henry David Thoreau*. Boston: Twayne, 1987.
A brief biography is followed by a treatment of the various aspects of Thoreau's complex personality as it is revealed in his major works. Thus, *A Week on the Concord and Merrimack Rivers* is used to reveal Thoreau as Transcendental artist while comments on *Walden* present him as seer. The poetry is barely acknowledged. Chronology and selected bibliography (with brief annotations).

Scudder, Townsend. "Henry David Thoreau." In *Literary History of the United States*, edited by Robert E. Spiller et al. 3d ed., rev. New York: Macmillan, 1963.
Remarks on the immense generative power of Thoreau's thought considering how little was published in his lifetime. Thoreau's literary work, opinions, and life were a seamless whole. Emerson encouraged Thoreau's poetry, and his own work served for a while as a model. Thoreau's problem of choosing a career was similar to Emerson's. Traces Thoreau's development as a stylist and praises his ability to communicate the joyful process of discovery.

Van Doren, Mark. *Henry David Thoreau: A Critical Study*. Reprint. New York: Russell & Russell, 1961.
The first to be largely founded on Thoreau's *Journal*, this study adds importantly to the chronological record as well as to our understanding of Tho-

reau's character and mind. For Van Doren, the journal reveals unattractive aspects of Thoreau. Here, his thoughts are less refined, yet more extravagantly elaborated. Discovers a "pungent" personality with an egotistic sensibility. Van Doren sees primarily the cynical side of Thoreau, or does he see Thoreau cynically?

Waggoner, Hyatt H. "Henry David Thoreau." In his *American Poets from the Puritans to the Present*. Boston: Houghton Mifflin, 1968.
Few of Thoreau's poems match the achievement of "Smoke." Many "are bare statements of opinion, rhymed doctrines, or poetry as artless prophecy omitting all those tensions that give his best work its unique tang." There is no distance between the poet and the speaker in Thoreau's work. Considers "Inspiration" and "Winter Memories" among Thoreau's best, the latter suggestive of Frost and Dickinson. Much of Thoreau's hymnlike verse is only "useful for the worshipper in the same church."

Wells, Henry W. "An Evaluation of Thoreau's Poetry." In *Thoreau: A Collection of Critical Essays*, edited by Sherman Paul. Englewood Cliffs, N.J.: Prentice-Hall, 1962.
Describes the careful revisions in Thoreau's poetry manuscripts. Thoreau wrote most of his poetry while a young man. He turned away from contemporary taste, favoring instead the metaphysical and neoclassical veins. His studies in Greek and Latin continued to inform his poetry. In some of his best work, poetic descriptions of smoke and clouds, he partakes of Romantic nature verse. A few of his poems look forward to the modernist period. "Thoreau found all schools of poetry his teachers, none his master."

JAMES RUSSELL LOWELL
(1819-1891)

General Studies

Allen, Gay Wilson. "James Russell Lowell." In his *American Prosody*. New York: American Book, 1935.
Provides detailed analysis of Lowell's lifelong work in the ode form. "Thredony" and the "Ode Recited at the Harvard Commemoration" are pseudo- Pindaric odes of irregular subdivisions and line lengths but in rhyme. Lowell used such structures for much of his best work. His contributions to American prosody include "a more varied placement of accents and the combination of different kinds of feet to produce a suggestiveness of tone and cadence." The metrical freedoms of "The Vision of Sir Launfal" influenced later nineteenth century practice.

Arms, George. "Lowell." In his *The Fields Were Green*. Stanford, Calif.: Stanford University Press, 1953. Also in *American Poetry to 1914*, edited by Harold Bloom. New York: Chelsea House, 1987.
Lowell suffers from misrepresentation in anthologies that pass him off as a "schoolroom poet." Poems such as "Agassiz" show Lowell's real strengths: "a quality of full-bodied talk, an educated man's mingling of the colloquial and the formal." Lowell's critical acumen on matters of form didn't carry over into his own poems. His best- liked poems, like *The Biglow Papers* and *A Fable for Critics*, are essentially nonpoetical. We admire them for their judgments and humor, not for their poetic stature. They are real, but limited, accomplishments. Lowell was best at the familiar verse essay, as in "The Cathedral."

Beatty, Richmond Croom. *James Russell Lowell*. Reprint. Hamden, Conn.: Archon Books, 1969.
A lively account of Lowell's life and times that benefits from some dramatic shaping of the documentary evidence. Considers Lowell's friendships, his travels, and his work on the *North American Review*. Summarizes the issues behind Lowell's major satirical efforts, outlining his place in the world of ideas. Assesses Lowell's value as critic and literary statesman. Novelistic treatment allows minimal intrusion of scholarly apparatus.

Clark, Harry Hayden, and Norman Foerster. Introduction to *James Russell Lowell: Representative Selections*. New York: American Book, 1947.
A comprehensive overview of the development of Lowell's thought as humanitarian, nationalist, and "natural aristocrat." The poems are presented as illus-

trations of Lowell's positions on various issues. Detailed discussion of Lowell's critical views includes such topics as the task of the critic, form and the ideal, imagination, and the function of literature. Chronological table and extensive bibliography.

Duberman, Martin. *James Russell Lowell*. Boston: Houghton Mifflin, 1966.
This comprehensive biography details each stage of Lowell's childhood, education, and career. Duberman's concern is not to revise the estimate of Lowell as a poet that "denies him the first rank," but rather "to restore him as a man." Duberman works against the stereotype of stiffness, smugness, and a lingering Puritan narrowness of vision. Stresses Lowell's loyalty to individuals, his striving to balance private and public responsibilities, his geniality, and his capacity for living. Illustrated.

Foerster, Norman. "Lowell." In his *Nature in American Literature*. Reprint. New York: Russell & Russell, 1958.
Lowell had an eighteenth century love of nature; "nature dominated by man gave him as much delight as he craved." The majesty of mountains and the vast solitude of the ocean seemed to repel him. Of all the seasons, he celebrated early summer most often: "He was the poet of June." Lowell admired nature categorically or in the aggregate; he was not a deft painter of particularities. "Science, romanticism, democracy—if he could not deny them, he could at least forget them in the gladness and repose of living nature."

Greenslet, Ferris. *James Russell Lowell: His Life and Work*. Reprint. Detroit: Gale Research, 1969.
First published in 1905, this study examines the formative environment that led Lowell to poetry, his employment of poetry in the service of politics, and his roles as teacher, editor, critic, and diplomat. A separate chapter on the poetry connects Lowell's earliest work with the vogue of Byronism. As Lowell developed, his poems became "increasingly bookish, yet decreasingly imitative." His first two volumes showed an extravagance in imagery. Admires the "freshly contemporary spirit" of Lowell's work as a whole.

Hale, Edward Everett. *James Russell Lowell and His Friends*. Boston: Houghton Mifflin, 1899.
This richly anecdotal biography examines the poet in the context of the important people in his life. Hale sketches a network of supportive relationships, along the way deepening our understanding of Boston literary life. He provides biographical sketches of many of these friends and relations, along with many photographs. The friendships Lowell made in Spain and England are also considered. Good for the flavor of the times and for the social dynamics of cultural leadership.

Heyman, C. David. *American Aristocracy: The Life and Times of James Russell, Amy, and Robert Lowell*. New York: Dodd, Mead, 1980.
The last three sections present critical biographies of the title subjects. The first section is "Backgrounds: The Lowell Landscape." The distinction of the Lowells among great American families is its triad of poets. Each was a founder or dominant figure in an important literary school or movement. James Russell Lowell is seen as "The Natural Aristocrat," yet a man whose life and achievement were marked by contradictions. Attractive discussion of how leaders emerge in a democracy.

Howard, Leon. *Victorian Knight-Errant: A Study of the Early Literary Career of James Russell Lowell*. Berkeley: University of California Press, 1952.
Howard's purpose "was to discover the extent to which a meticulous examination of an individual's entire literary output, within the context of its human origin, could improve one's understanding of the individual himself and of the age in which he lived." Lowell was driven by unusual inner energy but not pulled toward any consistent purpose. Thus his life patterns are chaotic, his career varied and discontinuous. Describes Lowell's commitment "to becoming a man of poetic action." Many poems and prose works examined.

Hudson, William Henry. *Lowell & His Poetry*. Reprint. New York: AMS Press, 1971.
First published in 1914, this is a compact volume of biographical criticism the original purpose of which was to introduce Lowell to British students. Extensive quotations, including whole works, are used to relate life and art. Hudson provides introductory notes on the period and on the Lowell family to prepare the way for the interweaving of poems and comment. Reviews the issues addressed in Lowell's first two volumes of poems and then introduces "The Vision of Sir Launfal." Little here on Lowell's satiric work. The clarity and sincerity of his more serious efforts are praised.

Kaufman, Marjorie R. Introduction to *The Poetical Works of James Russell Lowell*, edited by Kaufman. Rev. ed. Boston: Houghton Mifflin, 1978.
Explains why the nineteenth century Lowell canon did not wear well in the twentieth century. Argues that Lowell needs to be rediscovered for the wide range of his work and for the likely appeal in our time of poems that were not properly valued when Lowell was prominent. Praises "the accuracy, originality, and ingenuity of Lowell's use of vernacular speech," his ear for regional rhythms, and the force and dignity of his best serious poems.

McGlinchee, Claire. *James Russell Lowell*. New York: Twayne, 1967.
A concise yet rounded presentation of Lowell's life and achievements. The first chapter sketches the state of American literature at Lowell's birth. The next

two are biographical, while the third examines his early poetry. Then come treatments of his careers as Harvard professor, critic, and diplomat. Finally, the later poems are assessed. Lowell's work as a satirist and as a cultural emissary rivals his achievement as a poet. Chronology and selected bibliography.

Pearce, Roy Harvey. "James Russell Lowell." In his *The Continuity of American Poetry*. Princeton, N.J.: Princeton University Press, 1961.
Reviews Lowell's efforts to find a poetic manner that would both deal with the everyday and be an escape from it, would rise above mere verse but not so high as to lose his audience, would handle ideas without being preachy. Considers Lowell to be often "vague, sentimental, acutely tender," but in his best work penetrating and witty. *The Biglow Papers* and the later odes are his major achievements. Lowell fought against materialism as well as against the prevailing sentimentalism over nature.

Phelps, William Lyon. "Lowell." In his *Howells, James, Bryant and Other Essays*. Reprint. Port Washington, N.Y.: Kennikat Press, 1965.
A sound, if overly enthusiastic, introductory essay that reviews Lowell's privileged upbringing and his various contributions to our cultural and political life. Aside from his literary efforts, Lowell was famous as a speaker, correspondent, and conversationalist. Giving primary attention to *The Biglow Papers*, Phelps argues that Lowell was "like the Elizabethans in his overflowing vitality, in his essential manliness." He was "the finest representative of the modern republican gentleman." Useful characterizations of Lowell's style in prose and poetry. First published in 1924.

Scudder, Horace Elisha. *James Russell Lowell: A Biography*. 2 vols. Reprint. New York: AMS Press, 1974.
One of the most comprehensive early lives of Lowell, this study, first published in 1901, made use of the then-recently published *Letters of James Russell Lowell* edited by Charles Eliot Norton along with other letters independently discovered. A careful tracing of how Lowell's political allegiances developed and found voice in his writings. Separate chapters on *A Fable for Critics*, "The Vision of Sir Launfal," and *The Biglow Papers* elaborate upon circumstances leading up to publication. Detailed chapter on "Poetry and Prose 1858- 1872." An appendix provides a chronology of Lowell's publications.

Stewart, Charles Oran. *Lowell and France*. Nashville, Tenn.: Vanderbilt University Press, 1951.
Divides the French element in Lowell's writings into three categories. First, landscape, monuments, and events; second, individuals; third, literature. "The Vision of Sir Launfal" and some lesser works show the influence of French literature. Stewart provides detailed examinations of Lowell's work against

possible French sources, leading to a somewhat nervous summation regarding Lowell's strong "powers of assimilation." Appendices include Lowell's comments on French literature.

Underwood, Francis H. *James Russell Lowell: A Biographical Sketch*. Boston: James R. Osgood, 1882.
Lowell's prominence is attested by this early life written some ten years before his death. Though the whole career is in view, Underwood pays particular attention to the satire of *The Biglow Papers*, summarizing at length and stressing the sources and nature of the comedy as well as its "high aim and definite moral purpose." Underwood's section on "Yankee Humor and Pathos" is still useful after a hundred years. More comments on Lowell as poet than are found in many of the later biographies.

Wagenknecht, Edward. *James Russell Lowell: Portrait of a Many-Sided Man*. New York: Oxford University Press, 1971.
This critical biography plays down the idea that Lowell's fragmentation of his energies resulted in unrealized potential as a poet. Rather, Wagenknecht argues that Lowell was a man whose gift and need was to try his hand at everything and present himself in many roles. There is no guarantee that a one-sided poetic version of Lowell would have reached greater heights. His force of personality may have led his contemporaries to overestimate his abilities. The conditions of his life created as many opportunities as limitations. A colorful, persuasive assessment.

Waggoner, Hyatt H. "James Russell Lowell". In his *American Poets from the Puritans to the Present*. Boston: Houghton Mifflin, 1968.
Lowell was a much more thoughtful poet than Bryant or his other contemporaries. He had a richer sensibility. He tried his hand at long meditative verse, traditional odes, and satiric poems without making anything totally his own. In each area, including the retelling of Arthurian legend, he had a degree of success. Lowell's most readable poems, such as "The Cathedral," survive "because the thought in them is so firm." Lowell was caught between "a world he loved but could not quite believe and a world he understood but could not love."

Wurfl, George. *Lowell's Debt to Goethe: A Study of Literary Influence*. State College: Pennsylvania State College Studies, 1954.
Part 1 considers Lowell's knowledge of German and his interest in Goethe, including his frequent allusions to Goethe's work. Part 2 points up the direct parallels between the two writers in their theories of criticism, notions of originality, and conception of poetry. Views Lowell as "one of the champions of Goethe in America." Murky on how fully Lowell acknowledged the debt.

The Biglow Papers

Howard, Leon. *Victorian Knight-Errant: A Study of the Early Literary Career of James Russell Lowell*, 232-260. Berkeley: University of California Press, 1952.
Shows how this series grew out of Lowell's wish to unburden himself of an elevated poetic style that sought heroic ends. Wanting to be closer to the people, to make an immediate impact with effective social satire, Lowell adopted the persona of Hosea Biglow and spoke through his Yankee dialect. Other characters, usually represented through letters or comments on Biglow, populate an imaginary Boston. Through them, Lowell's political and moral positions are transformed into entertaining plain talk. Some of Lowell's intentions were compromised to meet publishing deadlines.

Phelps, William Lyon. "Lowell." In his *Howells, James, Bryant, and Other Essays*. Reprint, 102-111. Port Washington, N.Y.: Kennikat Press, 1965.
Lowell "represented the four main traits of the typical Yankee—Shrewdness, Caution, Humour, Moral Principle." Only the extreme topicality of its references to the Mexican War keeps this effort from being ranked with the great satires in world literature. Lowell used the Yankee dialect to fine artistic purpose, and he succeeded in stirring up Northern feeling against slavery and against war, declaring it to be incompatible with Christianity. Some verses are less satiric than pastoral. "The Courtin" is a superior poem in that vein, a "Yankee Eclogue."

Voss, Arthur. "Backgrounds of Lowell's Satire in *The Biglow Papers*." *New England Quarterly* 23 (March, 1950): 47-64.
A useful review of the historical circumstances and personalities lying behind Lowell's major achievement. Voss elucidates the incidents, events, and issues concerning slavery and the Mexican War that gave rise to this satiric endeavor. He reviews the contemporary response to *The Biglow Papers*, and he shows how and how well Lowell used all of the devices of the satirist.

Wortham, Thomas. Introduction to *James Russell Lowell's The Biglow Papers, first series*, edited by Wortham. DeKalb: Northern Illinois University Press, 1977.
Portrays Lowell's development as a reformer in an age of reform before turning to the means by which Lowell found the powerful vehicle of Hosea Biglow. Sketches the background of the Mexican War and then presents the method and design of the poem. Argues that the sustained ironic tone and the unique form are more important unifying factors than consistency in character. Samples early reactions to the book.

"A Fable for Critics"

Clements, Frances Marion. "Public and Private Reactions to Lowell's *Fable for Critics*." *ATQ*, no. 43 (Summer, 1979): 189-198.
Though Lowell's poem generated a good deal of enthusiastic public comment, there was a significant amount of negative reaction expressed privately. Of course, much of this came from Lowell's victims and their friends. Lowell tried to excuse himself by claiming that he never intended to publish the work; however, existing records prove otherwise. He did not dash it off, as he claimed, but worked on it for about a year.

Howard, Leon. *Victorian Knight-Errant: A Study of the Early Literary Career of James Russell Lowell*, 260-269. Berkeley: University of California Press, 1952.
Suggests that the poem was probably inspired by Lowell's irritation with the judgments made by Margaret Fuller in her essay on American literature, though Lowell insisted that the character of the critic was a composite. He borrowed the form and meter in which he chides his major contemporaries from Leigh Hunt's milder *The Feast of the Poets*. Composed over various sittings, the satire shows shifts in mood. The poem's "lively impressionism" presents "more human and thus more lasting critical judgments" than are to be found in many traditional critical assessments. Thousands of copies were sold in a few months.

HERMAN MELVILLE
(1819-1891)

General Studies

Aaron, Daniel. "Melville: The Conflict of Convictions." In his *The Unwritten War: American Writers and the Civil War*. New York: Alfred A. Knopf, 1973.
Unlike Whitman, Melville did not find the outcome of the war conducive to a happy vision of America's future. He, too, voiced antislavery opinions, but he distrusted doctrinaire abolitionism. Aaron explores the design of *Battle-Pieces*, which he considers a carefully patterned sequence beginning with references to John Brown and responding to key battles. The replacement of wood by metal in warships is emblematic of the passing of a Romantic age and the coming of a mechanical, utilitarian one.

Adler, Joyce Sparer. *War in Melville's Imagination*. New York: New York University Press, 1981.
Traces the "war or peace theme" from its first appearance in *Typee* through its final discussion in *Billy Budd* and the later poems. Melville's works not only cry out against war, but they probe the individual and cultural dynamics that lead to war. *Moby Dick* is viewed "as a symbolic poem of war and peace," while *Billy Budd* is considered the most philosophical presentation of this issue. A separate chapter on *Battle-Pieces* links this sequence of poems to tragic drama.

Arvin, Newton. *Herman Melville: A Critical Biography*. Reprint. New York: Macmillan, 1957.
One of the most engaging and sensible studies of the interaction between Melville's life and work. Arvin's feeling for his subject makes for a more persuasive exploration than many later studies based on more comprehensive documentary evidence. The "Trophies of Peace" chapter examines the late prose and the poetry. Arvin addresses Melville's poetic diction and his idiosyncratic imagery. Praises characterization in *Clarel*, calling it "a novel of ideas in verse."

Barrett, Laurence. "The Differences in Melville's Poetry." *PMLA* 70 (September, 1955): 606-623.
Melville's earliest poetry, scattered through *Mardi*, was not a serious effort. His later poetry was earnest and innovative, with much of it being about poetry itself. Changes in Melville's poetry stem from changes in his use of symbols. In his later poems, he moves away from allegory and employs "a highly personal symbolism developed from metaphor." This symbolism, because it

makes sense on the surface level and often reads like conventional poetic idiom, is often overlooked. Melville's poems show the process of discovering form.

Bercaw, Mary K. *Melville's Sources*. Evanston, Ill.: Northwestern University Press, 1987.
A checklist, "keyed to Melville's works, of all the sources scholars have suggested that Melville used." The evidence is not merely the availability of the source, but the internal evidence of his writings. Bercaw credits the scholars who have made the various attributions. Her introduction contains "A History of Melville Source Study" and "Melville's Acquisition and Use of His Sources." The checklist is alphabetical by author of source, keyed to the chronological list of scholarship that follows.

Bernstein, John. *Pacifism and Rebellion in the Writings of Herman Melville*. London: Mouton, 1964.
Treats the themes of pacificism and rebellion as polarities that emerge in virtually all Melville texts. These terms or concepts are not so much antithetical as they are complementary. After exploring the fiction, Bernstein examines this theme in paired poems from *Battle-Pieces* and in the characters of Derwent and Ungar from *Clarel*. Melville's late message is that "man's ultimate expression of defiance against the universe is to continue to live."

Berthoff, Warner. *The Example of Melville*. Princeton, N.J.: Princeton University Press, 1962.
"The concern of this book is with the example Melville presents as a writer, as it still lies before us in his work." Focus is less on the particulars of "themes, ideas, procedures, forms" than on the "continuous imaginative presence and energy sustaining these particulars and positively generating them." Chapters on setting, character, narrators, and style. Scattered references to the poems. Melville's storytelling moves toward "the free suggestiveness, the profounder creativity, of myth."

Bloom, Harold, ed. *Herman Melville*. New York: Chelsea House, 1986.
A representation of modern critical views on Melville's work that focuses more on thematic and stylistic concerns than on rounded overviews of individual works. Elaine Barry's essay on Melville's comic sense and Richard H. Brodhead's discussion of *Mardi* as a key stage in Melville's creative development are useful for all Melville students. Robert Penn Warren's "Melville the Poet" is collected here, as is Bryan C. Short's "Form as Vision in *Clarel*." Bloom's introduction meditates on the shifts in Melville's religious outlook.

Boswell, Jeanetta. *Herman Melville and the Critics: A Checklist of Criticism, 1900-1978*. Metuchen, N.J.: Scarecrow Press, 1981.

The checklist is a numbered, alphabetical listing of assessments and analyses of Melville's work. It is not annotated, and it does not consider works that are solely biographical. The 3,215 items are selected from books, newspapers, and periodicals. Dissertation abstracts are also included. There is an author index and a subject index, the latter making it possible to locate criticisms of particular works by Melville or topics he treated.

Bowen, Merlin. *The Long Encounter: Self and Experience in the Writings of Herman Melville*. Chicago: University of Chicago Press, 1960.
"This study calls attention . . . to the part played by the concept of selfhood in the writings of Herman Melville and attempts to show, in an examination of particular works, how this persistent concern helped to determine his subject matter, his imagery, his view of character, the shape of his narratives, and his at times equivocal attitude toward his material." *Clarel* is quoted extensively throughout the study, especially in the final chapter.

Branch, Watson G. *Melville: The Critical Heritage*. London: Routledge & Kegan Paul, 1974.
A rich sampling of comment on Melville's works in his own day. The survey presents reviews, articles, and notices on the major novels, *The Piazza Tales*, and the volumes of poetry in a chronological arrangement. Interspersed in the chronology are general assessments of Melville's achievement, with a larger grouping of such estimates for the period 1889-1892. Branch's introduction gives a detailed overview of Melville's critical reputation.

Braswell, William. *Melville's Religious Thought*. Reprint. New York: Pageant Books, 1959.
First published in 1943, this study traces Melville's complex religious development. His upbringing in a religious household planted in him an early faith and a firm knowledge of the Bible. As an adult, he became acquainted with the writings of religious philosophers as well as cynics and skeptics. Some of these writings echoed the teachings of personal experience that led Melville to a period of doubt. His later works, including *Timoleon* and *Clarel*, reflect his long search for peace of mind and the restoration of lost faith.

Bryant, John, ed. *A Companion to Melville Studies*. New York: Greenwood Press, 1986.
A series of essays that survey and assess the various branches of Melville scholarship, combining criticism and biography. Includes several chapters that focus on individual works and others that relate the Melville canon to a particular sphere of inquiry. Chapters include "Melville's Poems: The Late Agenda" by William H. Shurr and "*Clarel*" by Vincent Kenny. Probably the one indispensable guide for Melville students.

Budd, Louis J., and Edwin H. Cady, eds. *On Melville: The Best from American Literature*. Durham, N.C.: Duke University Press, 1988.
As in other titles in this series, the editors reach back through the volumes of this prestigious journal and make a generous, engaging selection. Includes Bryan C. Short's essay on *Clarel* (listed separately below) as well as many excursions into Melville's novels, stories, themes, techniques, and symbols. Representing more than fifty years of Melville criticism, this volume provides a map of Melville's critical fortunes in the twentieth century.

Chase, Richard. *Herman Melville: A Critical Study*. New York: Macmillan, 1949.
Viewing Melville as a founding father of American thought, Chase examines his life and work in the light of the emerging "new liberalism" that followed the Great Depression and World War II. Chase sees parallel movements toward liberalism and progressivism in Melville's day, and he positions Melville within the liberal spectrum of ideas. Separate chapters on *Battle-Pieces* and *Clarel*.

—————————, ed. *Melville: A Collection of Critical Essays*. Englewood Cliffs, N.J: Prentice-Hall, 1962.
Represents various approaches to Melville's work. Most of the essays treat particular novels or clusters of novels, while others delve in more general matters of craft or outlook. Marius Bewley's "Melville and the Democratic Experience" and Robert Penn Warren's "Melville the Poet" are noteworthy. Chase's introduction traces the history of Melville criticism and comments briefly on the nature of his art and philosophy. Chronology and selected bibliography.

Coffler, Gail H. "Form as Resolution: Classical Elements in Melville's *Battle-Pieces*." In *American Poetry Between Tradition and Modernism*, edited by Roland Hagenbuchle. Regensburg, W. Germany: Friedrich Pustet, 1984.
Simplicity, restraint, and harmony are among the classical characteristics of Melville's style in these Civil War poems. There is a duality in Melville's poems that both distinguishes the actual from the ideal and identifies them as one. The classical manner contributes to that duality.

—————————. *Melville's Classical Allusions*. Westport, Conn.: Greenwood Press, 1985.
This is a "comprehensive index and glossary" that locates references to classical literature, culture, and myth in Melville's writings. The alphabetical master list can help a student locate an allusion in a particular work, locate all instances of an allusion, determine the frequency of particular allusions both generally and by work or period of Melville's career. Such allusions are frequent in works written after Melville's visits to Greece and Italy. *Clarel* and *Timoleon* are heavily dependent on such references.

Cohen, Hennig. Introduction to *The Battle-Pieces of Herman Melville*, edited by
Cohen. New York: Thomas Yoseloff, 1964.
"The central theme of *Battle-Pieces* is one of opposition and reconciliation."
The raw materials include Melville's readings in the Old Testament, Milton,
and Shakespeare as well as Civil War accounts from friends and newspaper
reports. Melville's visit to a cousin at the front provided additional insights.
The title, along with its subtitle, "Aspects of the War," reveals Melville's pic-
torial intention. Cohen examines various kinds and techniques of order that
Melville manipulated, including the creation of distinct sequences.

Donoghue, Denis. "Herman Melville." In his *Connoisseurs of Chaos: Ideas of
Order in Modern American Poetry*. 2d ed. New York: Columbia University
Press, 1984.
Makes comparisons and contrasts with two other great novelist-poets: Hardy
and Lawrence. Donoghue feels that "after 1857, when he had driven himself to
distraction with private visions, elemental forms, and strange obliquities,
[Melville] craved the comfort of simplicity" and thus turned to poetry. Melville
tried to work in conventional forms, in fact, to be a conventional man in his
advancing years, but his restless, nonconformist nature was at odds with these
self-imposed boundaries. Useful treatment of *Battle-Pieces*.

Finkelstein, Dorothy Metlitsky. *Melville's Orienda*. New Haven, Conn.: Yale University Press, 1961.
A thorough investigation of the non-Christian elements in Melville's use of the
history, creeds, and mythologies of the Bible lands—the Islamic Orient.
Finkelstein shows how Melville participated in the vogue for Near Eastern
material that colored the American literary scene. This study of Melville's
sources and how he used them aids the interpretation of many individual
works. Melville's own travels in the region are fed into the picture of his
overall conception of the Near East.

Fogle, Richard Harter. "The Themes of Melville's Later Poetry." In *Critics on
Melville*, edited by Thomas J. Rountree. Coral Gables, Fla.: University of
Miami Press, 1972.
Emphasizes Melville's constant imaginative return to the sea as the source of
metaphor and illustration in *Clarel* and other late poems. Melville's chosen
protagonists "are men who have been tried and almost broken, who have
learned to accept the burden of life with patience, humility, and—in some
fortunate cases—faith." Melville's last poems revel in ironic complexities regarding the Christian belief in immortal life and the "counter-theme" of a
golden age. Fogle reviews each volume of poems succinctly.

Gale, Robert L. *Plots and Characters in the Fiction and Narrative Poetry of Herman Melville*. Hamden, Conn.: Archon Books, 1969.

Although most useful for Melville's fiction, this handbook provides plot summaries and brief character sketches (often merely identifications) for the narrative poetry as well. The titles of poems treated in the two alphabets ("plots" and "characters") are listed in an appendix. This guide can be used to preview, review, and make comparisons among works. The *Clarel* summary takes thirteen pages. Treats poems from each of Melville's collections.

Georgovdaki, Catherine. "*Battle-Pieces and Aspects of the War*: Melville's Poetic Quest for Meaning and Form in a Fallen World." *ATQ*, n.s., 1 (March, 1987): 21-32.

Sees *Battle-Pieces* as the climactic work in Melville's growing "disillusionment with the American Dream." Melville's references to landmarks, personages, cultural objects, locations, and landscape features—materials reworked from his travel journals —"enrich the setting, atmosphere, themes, imagery, and symbols of his poems." These references are part of Melville's attempt "to create aesthetic order and unity out of disorder."

Higgins, Brian. *Herman Melville: An Annotated Bibliography*. Vol. 1, *1846-1930*. Boston: G. K. Hall, 1979.

An exhaustive listing, with descriptive comment, of all writings on Herman Melville and his works. The plan is a yearly calendar that first lists books and then shorter writings (chapters, articles, and so forth) in chronological order. The annotations vary according to the importance of the entry. Titles of Melville's works are listed in the index. Later volumes will bring the list up to date.

Hillway, Tyrus. *Herman Melville*. Rev. ed. Boston: Twayne, 1979.

Presents introductory materials on Melville's life and work for a student audience. Chapter 1 relates Melville's discovery of his vocation and the development of his craft. Chapters 2-4 trace the main contours of his career. The next four chapters explore the major works chronologically. Melville's poetry is discussed in a chapter on his last published works. The final chapter reviews the Melville revival. Chronology and selected bibliography.

Hook, Andrew. "Melville's Poetry." In *Herman Melville: Reassessments*, edited by A. Robert Lee. Totowa, N.J.: Barnes & Noble, 1984.

Questions the general lack of interest of Melville's poems considering how little poetry of the first rank was written in nineteenth century America. The idea that a great prose writer became burnt out, quit, and fell to poetry has colored assessments of Melville's achievement. Melville's poetry establishes "an aesthetic of undecorated plainness" to deal with the Civil War. The poetry as a whole develops "the theme of an America corrupted by materialism and utilitarianism, and descending into civic barbarism." Brief comments on the weakness of *Clarel*. Suggests that the later collections reveal a qualified acceptance, a hesitant movement toward peace of mind.

Howard, Leon. *Herman Melville*. Minneapolis: University of Minnesota Press, 1961.
A well-balanced pamphlet treatment of Melville's life, literary career, and major works. Examines Melville's growing ambitions and sophistication as he struggled endlessly with the problem of evil: its source, its nature, and its power. Discusses Melville's relationship with Nathaniel Hawthorne. Treats the poetry and later fiction as projects unpressured by professional concerns. Melville's "imaginative development kept abreast of the times—despite neglect and adversity . . . the acuteness and depth of his sensitivity never failed."

——————— . *Herman Melville: A Biography*. Berkeley: University of California Press, 1951.
This conventional narrative biography pays close attention to the business of authorship, detailing Melville's experience in the literary marketplace. Howard examines Melville's motives and particularly his methods. Assesses Melville's own autobiographical works in terms of their reliability. Fascinating glimpses of Melville's career frustrations.

Kaplan, Sidney. Introduction to *Battle-Pieces and Aspects of the War* by Herman Melville, edited by Kaplan. Amherst: University of Massachusetts Press, 1972.
Presents a thorough history of the genesis of these poems, both in subject and in style. While planning the project, Melville was educating himself as a poet by reading and marking the work of others. He was also concerned with the role of the poet, especially as argued by Emerson and Madame de Stael. The poems become illustrative of Melville's developing theory of poetry. Kaplan provides a list of Melville's revisions and a sampling of contemporary comment.

Karcher, Carolyn L. *Shadow Over the Promised Land: Slavery, Race, and Violence in Melville's America*. Baton Rouge: Louisiana State University Press, 1980.
A thematic study of Melville's work showing how his vision of America was affected by the social and moral evils he perceived. Melville's democratic and religious ideals kept him returning to these issues throughout his career. While the focus here is on Melville's fiction, there are plentiful references to the poems in the chapter "Fratricidal Strife in the Postwar Writings." Melville's guilt was responsive both to the enslaved Negro and the defeated southerner.

Kazin, Alfred. "Melville Is Dwelling Somewhere in New York." In his *An American Procession*. New York: Alfred A. Knopf, 1984.
Explores Melville's period of obscurity in New York as a custom's inspector and part-time writer. Melville's personal life put him under great strain. After looping back to trace Melville's earlier career, Kazin returns to the older novelist-turned-poet and explores the themes, tones, and techniques of representative passages. Melville's anonymity opened new possibilities for experiment. His less frantic, but still strenuous, pursuit of ideas led him to the condensation demanded by poetry.

Lee, A. Robert, ed. *Herman Melville: Reassessments*. Totowa, N.J.: Barnes & Noble, 1984.
New readings of Melville's major works by British and American scholars. The essays attest to the astonishing intellectual richness and artfulness of Melville's work. Lee's own contribution on voice in *The Confidence-Man* has utility for the student of poetry. All the pieces clarify Melville's vision of the world. One, by Andrew Hook, surveys the poetry.

Lewis, R. W. B. "Melville after *Moby Dick*, I: Tales and Poems." In his *Trials of the Word*. New Haven, Conn.: Yale University Press, 1965.
During the period in which Melville wrote *Battle-Pieces*, "American poetry was getting worse, not better." It was following the other arts into decline. Thus, Melville worked without useful contemporary models. In private, he found his own way. The tragic hero of *Battle-Pieces* is America, and the poetic sequence is "a tragic drama expanding in the direction of tragic epic." Over and over, enlightenment is born of horror and death, as in traditional tragedy. "One of the great qualities of *Battle-Pieces* is its powerful rise to a comprehensive pity."

Leyda, Jay. *The Melville Log: A Documentary Life of Herman Melville 1819-1891*. Enl. ed. 2 vols. New York: Gordian Press, 1969.
First published in 1951, this chronology of documentary references to Melville is broken down into chapters covering five- or ten-year periods. As with other works in this format, the reader has the opportunity to do the interpreting—to become the biographer. Leyda brings together all written and printed contemporary evidence: letters, newspaper items, legal documents, expense accounts, and so forth. Includes biographical notes on Melville's associates. Indexed by subject for quick reference to Melville's individual works.

Mason, Ronald. *The Spirit Above the Dust: A Study of Herman Melville*. 2d ed. Mamaroneck, N.Y.: Paul P. Appel, 1972.
A critical study with only skeletal biographical references, focusing on the "embodiment" of Melville's perceptions in his work. Melville's imaginative

life is explored as a spiritual quest. One or more chapters on the major novels, a chapter on *Clarel*, and another on the other poems. Mason sees the poems as marking the final stages of "a new and stable philosophy."

Matthiessen, F. O. "Melville." In his *American Renaissance: Art and Expression in the Age of Emerson and Whitman*. New York: Oxford University Press, 1941.
Matthiessen's classic study has four chapters that are largely concerned with Melville's formal inventions and his experiments with language. Matthiessen calls Melville "the American with the richest natural gifts as a writer." Examines the relationship between autobiography and art, Melville's social vision, his tragic sensibility, his outsider stance, and his late reaffirmation of the human heart's redeeming value. Many parallels to Shakespeare developed.

Metcalf, Eleanor Melville. *Herman Melville: Cycle and Epicycle*. Reprint. Westport, Conn.: Greenwood Press, 1970.
Melville's oldest grandchild attempts to recapture the living human being by drawing upon family letters, other correspondence, diaries, and memories of conversations with those who knew him. This is an intimate portrait of Melville in the family setting, with little concern for addressing critical issues or studying his career. As much as possible, Metcalf lets the documents speak for themselves.

Miller, Edwin Haviland. *Melville*. New York: George Braziller, 1975.
A psychoanalytic portrait of a man who revealed "his longings, his depressions, his hunger, his excitement, in the pages of his books." Miller explores the creative works in order to imagine and re-create the man behind them, a man who "dared to peer into the abysses of his own troubled, sensitive nature and to examine old wounds and old hurts." Under the surface of Melville's works runs "an almost manic depressive rhythm." Separate chapters on *Battle-Pieces* and *Clarel*, as well as comments on Melville's other poetry.

Miller, James E., Jr. *A Reader's Guide to Herman Melville*. New York: Farrar, Straus & Giroux, 1962.
Establishes the patterns of meaning that run through Melville's work. The interpretation of each work sheds light on the others. The novels are either paired or given separate chapters. In the world of Melville's imagination, men don masks of innocence with which to deny society's evil and duplicity. Melville explores what is hidden behind these masks. "Melville's drama of masks might be likened to one prolonged morality pageant." A coherent, engaging reading of the Melville canon. Selected bibliography.

Phelps, Leland R. *Herman Melville's Foreign Reputation: A Research Guide*. Boston: G. K. Hall, 1983.

Presents "a comprehensive and systematic bibliography of the non-English-speaking world that will permit scholars to trace the course of interest in and critical reaction to Melville's life and works in various foreign languages." The major plan is an alphabetical arrangement of language names under which comments on various works or groups of works ("Poetic works," for example) are listed chronologically. Includes English language materials written in foreign countries.

Pommer, Henry F. *Milton and Melville*. Reprint. New York: Cooper Square Publishers, 1970.
First published in 1950, this detailed influence study strives to determine the nature and degree of Melville's debt to Milton. Even though Melville drew in large measure upon his physical environment and upon his own life, an enormous amount of his writing relies on literary sources. Melville drew upon Milton both directly and indirectly. Chapters on the influence of Milton's minor works, of *Paradise Lost*, of his vocabulary and sentence structure, of his concept of Satan. Treats both Melville's prose and poetry.

Pullin, Faith, ed. *New Perspectives on Melville*. Kent, Ohio: Kent State University Press, 1978.
These essays represent the Anglo-American view of Melville; half of the twelve contributors are British. The focus of the collection concerns Melville's attitudes toward society and language as well as his concepts of nature and civilization. Some essays explore individual works while others are oriented toward themes or issues. "Shakespeare and Melville's America," "Melville's England," and "Orpheus and Measured Forms" (on law and convention) are examples of the latter.

Ricks, Beatrice, and Joseph D. Adams. *Herman Melville: A Reference Bibliography, 1900-1972*. Boston: G. K. Hall, 1973.
The first section is "a masterlist of bibliographic items alphabetically arranged, the items consecutively numbered." The second part is an index of works and topics keyed to the numbers in the masterlist. Brief annotations "indicate the principal areas of study, or pertinent issues raised." The 3,500 items represent the range of approaches to Melville in the twentieth century, while selected nineteenth century items "indicate Melville's place in his contemporary culture and literary milieu."

Robillard, Douglas. Introduction to *Poems of Herman Melville*, edited by Robillard. New Haven, Conn.: College & University Press, 1976.
Examines Melville's view of the creative struggle and traces the path by which Melville shifted his attention from fiction to poetry. Robillard addresses the

structure of the three collections of short poems that Melville saw through the press. He contends that Melville wanted these collections to be read as wholes, although many individual poems stand on their own merit and are worthy of separate study. *Timoleon* is the least unified of the three collections.

Rogin, Michael Paul. "The Iron Dome." In his *Subversive Genealogy: The Politics and Heart of Herman Melville*. New York: Alfred A. Knopf, 1983.
This chapter attends to Melville's poetic period. "The poetry completed Melville's evolution from sprawling stories of artistic and experiential variety to grim, carefully crafted aesthetic objects." *Battle-Pieces* and *Clarel* have little in common with either "the flowery tropes of . . . American poetic convention" or the exuberant, antiformalist efforts of Whitman. In *Battle-Pieces*, Melville works in a minimalist direction. After a period of detachment, the Civil War reconnected Melville to public events in America.

——————— . *Subversive Genealogy: The Politics and Heart of Herman Melville*. New York: Alfred A. Knopf, 1983.
Melville's writings are simultaneously a family history and a symbolic rendering of American history. The crises of race and slavery in American society "called into question the ideal realm of liberal political freedom." Because of the political prominence and the history of his family, Melville was especially sensitive to these crises. Rogin's study is divided into chapters on societal issues, each explored by references to Melville's family and his literary works. The three major divisions are "Politics," "Society," and "The State."

Rosenberry, Edward H. *Melville*. London: Routledge & Kegan Paul, 1979.
A chronological account of Melville's works seen against their background of time and place. Rosenberry attempts to sort through the various schools of thought about Melville's writing and to present whatever can be called a consensus view in plain language. This discussion is aimed at students rather than specialists. Melville's poetry, treated in a separate chapter, is viewed as essentially an outgrowth of the Romantic tradition. Useful summaries of *Clarel*, *Battle-Pieces*, *John Marr*, and *Timoleon*.

——————— . *Melville and the Comic Spirit*. Reprint. New York: Octagon Books, 1969.
First published in 1955, this study explores the range of comic ingredients and tones in Melville's work. Melville's early semi-autobiographical romances are "predominantly comic in the jocular-hedonistic vein." Other works show "picaresque gaiety," "demonic laughter," or "native humor." Though the poems are not treated, it is worth testing Rosenberry's assertion that Melville "ceased to write humorously after 1856." Brief reference to "Jack Roy" from *John Marr*.

Rountree, Thomas J., ed. *Critics on Melville*. Coral Gables, Fla.: University of Miami Press, 1972.

A representation of the many faces and angles of Melville criticism divided into three sections. First come early reviews by Hawthorne, Bayard Taylor, and others. Next, a series of general essays provides perspectives on the Melville canon. The last and largest section includes essays that examine particular works. Includes Richard Harter Fogle's "The Themes of Melville's Later Poetry." Chronology and selected bibliography.

Sealts, Merton M., Jr. *The Early Lives of Melville*. Madison: University of Wisconsin Press, 1974.

Presents and comments on the nineteenth century biographical sketches of Melville and their authors. Sealts provides the material on Melville that was available to nineteenth century readers, allowing us to see how Melville was perceived by his contemporaries. Materials include encyclopedia entries, family reminiscences, and retrospective essays. Subject index includes Melville's works; thus we can examine early references to his poetry.

——————— . *Melville's Reading*. Rev. and enl. Columbia: University of South Carolina Press, 1988.

This study is organized into chapters that bring Melville's library and borrowed books into connection with his own writings. Sealts has not simply created lists but has also developed insights into how Melville used his readings. Two chapters focus on what Melville was reading while working on his poetic projects. To know what literary materials might have fed the composition of *Battle-Pieces* or *Clarel* is most useful to the scholar. Includes a "Check-List of Books Owned or Borrowed."

——————— . *Pursuing Melville 1940-1980*. Madison: University of Wisconsin Press, 1982.

A selection from Sealts's Melville scholarship focused on explorations of Melville's personality, his relationships, his readings in philosophy and other topics, and his short fiction. Part 2, "A Correspondence with Charles Olson," is an exciting interchange between two enthusiastic professionals. Frequent references to *Battle-Pieces*, *Clarel*, and *John Marr*. A smorgasbord from a prominent Melville scholar.

Seelye, John. *Melville: The Ironic Diagram*. Evanston, Ill.: Northwestern University Press, 1970.

Melville inherited the technique of stylistic indirection from Romantic criticism of Shakespeare. He creates polarities of outlook and method that do not easily reconcile themselves. "His use of stylistic indirection, shaped by diagrammatic confrontation, is . . . useless as a guide to intention." Seelye examines this dynamic in several novels. A chapter on "The Endurance of Form: Melville's Poetry" deals mainly with *Battle-Pieces* and *Clarel*: "a composite of antitheses whose terms, in their very contrariety, put forth a puzzling consistency."

Sedgwick, William Ellery. *Herman Melville: The Tragedy of Mind*. Reprint. New York: Russell & Russell, 1962.
    First published in 1944, this study is focused on five major novels, *Clarel*, and *Billy Budd*. Sedgwick examines these works by raising their ultimate questions: "What is truth? What is the nature of human life? How are human beings to accommodate themselves to the external creation in which we find ourselves?" A tragic "drama of human growth" emerges in Melville's writings.

Shetley, Vernon. "Melville's 'Timoleon.'" *ESQ* 33 (2nd Quarter, 1987): 83-93.
    In adapting the Timoleon story from Plutarch's *Parallel Lives*, Melville shifts the focus from the last phase of Timoleon's career to the assassination and its aftermath. Like much of Melville's late work, the dominant mood of "Timoleon" is one of interrogation. The questions regarding Timoleon reflect back on Melville's own difficulties. The fate of Melville, who became "a literary island unto himself," is paralleled in Timoleon's self-exile. Shetley's thematic and prosodic analysis supports the consensus about Melville's withdrawal in his later years.

Shurr, William H. "Melville's Poems: The Late Agenda." In *A Companion to Melville Studies*, edited by John Bryant. New York: Greenwood Press, 1986.
    This is a general review of tendencies in criticism of Melville's poetry. Since the poetry was discovered by critics late in the process of the Melville revival, Shurr can not point to a critical tradition. After discussing estimates of Melville's poetry as a whole, he provides separate sections on *Battle-Pieces*, *Timoleon*, *John Marr*, the posthumously published *Weeds and Wildings*, and the scattered poems that Melville left unfinished or unpublished at his death. The poetry remains the least studied area of Melville's work. Extensive works-cited list.

——————— . *The Mystery of Iniquity: Melville as Poet, 1857-1891*. Lexington: University Press of Kentucky, 1972.
    The first full-scale attempt to see Melville's poetry as a separate enterprise, not subsidiary to a consideration of his fiction. Shurr argues against the theory that Melville's later decades were a long decline into obscurity. Rather, he discovers a complex, difficult body of work that in its own way is as original and rewarding as anything in Melville's fiction. Melville showed prosodic flexibility and resourcefulness and orchestrated significant structures in patterns of imag-

ery and meaning. "Melville is for all practical purposes a new American poet."

Stein, William Bysshe. *The Poetry of Melville's Later Years* Albany: State University of New York Press, 1970.
Melville wrote mostly poetry for the last thirty-five years of his life. The late works are marked by matter-of-fact situations, though many are "characterized by sudden shifts in style and tone and by unexpected dislocations of syntax and meter." These features announce Melville's rebellion against the Romantic sensibility, a rebellion requiring original stances and tonalities. Stein draws upon Freudian and Jungian insights to explore Melville's archetypal symbols.

Stone, Geoffrey. *Melville*. New York: Sheed & Ward, 1949.
This popular biography eschews footnotes in addressing the general reader. Stone places Melville within the context of the Romantic revolt: "The Romantic insistence on absolute freedom resulted . . . in the conviction that human existence was a trap" which required one of a number of escapes. Melville struggled within this intellectual and moral climate both inside and outside his writings. Stone provides an elaborate discussion of Melville's later career and the philosophical import of the poems. Useful paraphrase of *Clarel*.

Sweeney, G. M. *Melville's Use of Classical Mythology*. Amsterdam: Rodopi, 1975.
Though the poetry is not meaningfully treated here, these chapters present necessary understandings of the extent and nature of Melville's mythological parallels and allusions. There is an index to mythological characters that directs readers back to their use in Melville's works. This contains several references to *Clarel*. Sweeney hopes to discover which sources provided Melville's understanding of the various myths. Focus is on Ahab in *Moby Dick*.

Tolchin, Neal L. *Mourning, Gender, and Creativity in the Art of Herman Melville*. New Haven, Conn.: Yale University Press, 1988.
"This book traces the emergence of unresolved grief in Herman Melville's fiction." Tolchin argues that "the conflicting images of Allan Melville in his wife Maria's Calvinist and genteel style of bereavement crucially influenced the outcome of Melville's adolescent mourning." It remains for students of the poetry to see if this analysis of Melville's "chronic grief," which had cultural as well as personal origins, can be applied further.

Warren, Robert Penn. "Melville the Poet." In his *Selected Essays of Robert Penn Warren*. New York: Random House, 1958.
Also in Bloom and in Chase. Examines samples of Melville's verse to show that he had mastered the poetic conventions of his day and that his deviations

were purposeful exhibitions of dissatisfaction with those conventions. Melville's shifts in rhythm within poems accompany, announce, and evoke shifts in tone. Explores the management of "dualities and dubieties" in Melville's poetry as well as the effort toward resolution. Insists on an "astonishing continuity" in outlook between the early poems and *Clarel*.

Weaver, Raymond M. *Herman Melville: Mariner and Mystic*. New York: George H. Doran, 1921.
> Published at the outset of Melville's rediscovery, this biography draws a vivid picture of his life and times. Weaver recognizes the importance of whaling industry details to the study of Melville, and he provides a good beginning. He also sketches vividly the dangers of life at sea, attesting the authenticity of Melville's voyage narratives. Melville's works are addressed mainly to illustrate the contours of his outer and inner life. Colorful, and scholarly without seeming so.

Clarel

Bezanson, Walter E. Introduction to *Clarel*, by Herman Melville, edited by Bezanson. New York: Hendricks House, 1960.
> An astoundingly detailed and complete exploration of the circumstances that produced *Clarel* and of the poem's main features. Bezanson reviews Melville's journey to Palestine, examines the sources and structure of the poem, and elucidates its major symbols. *Clarel* incorporates the contemporary debate over the crisis in religion and the impact of science on belief. "The loss of faith is the basic assumed fact of the poem, and its largest problem is how to endure the overwhelming sense of a shattered vision."

Chase, Richard. "'Just Reason, and Appeal for Grace.'" In his *Herman Melville: A Critical Study*. New York: Macmillan, 1949.
> *Clarel* sits "squarely in the tradition of Victorian thought" and reminds us of the work of Matthew Arnold and Arthur Hugh Clough. Clarel's education comes from witnessing extreme modes of behavior and through his relationship with Ruth. Their prospective marriage "would be a symbolic union of America and the Old World," a marriage for which Clarel must be prepared by separation and pilgrimage. Clarel must reject other representative characters to accept Rolfe, "a secular liberal" and "Melville's ultimate humanist."

Dettlaff, Shirley. "Ionian Form and Esau's Waste: Melville's View of Art in *Clarel*." *American Literature* 54 (May, 1984): 212-228.
> In *Clarel*, Melville incorporates a coherent and basically classical aesthetic discussion. The poem reveals his response to the leading Hellenist thinkers— Goethe, Schiller, and Matthew Arnold. Written at the end of Melville's decade-

long interest in Arnold, the poem shows that Arnold's influence on Melville's view of art was essentially negative. "Melville . . . did not believe that beauty was the primary goal of art, nor did he consider it an avenue to truth."

Finkelstein, Dorothy Metlitsky. "Material for *Clarel*." In her *Melville's Orienda*. New Haven, Conn.: Yale University Press, 1961.
Melville's most programmatic reading on the Near East occurred after his journey there. *Clarel* was his only sustained attempt to use his direct experience of the region, though it was published two decades after his visit to Palestine. Much of Melville's reading eventually was put to use in the poem, including such works as William McClure Thomson's *The Land and the Book*, Dean Stanley's *Sinai and Palestine*, and various titles by William Henry Bartlett. Finkelstein reveals how Melville used his sources.

Flibbert, Joseph. "The Dream and Religious Faith in Herman Melville's *Clarel*." *ATQ*, no. 50 (Spring, 1981): 129-137.
Moving through a bleak, depressing landscape, most of Melville's pilgrims do not attain spiritual fulfillment. They mistake the outward condition of the Holy Land as a sign of spiritual desolation. Clarel denies this connection. As he becomes more independent in his outlook, "he relies more and more upon the transformative power of the dream-vision to create a temporary, personally-meaningful world of limited spiritual and aesthetic satisfaction." Melville suggests that this is all we can hope for.

Kenny, Vincent "*Clarel*." In *A Companion to Melville Studies*, edited by John Bryant. New York: Greenwood Press, 1986.
After giving some background on the place of *Clarel* in Melville's career, Kenny proceeds to trace the history of critical responses to the poem. The first reviews were almost uniformly negative, and the book sold poorly. Explanatory notes were needed to decipher Melville's erudition. Kenny outlines the poem and samples the commentary, paying particular attention to the detailed assessments that began in the 1940's. He concludes with an independent analysis that stresses Melville's imagery and characterizations. Extensive works-cited list.

_____ . *Herman Melville's Clarel: A Spiritual Autobiography*. Hamden, Conn.: Archon Books, 1973.
A detailed examination of the enormous, late poem that is the culmination of Melville's philosophical, political, social, and religious views. "The subject matter circles almost endlessly around a modern pilgrim's search for truth and blisters all of the popular nineteenth-century notions of progress, optimism, and meliorism." The form is "a fairly consistent iambic tetrameter pattern of irregular, hooked rhymes." *Clarel* projects a battle between the forces of faith and despair.

Knapp, Joseph G. "Melville's *Clarel*: Dynamic Synthesis." *ATQ*, no. 7 (Summer, 1970): 67-75.

In *Clarel*, Melville struggled toward the principle that would "integrate the manysidedness of things," and he finally succeeded. *Clarel* has an internal rhythm with an antiphonal call-and-response pattern. Each canto contains this pattern, which also relates canto to canto. "The struggling dissonance, sharpened by the diction and rhyme, melts into single harmonies in successful metaphors." The ultimate harmony of the work is achieved in its imagery. A patient and persuasive discussion of structure, theme, and technique.

Mason, Ronald. "*Clarel.*" In his *The Spirit Above the Dust: A study of Herman Melville*. 2d ed. Mamaroneck, N.Y.: Paul P. Appel, 1972.

"The poem is divided into four main books, each of which in turn is split into short sections each presenting a scene, a conversation, an incident, a mood, sometimes an almost unrelated lyric." The effect is one of "a series of headlong rushes . . . rather than the intended one of cumulation" and purposeful sequence. Clarel reaches a point where "he salves desolation in community and not in solitude. He has reached a point where it is no longer in his nature to reject." The poem is concerned with the reestablishment of innocence.

Matthiessen, F. O. "Melville." In his *American Renaissance: Art and Expression in the Age of Emerson and Whitman*, 494-497. New York: Oxford University Press, 1941.

The poem accentuates Melville's blacker visions of society, following the path of his doubts more than that of his faith. In Rolfe, Melville questions freedom of thought and presents a man of action. Through Unger, he addresses the brutality of technological progress that fosters regression and makes demagoguery possible. Clarel's doubts are not reconciled by his pilgrimage, and through him Melville remains poised between optimism and pessimism. This same mood is articulated in his poem "Commemorative of a Naval Victory," which "conveys his special perception of the unavoidable lurking terror in life."

Miller, James E., Jr. "*Clarel.*" In his *A Reader's Guide to Herman Melville*. New York: Farrar, Straus & Giroux, 1962.

The long poem shares many characteristics of Melville's prose fiction: the young seeker, the temptation to withdrawal, the presence of titans and rebels, the problem of hypocrisy, and the motif of foreshadowed "deprivation in the very promise of paradise." Derwent is parallel to the confidence man; Vine is a typical Melvillian recluse; Mortmain the master despairer; and Ungar the scourge of mankind. Rolfe, who is a rare maskless character, balances heart and intellect.

Sedgwick, William Ellery. "*Clarel.*" In his *Herman Melville: The Tragedy of Mind*. Reprint. New York: Russell & Russell, 1962.

Uses Melville's pilgrimage journal as a starting point for examining the spiritual quest in *Clarel*. Clarel, a seeker of truth, is bewildered by the "multiplicity of different religions and different shrines all over the world." What links these bodies of experience and knowledge? "*Clarel* is religious because it takes the opposite direction to Melville's radical Protestantism." In this poem, "Melville has accepted the tragedy implicit in human nature, because he has identified it with a positive and universal necessity."

Short, Bryan C. "Form as Vision in Clarel." In *Herman Melville*, edited by Harold Bloom. New York: Chelsea House, 1986. Also in Budd.
"A reverence for organic unity pervaded Romantic poetics in America; Melville's changing interpretation of this doctrine determines the adapting of versification to the narrative purpose which gives *Clarel* its unique shape." Here and in other late works, Melville was motivated more by artistic considerations than by philosophical ones. He carries over from *Battle-Pieces* the strategy of a disciplined objectivity. Within *Clarel* is a shifting aesthetic that is in constant, positive reaction to Melville's reservation about his initial approach. "*Clarel* can be called America's greatest Victorian poem."

Shurr, William H. "*Clarel*: The Static Elements" and "*Clarel*: The Dynamics of the Symbol." In his *The Mystery of Iniquity: Melville as Poet, 1857-1891*. Lexington: University Press of Kentucky, 1972.
Reviews the reception of the poem and accounts for negative reviews by describing the poem's frustrations: inconclusiveness and the simultaneous operation of several symbol-systems. Three major static elements are "the city, the landscape of the Holy Land, and the Dead Sea." These are emblems made dynamic by Melville's infusion of various literary modes (pastoral among them) and a historical vision. The dynamic relationships among symbols orchestrates Melville's answer to the question of whether good or evil dominates the universe.

WALT WHITMAN
(1819-1891)

General Studies

Aaron, Daniel. "Whitman: The 'Parturition Years.'" In his *The Unwritten War: American Writers and the Civil War*. New York: Alfred A. Knopf, 1973.

While the first two versions of *Leaves of Grass* subordinated politics to personality, later editions closer to and following the war had stronger political overtones. Aaron reviews Whitman's attitudes on racial amalgamation, slavery, and states' rights by reference both to his poetry and prose. The effect on Whitman of his hospital visits is outlined, as well as the dramatic charge of wartime events on his imagination. Addresses the stature of *Drum-Taps*, Whitman's myth of Lincoln, and his optimistic view of national reconciliation.

Allen, Evie Allison. "A Check List of Whitman Publications, 1945-1960." In *Walt Whitman as Man, Poet, and Legend*.

All other materials by Gay Wilson Allen (see below). This reference guide is divided into the following sections: (1) bibliography and reference books, (2) editions and selections, (3) uncollected writings, including poems, letters, and essays, (4) translations, (5) books about Whitman, (6) articles on Whitman, and (7) theses. Continued by Tanner (see below) and in the *Walt Whitman Review*. This bibliography is also found in an enlarged edition of Gay Wilson Allen's book, retitled as *Aspects of Walt Whitman*.

Allen, Gay Wilson. *The Solitary Singer: A Critical Biography of Walt Whitman*. New York: Macmillan, 1955.

This is Allen's primary work, upon which his many shorter introductions and handbooks rest. Moves back and forth between the known facts of Whitman's life and the development of his career, persona, and art. Tends to evaluate rather than interpret individual poems, but significant interpretive comments are found throughout. Excellent at discovering the life sources of Whitman's symbolism and at re-creating Whitman's experience of a burgeoning America.

───────────── . *Walt Whitman as Man, Poet, and Legend*. Carbondale: Southern Illinois University Press, 1961.

A collection of essays including "Mutations in Whitman's Art," "The Man," "The 'Long Journey' Motif," and "Whitman's Image in the Twentieth Century." Includes Evie Allison Allen's "A Check List of Whitman Publications" (see above). Revised and expanded in 1978 as *Aspects of Walt Whitman* (Norwood Editions) to include "Walt Whitman's Reception in Scandinavia," "Walt Whitman's Inner Space," and "The Problem of Metaphor in Translating *Leaves of Grass*."

_____ . *Walt Whitman*. Rev. ed. Detroit: Wayne State University Press, 1969.
Written for nonspecialists, this book is primarily biographical but responds to the poems to illustrate Whitman's sense of self, history, and environment. Considers Whitman's poetic motives: "to celebrate himself and exploit his own real or imagined personality . . . to celebrate his nation . . . and an intuition of the meaning of the great mysteries: birth, death, and the hope of resurrection." Whitman's responses to his changing critical fortunes handled well.

_____ . *A Reader's Guide to Walt Whitman*. New York: Farrar, Straus, & Giroux, 1970.
An authoritative introductory volume that reviews changes in Whitman's critical fortunes and then offers a personalized articulation of the critical consensus at Whitman's sesquicentennial. Explores Whitman's prevailing metaphors and symbols in terms of both vision and structure. Treats structure on all levels: the entirety of the evolving *Leaves of Grass*, individual poems, and components of poems—passages, sentences, and the like. Whitman's "expressive form" also involves his characteristic cadences and musicality.

_____ . *The New Walt Whitman Handbook*. New York: New York University Press, 1975.
Separate chapters on the life, the development of *Leaves of Grass*, literary technique, and Whitman's place in world literature. Explains the essence of Whitman's work in terms of "analogous form" and through examination of parallelism. Sees Whitman's gradual simplification of punctuation as a sign of his growing control and confidence in handling rhythms. Treats foreign estimates of Whitman's achievement.

_____ , ed. *The Merrill Studies in Leaves of Grass*. Columbus, Ohio: Charles E. Merrill, 1972.
This slender collection aims to gather opinions on the kind of poet Whitman is and on what aesthetic or technical principles underlie his poems. Most of the selections are readily available elsewhere, but this anthology has a sharper focus than most so that the contributors seem engaged in a debate. Herbert Read's "The Figure of Grammar" is especially provocative. Includes a poem addressed to Whitman by Stanley Burnshaw.

Arvin, Newton. *Whitman*. Reprint. New York: Russell & Russell, 1969.
First Published in 1938, this is an early attempt to trace the intellectual life of Whitman, to locate the sources of ideas that find their way into the poetry. Strives to re-create the historical context surrounding Whitman's emergence: the economic, scientific, technological, religious, and political dimensions of his environment. What did Whitman care and know about these matters? How did he develop and reveal his opinions? Arvin explores such questions.

Aspiz, Harold. "Walt Whitman: The Spermatic Imagination." *American Literature*
   56 (October, 1984): 379-395.
   Shows how Whitman combined "the images of the hero-poet as sexually
   charged begetter, fantasizer, and speaker with some bizarre notions about the
   nature of sperm as the quintessential distillation of the body and the mind." In
   this spermatic trope, "sexual arousal and visionary fervor" combine in a vocal
   utterance that parallels orgasm. Examines ideas about the properties of sperm
   available to Whitman.

_____ . *Walt Whitman and the Body Beautiful*. Urbana: University of
   Illinois Press, 1980.
   Explores Whitman's literal and metaphoric depictions of the human body.
   Special concerns are the poses of the Whitman persona, the experience of
   medical practice and hospitals, medical pseudosciences such as phrenology
   and pathognomy, and the Whitman persona as a sexual-genetic prototype. Sees
   Whitman's "gospel of the body" as the essential complement to his "gospel of
   the soul." The poet's response to the new science of electricity is related to
   these issues.

_____ . "Walt Whitman, Feminist." In *Walt Whitman Here and Now*,
   edited by Joann P. Krieg. Westport, Conn.: Greenwood Press, 1985.
   "Whitman's ideal of athletic, self-reliant women, eligible to participate on
   equal terms with men in all phases of public life and to become happy wives
   and the mothers of well-conceived, painlessly birthed children and to grow into
   magnificent old age, harmonizes with the avant-garde feminist opinion of his
   era." Aspiz provides Whitman's assertions along with the positions of such
   feminist writers as Margaret Fuller, H. C. Wright, Elizabeth Cady Stanton, and
   Eliza W. Farnham.

Asselineau, Roger. *The Evolution of Walt Whitman*. Vol. 2, *The Creation of a Book*.
   Cambridge, Mass.: Harvard University Press, 1962.
   Studies *Leaves of Grass* from two perspectives: themes and artistic growth. In
   part 1, mysticism, metaphysics, esthetics, sexuality, patriotism, democracy, and
   industrial civilization receive separate chapters. Part 2 considers Whitman's
   style, his language innovations, and his prosody. Argues that Whitman's original intention was to present a visual poetry. Revisions show his developing
   craft and concern for the auditory features. Useful discussion of Whitman's
   attitude toward science.

Baily, John. *Walt Whitman*. Reprint. St. Clair Shores, Mich.: Scholarly Press, 1970.
   First published in 1926, this study attempts to define Whitman through comparison and contrast with major British writers and accommodate his achieve-

ment to Western tradition. Baily draws parallels to Milton, Wordsworth, and Macaulay. His discussion of language and meter contains an argument on the evolution of English verse. Observes Whitman's faults and failures from a conservative perspective, yet appreciates the spirit of freedom in Whitman's work.

Bauerline, Mark. "Whitman's Language of the Self." *American Imago* 44 (Summer, 1987): 129-148.
The presentation and celebration of an original self in unique, vital surroundings is Whitman's essential project. However, the act of glorification is accompanied by "gestures that obscure and even censure the self." Whitman's efforts "to subsume his life and his self into a poetic fiction became such an obsession that they supplanted the historical 'Personality' Whitman claimed was to occupy the center of his poetry." In the end, the poetry structures the personality, and its publication "spells the death of the self."

Beach, Joseph Warren. "Whitman." In his *The Concept of Nature in Nineteenth-Century English Poetry*. New York: Pageant Books, 1956.
"Nowhere perhaps, in the range of poetry written in English, is the thought of nature more confidently called to the support and inspiration of the spirit." Whitman was influenced by popular abstracts of German philosophers as well as by Rousseau and Thomas Paine. Beach discusses "Idealism," "Religious Optimism," and "The Democracy of Nature" while attending to key passages in Whitman's poetry. After Whitman, nature poetry responded to Darwinian theory rather than to Transcendentalist thought.

Beaver, Joseph. *Walt Whitman—Poet of Science*. Reprint. New York: Octagon Books, 1974.
First published in 1951, this study argues that Whitman was the first American poet to contend with and largely resolve the historical dichotomy between poetry and science. "His attitude toward science was one of faith," as it was toward everything else. Contends that Whitman's thought on science was much more informed than has been previously held. "Whitman regarded the universe from a consistently modern point of view, and this figures prominently and functionally in his poetry." Emphasis on astronomy and evolution.

Bedient, Calvin. "Walt Whitman." In *Voices and Visions: The Poet in America*, edited by Helen Vendler. New York: Random House, 1987.
Whitman's poetic subjects and formal inventions are responses to the American experience as envisioned by Alexis de Tocqueville, who felt that democracy would force poets in new directions. Bedient traces the ramifications of the principle of equality in Whitman's cataloguing, his liberated metrics, and his concern with the individual and all-encompassing life force. "Organicism, dynamism, and diversitarianism" are the tenets of Whitman's work. Whitman's

poetic manner has affinities with the work of his contemporaries in the visual arts.

Black, Stephen A. *Whitman's Journey into Chaos: A Psychoanalytic Study of the Creative Process*. Princeton, N.J.: Princeton University Press, 1975.
Focuses on Whitman's inner poetic processes between 1855 and 1865. The poems represent a journey into the chaos of the unconscious. Whitman's patterns of fantasy and symbol reveal someone "chiefly autoerotic in his sexual expressions." Argues that Whitman hid his "homosexual impulses and his sexual confusions" even from himself, and that the poems rarely resolve conflicts or relieve anxieties. Period covered deals with composition of the major poems.

Blasing, Mutlu Konuk. "The Coinciding Leaves of Walt Whitman." In her *American Poetry: The Rhetoric of Its Forms*. New Haven, Conn.: Yale University Press, 1987.
"Since past, present, and future coincide in a synchronic identity, nature is not a blank slate for Whitman but a palimpsest. It is a tissue or fiber woven through the ages that even now conveys actual conversions and metamorphoses of all ages and forms." Language is inherently metaphoric, and as a generative process recycles nature and its own texts. Sees coincidence of form and content as Whitman's main poetic project.

Bloom, Harold. "Whitman's Image of the Voice: To the Tally of My Soul." In *American Poetry to 1914*, edited by Bloom. New York: Chelsea House, 1987.
Briefly traces the problem of voice in Bryant and other early nineteenth century American poets before examining the nature and extent of Whitman's confrontation of the issue. Whitman does not just say "hear my voice" but "hear me *as* voice." Bloom examines the key word "tally" in "When Lilacs Last in the Dooryard Bloom'd" and makes connections between the notions of voice in Whitman, Wallace Stevens, and John Ashbery. Eclectic, elliptical, and finally as much about criticism as about poetry.

Bradley, Scully. "The Fundamental Metrical Principle in Whitman's Poetry." *American Literature* 10 (January, 1939): 437-459.
The feature that recurs regularly and markedly in Whitman's poetry is nothing other than the stressed syllable. Whitman uses an evolved form of the strong-stress line that characterizes Old English verse and that has persisted, despite the overlay of other schemes, through the centuries. Various poems and passages are built on a stress-count prosody that depends on the use of hovering accents. Like the Old English poets, Whitman employs a strong medial caesure. Detailed exemplification.

Briggs, Arthur E. *Walt Whitman: Thinker and Artist*. Reprint. New York: Greenwood Press, 1968.
"The key to Whitman is his conception of personality." An attempt to use but go beyond the Whitman cults to the "personalistic humanism" that "harmonizes sex, science, religion, and government without sacrifice of man or men." Treats love and comradeship, social morality and democracy, and the created persona. Chapter on "Dickinson and Whitman" reveals significant parallels. Another measures Whitman against Gerard Manley Hopkins.

Broderick, John C., ed. *Whitman the Poet*. Belmont, Calif.: Wadsworth, 1962.
A casebook for study with a selection of Whitman's poems, a series of prefaces by Whitman to his own work, samples of Whitman's revisions, and some of his critical pronouncements. Writings about Whitman include his contemporaries' estimates and then groupings on form and technique, prosody, style and language, and the Whitman personae. Special sections on the design of *Leaves of Grass* and on "Approaches to 'Passage to India.'"

Brooks, Van Wyck. "Whitman: *Leaves of Grass*." In his *The Times of Melville and Whitman*. New York: E. P. Dutton, 1947.
Emphasizes the theories of scientific breeding that were current when Whitman wrote. Whitman's attitude toward the perfectibility of the body of the species called for a healthy sexuality through which the American type could continue its progressive evolution. Brooks assays Whitman's attempt to marry science and democracy, to spiritualize democracy, and to foster an American culture of widely varied "comrade-apostles." Highlights the Quaker impulse in Whitman. (Includes other chapters on Whitman.)

Cady, Edwin H., and Louis J. Budd, eds. *On Whitman: The Best from American Literature*. Durham, N.C.: Duke University Press, 1987.
A selection from fifty years of the prestigious journal *American Literature* rescues sixteen striking essays from possible oblivion. These cover Whitman's imagery, metrics, and rhetoric as well as such topics as Quaker influence, Whitman's notion of spiritual democracy, and his standing with contemporary periodical editors. Included are Emory Holloway's "Whitman Pursued" and David W. Hiscoe's "Whitman's Use of the Middle Ages." Most of the Whitman articles cited from *American Literature* in this bibliography are included here.

Cady, Joseph. "*Drum-Taps* and Nineteenth-Century Male Homosexual Literature." In *Walt Whitman Here and Now*, edited by Joann P. Krieg. Westport, Conn.: Greenwood Press, 1985.
Considers these poems "documents of nineteenth-century male homosexual

literature." The homosexual affirmations are not so open as in the *Calamus*
poems, yet they are clearly conveyed by the motif of "soldier-comradeship"
and by elegiac conventions. Cady develops the context of gay experience in
Whitman's time before analyzing "Vigil Strange I Kept on the Field One
Night" and "As I Lay with My Head in Your Lap Camerado." Suggests that
the war's conditions permitted seemingly innocent formulations that masked
the homosexual content and protected Whitman from exposure.

Canby, Henry Seidel. "Walt Whitman." In *Literary History of the Unites States*,
  edited by Robert E. Spiller et al. 3d ed., revised. New York: Macmillan, 1963.
  The notion of expansiveness dominates Whitman's way of relating to his
  world. He fought for a vision of vast inclusiveness, a harmony of various self-
  interests. In proposing to be the voice of democracy, unelected, he anointed
  himself as the nation's prophet and as its "divine average." But Whitman was
  in most ways not ordinary. His homosexual sensibility, his outdoor personality,
  and his egocentric celebrations were outside the mainstream—yet finally enormously successful.

——————— . *Walt Whitman: An American*. Reprint. Westport, Conn.: Greenwood Press, 1970.
  Sees *Leaves of Grass* as the symbolic autobiography which must be interpreted
  along with the impact of the variegated America in which Whitman lived.
  Whitman's commitment to the dream of an American poem is the center of
  Canby's study. Canby appreciates the large patterns of Whitman's rhythms and
  the poet's ability to find rhythmic equivalents for emotional tides. Keen insights on how Whitman's free verse functions.

Carlisle, E. Fred. *The Uncertain Self: Whitman's Drama of Identity*. East Lansing:
  Michigan State University Press, 1973.
  Explores the personality as it engages varieties of experience that leave it
  uncertain "about the nature of the self and the world." Disagrees with those
  who consider Whitman's identity to have been fixed early or who feel it was
  never an important problem for him. The voices in Whitman's poems reaffirm
  and extend one another so that "each poem becomes a moment in a continuing
  dialogue between the poet and his reader." This is a biography of the poetic
  persona, not a treatment of the life.

Carpenter, George Rice. *Walt Whitman*. Reprint. Detroit: Gale Research, 1967.
  First published in 1909, this is an early career biography that sees Whitman
  less as a miracle worker and more as a literary professional trying to succeed
  in his craft, with the literary marketplace, and with the public. Carpenter
  considers the role of literal and figurative "comradeship" in Whitman's life
  and art while celebrating the poet as a great voice of unification.

Cavitch, David. *My Soul and I: The Inner Life of Walt Whitman*. Boston: Beacon Press, 1985.

Cavitch summarizes his argument as follows: "Whitman gained his full power to write when he learned how to re-create his family relationships in the voice and the structure of his poems, and then in being a poet he struggled against his poetry just as he had spent his entire life in loving conflict with his family." Whitman's "commonness" was a constant delight to him and the basis of his relationship with his readers.

Chari, V. K. *Whitman in the Light of Vedantic Mysticism*. Lincoln: University of Nebraska Press, 1971.

Whitman's Vedantic mysticism "is the clue to his democratic idealism." The Vedantic outlook is nondualistic, thus Whitman can view all of creation as a "spectrum analysis" of the individual soul. Chari's chapters emphasize the "nature of consciousness," "the dynamic self," and "the paradox of identity." Whitman a "thoroughgoing idealist" whose mysticism is unlike the Brahminical strand that finds fulfillment in self-obliteration and the "deprecation of the individual." The Vedantic vision, like Whitman's, is dynamic.

Chase, Richard. *Walt Whitman*. Minneapolis: University of Minnesota Press, 1961.

A pamphlet essay that introduces the major issues in Whitman's poetry and personality. Examines the ways in which the self-proclaimed anti-intellectual poet was, in fact, a kind of intellectual. Whitman's pose of simplicity and openness masks the real complexity and nuance of his work. The essential Whitman paradox: "the individual becomes integral in his separateness to the extent that he is absorbed into the indissoluble union of all men." Perhaps the best forty pages available on this poet.

——————. *Walt Whitman Reconsidered*. New York: William Sloane, 1955.

A critical examination of *Leaves of Grass* follows a biographical chapter. Chase pays most attention to "Song of Myself," calling it "a profound and lovely comic drama" that uses the strategies of the tall tale. Chase finds Whitman's exuberant tone to be linked to the uninhibited comic flavor that gives his work its signature. This poem, like the critic who admires it, is "committed to the radical literary and cultural values of its time."

Daiches, David. "Walt Whitman as Innovator." In *The Young Rebel in American Literature*, edited by Carl Bode. New York: Frederick A. Praeger, 1960.

Examines, from a British perspective, the nature of Whitman's rebellious stance. Against the European model of counterpointing personal aesthetic experience and tradition, Whitman's rebellion could be more radical because his culture and its traditions were less rigorously defined. For Whitman, whatever he sees becomes part of him before it becomes shaped into an available form. The poem, then, is truly an expansion of his sensibility, not a contraction of it to fit a traditional formula.

De Selincourt, Basil. *Walt Whitman: A Critical Study*. Reprint. New York: Russell & Russell, 1965.
First published in 1914, this is an early analysis of form in Whitman, and still a useful one. Its focus is on "constructive principles," types of unity, style, and plan with later sections on thematic issues. Before free verse and its attendant theories were commonplace, this critic made good sense of Whitman's use of the line, adapting traditional prosodic thinking to this unconventional material. A sense of discovery charges this study of now-familiar issues.

Deutsch, Babette. *Walt Whitman: Builder for America*. New York: Julian Messner, 1941.
A popular biography seemingly written with young readers in mind, this treatment uses novelistic devices to attract us to Whitman's personality and to engage us in his poems. Episodes with colorful people and stimulating settings abound. Many passages from the poetry are introduced into the narrative, and the life proper is followed by a generous selection of Whitman's poems. "Suggested Readings" lists poems to be reviewed in conjunction with Deutsch's chapters.

Diggory, Terence. "Armored Women, Naked Men: Dickinson, Whitman, and Their Successors." In *Shakespeare's Sisters: Feminist Essays on Woman Poets*, edited by Sandra M. Gilbert and Susan Gubar. Bloomington: Indiana University Press, 1979.
Diggory examines representative passages from Dickinson and Whitman to point out distinctions between "male and female traditions in American poetry that have their roots in these two great contemporaries." Armor and its function of concealment are treated with repugnance by Whitman but are highly valued by Dickinson. "Dickinson and Whitman agreed that any utterance could be a disclosure of identity, but they disagreed about the desirability of the disclosure." Diggory follows this dichotomy in the works of Robert Frost and Sylvia Plath.

Donoghue, Denis. "Whitman." In his *Reading America: Essays on American Literature*. New York: Alfred A. Knopf, 1987.
Observing that Whitman's verse cadences must be read "in long, rolling stretches," Donoghue notes that Whitman depends on the natural flow of breath for his rhythmic and semantic structures—a moving vehicle for thought and image. Concludes, however, that Whitman's rejection of the past was uninformed and unearned, and that his freedom therefore lacks authority.

Eby, Edwin Harold. *A Concordance of Walt Whitman's Leaves of Grass and Selected Prose Writings*. Reprint. New York: Greenwood Press, 1969.
This alphabetical listing of all words except function words gives usage citations. From such a reference students can explore Whitman's stylistic habits, discover key words, determine from context which meanings are emphasized, and so forth. This concordance is keyed to the 1902 *Complete Writings of Walt Whitman*. The prose and poetry are treated in separate alphabets. First published in 1955.

Ehrenpreis, Irvin. "Whitman." In *Poetries of America*, edited by Daniel Albright. Charlottesville: University Press of Virginia, 1989.
In the first of these "Essays on the Relation of Character to Style," Ehrenpreis focuses on the self- definition that lies behind and within the works of Whitman. Whitman tended to evade "the problem of selfhood and clung to unfocused potentiality" by identifying his poetic self with his nation." He found that he could trust his genius and reject the schemes of conscious art. Ehrenpreis examines the relationship between persona and free verse mode.

Erkkila, Betsy. *Whitman the Political Poet*. New York: Oxford University Press, 1989.
Views Whitman's work in relation to the political struggles of the century, presenting the poems as products and as agents of political change. Topics include the politics of race, gender, class, capital, technology, and expansion. Relates the dominating image of the sexual body to the metaphor of the body politic. Suggests that the effects of the Civil War led Whitman to reordering the parts within *Leaves of Grass*: "Whitman is one of America's most overtly political poets."

Faner, Robert D. *Walt Whitman and Opera*. Philadelphia: University of Pennsylvania Press, 1951.
A detailed look at what had become an unexplored critical cliché, this study has two parts. First, Faner reviews all the sources of musical knowledge available to Whitman, stressing what he actually heard and knew during the evolution of *Leaves of Grass*. The second part examines representative poems to show how various aspects of opera influenced form and content. According to Faner, grand opera made a poet out of Whitman.

Fast, Robin Riley. "Structure and Meaning in Whitman's *Sea-Drift*." *ATQ*, no. 53 (Winter, 1982): 49-66.
This significant sequence in *Leaves of Grass* is arranged so as to develop the themes of confrontation with power and vastness, reconciliation in individuality, and recognition of emerging powers of vision. "Out of the Cradle End-

lessly Rocking" begins the sequence and previews the entire structure that is elaborated and deepened in the following poems. These trace a progress of resolution and discovery through which the poet transcends fears of fragmentation. Seeing anew, he transforms his natural surroundings and the cosmos. Each poem builds on or responds to those which precede it.

Fausset, Hugh l'Anson. *Walt Whitman: Poet of Democracy*. Reprint. New York: Haskell House, 1966.
First published in 1940, this biographical and critical appreciation was prepared for British readers. Fausset explores Whitman's roots, the Long Island culture of his boyhood, and the bustle of his newspaper work. Whitman's "obtrusive egotism" is almost always present, but is balanced or overwhelmed by the more congenial aspects of his art. Whitman's sense of mission led him to be a poet and to invent both his style and the phenomenon of *Leaves of Grass*. Changes in successive editions reflect modifications of that mission as well as Whitman's long decline after the Civil War.

Fussell, Edwin. "The Birth of Death in Whitman." In his *Lucifer in Harness*. Princeton, N.J.: Princeton University Press, 1973.
Addresses the problem of finding an appropriate diction for American poetry. Discusses Whitman's movement from a "psychedelic eclecticism" in his early poems to a purer vernacular in his "breakthrough" year of 1859. "As I Ebb'd With the Ocean of Life" and "Out of the Cradle Endlessly Rocking" solve the problem. Whitman argued and practiced the elimination of abstract, haughty, and rhetorical address current in British poetic style. He gave birth to an idiom of "a wild land noisy with natural and human dissonance and dislocation."

Gelpi, Albert. "Walt Whitman: Self As Circumference." In his *The Tenth Muse: The Psyche of the American Poet*. Cambridge, Mass.: Harvard University Press, 1975.
Whitman's persona of prophet and mythmaker projects a "tremendous range of diction and rapid shifts of levels and tone . . . blending slang and philosophical abstractions with coinages and foreign borrowings." Whitman is forging "an all-inclusive language to convey the mystery of identity in the eternal flow of bodies." In Whitman's experience, art becomes indispensable to life. By exploring "his highest and deepest possibilities," Whitman gives us an identity truer than that of "the observable data of his existence."

Hindus, Milton, ed. *Walt Whitman: The Critical Heritage*. New York: Barnes & Noble, 1971.
Reviews and excerpts from the early decades of response to Whitman's achievement are divided into three eras: "The Battle for Recognition:

1855-60," "After the Civil War: 1865-92," and "Canonization, Kindnesses, and Some Brickbats: 1892-1914." Introduction synthesizes the material. The European responses especially illuminating. Foreign critics accepted and praised Whitman well before praise at home was unanimous.

Hollis, C. Carroll. *Language and Style in Leaves of Grass*. Baton Rouge: Louisiana State University Press, 1983.
Considers the "oratorical impulse" that lies behind the poetic style. Vocal utterance fascinated Whitman, who was well aware of lecture techniques. Studies on the cadence of oratory are applied to Whitman's lines. Other interests include negation, metonymy, and journalistic technique. A lively, witty exposition whose implicit argument is that Whitman wrote for performance.

Holloway, Emory. *Whitman: An Interpretation in Narrative*. Reprint. New York: Biblo and Tannen, 1969.
First published in 1926, this study begins with Whitman's career as a journalist in Brooklyn. Holloway points out the ways in which Whitman's early work kept him abreast of the facts and issues of contemporary America. He considers Whitman's literary and imaginative travels as the sources for his invention of the American type held forth in his poetry as spokesman, exemplar, and companion. The spirit of spiritual discovery links Whitman with the genius of American pioneering history and the worldwide saga of human liberation.

Hutchinson, George B. *The Ecstatic Whitman: Literary Shamanism and the Crisis of Union*. Columbus: Ohio State University Press, 1986.
Uses shamanistic ecstasy as it was popularized in the nineteenth century as a way of seeing Whitman's stance and method in the pre- and postwar poems. Whitman's ecstatic vision would provide healing power for the nation's political crisis. An interesting alternative to those studies that view Whitman's mysticism through other lenses. "The Sleepers" and "Song of Myself" treated in detail; many other poems given brief explications.

Jannacone, Pasquale. *Walt Whitman's Poetry and the Evolution of Rhythmic Forms and Walt Whitman's Thought and Art*. Translated by Peter Mitlineos. Washington, D.C.: NCR/Microcard Editions, 1973.
Comprises two essays. The essay on rhythmic forms was first published in Italy in 1898. Jannacone reveals the high degree of conventional metrics in Whitman's work as well as the characteristic repetitions of sound, of grammatical units, and of a word or words at the beginning of lines. Argues that the most important unit is not the line, but the group of lines marked by a period. The second, less original essay on Whitman's thought first appeared in 1920.

Jarrell, Randall. "Some Lines from Whitman." In his *Poetry and the Age*. New York: Alfred A. Knopf, 1953.

While observing the tendency to value Whitman for his outlook, Jarrell insists that Whitman's poetic skills are enormous. Although Whitman wrote some very bad poetry, at his best he is "a poet of the greatest and oddest delicacy and originality and sensitivity, as far as words are concerned." Whitman's wit is illustrated, as is his engagement with complex issues that demand and receive appropriately complex verbal structures. The "feeling of raw hypnotic reality" is one consequence of Whitman's manipulation of parallel structure.

Kaplan, Justin. *Walt Whitman: A Life*. New York: Simon and Schuster, 1980.

A comprehensive biography that presents Whitman as the foremost poetic chronicler of democracy and progress, scientific and otherwise. Re-creates the milieu of Whitman's formative years, the New York of his newspaper days, and the suffering he witnessed during the Civil War. Explains how and why the writing and rewriting of *Leaves of Grass* became the center of Whitman's life. Reviews Whitman's difficulties with editors even after receiving Emerson's influential praise. Illustrated.

Kazin, Alfred. "A More Perfect Union: Whitman to Lincoln." In his *An American Procession*. New York: Alfred A. Knopf, 1984.

Considers the theme of longing and the strategic suspension of its fulfillment. The reader must join in, must somehow help the realization of completeness. Whitman's greatest longing, the longing for unity, has personal, philosophical, and political dimensions. The "Union" of the United States, represented by the figure of Lincoln, is a quest parallel to that for sexual union and spiritual accord. Whitman seeks techniques to resolve the obvious fragmentation of the nation, of the burgeoning cities, of modern life.

Keller, Karl. "Walt Whitman and the Queening of America." *American Poetry* 1 (Fall, 1983): 4-26.

Keller tries to understand how "that kind of poet-prophet—the faggot-guru— could become part of the American mainstream," especially in Victorian America. He examines the European tradition of the dandy turned queen, and he relates this mode of personality to Whitman's role as a "field . . . a space into which many things can fit." Keller believes that "the Self conceived of as space . . . is Whitman's greatest invention. Argues that the polymorphous poet ushered in the modern literary era of the "holy creep" and genderless sensuality.

Killingsworth, Myrth Jimmie. "Whitman and Motherhood: A Historical View." *American Literature* 54 (March, 1982): 28- 45.

Whitman's treatment of motherhood has a decidedly Victorian slant. He is always at war, but never free from, "the characterization of the ideal mother as his culture depicted her" in ladies' magazines and elsewhere. Selflessness is a major trait of this ideal. Whitman's memorialization of his own mother is fully conventional. Orson Fowler's writings influenced Whitman's view of motherhood.

Kinkead-Weeks, Mark. "Walt Whitman Passes the Full-stop by . . ." In *Nineteenth-Century American Poetry*, edited by A. Robert Lee. Totowa, N.J.: Barnes & Noble, 1985.
Examines the blend of organic form and democratic syntax in Whitman's major poems. This syntax, which holds no one thing above another, "has to be radically coordinative rather than subordinative." In "Song of Myself," this technique is self-cancelling: nothing stands out. Moreover, the technique allows the poem no resolution. In "When Lilacs Last in the Dooryard Bloom'd" and "Out of the Cradle Endlessly Rocking," Whitman develops his material by rewritings of the poems' first movements. Symbolic structures provide shape and containment.

Krieg, Joann P., ed. *Walt Whitman Here and Now*. Westport, Conn: Greenwood Press, 1985.
Collects papers presented at the Walt Whitman Conference held at Hofstra College (125th anniversary of *Leaves of Grass*). The introductory remarks by William White survey the "Whitman Industry." Groupings include "Biographers and Critics," "Here and Now: Contemporary Views," "Whitman's Poetics," "Whitman and America," and "Whitman and the World of Literature." Most of these essays are concise, well-focused discussions. The conference program is appended.

Lawrence, D. H. "Whitman." In his *Studies in Classic American Literature*. Reprint. New York: Viking Press, 1964.
Considers Whitman's exuberance forced and false, his alleged inclusiveness the key to a fundamental lack of sure identity. Whitman a "great post-mortem poet" whose real subject is the end of life and whose optimism is paradoxically and futilely death-directed. Appreciates Whitman's pioneering spirit, his insistence on venturing down the open road into the unknown. However, the traditional known is what he reaches: a Christian vision without the language of Christianity. First published 1923. Often anthologized.

Lewis, R. W. B., ed. *The Presence of Walt Whitman*. Selected Papers from the English Institute. New York: Columbia University Press, 1962.
Four of the essays are on "Out of the Cradle Endlessly Rocking." These are by Whicher, Chase, Fussell, and Pearce. The other essayists are James E. Miller, Jr., on "Whitman and Thomas: The Yawp and the Gab"; Samuel Hynes on

"Whitman, Pound, and the Prose Tradition"; and James A. Wright on "The Delicacy of Walt Whitman." Lewis' foreword places the essays within the larger context of Whitman criticism.

Loving, Jerome. *Emerson, Whitman, and the American Muse*. Chapel Hill: University of North Carolina Press, 1982.
Examines how the main lines of American poetry became established in the complex relationship between these two men. Asserts that for all their differences in background and culture, the two were much alike in temperament and talent. Assesses their major works as a figurative correspondence between them: an imaginary conversation in which each fired the other's imagination. A provocative exploration of how the two poets dealt with the conflict between the law of the group and the freedom of the individual.

Marinacci, Barbara. *O Wondrous Singer! An Introduction to Walt Whitman*. New York: Dodd, Mead, 1970.
An inspired literary adventure story with Whitman as the hero, this book develops the innocent thesis that there is something in Whitman for everyone. While the tone and diction suggest a biography for young readers, the detail and length of this book are larger than most projects of that kind. Colorful, enthusiastic, and uncritical, this treatment has a vitality that suggests just how infectious Whitman can be.

Martin, Robert K. "Walt Whitman." In his *The Homosexual Tradition in American Poetry*. Austin: University of Texas Press, 1979.
Whitman used his poetry to announce and define his homosexuality. Martin contends that few critics have been able to take Whitman at his word, probably because in their view being great means being heterosexual. Martin reviews the poems carefully and makes a compelling case for Whitman's agenda of self-revelation. The "Calamus" group receives the most attention. Here, "he has revealed the pleasures and pains of life as a homosexual in nineteenth century America." Traces transition in emphasis from longing to response.

Masters, Edgar Lee. *Whitman*. New York: Charles Scribner's Sons, 1937.
A straightforward, cautiously appreciative biography and assessment of one major American voice by an important minor one. Masters stresses Whitman's total emergence in the project of finding the language and poetic manner for the unique American experience. He is impressed by Whitman's remarkable productivity, yet he judges that Whitman did not possess the kind of genius needed to create the distinctive American poetry he sought. He lacked architectural and logical powers; his expansive, mystical outlook never penetrated through the seen to the unseen.

Marx, Leo, ed. *The Americanness of Walt Whitman*. Boston: D. C. Heath, 1960.
Readings "selected to assist students in forming a more precise idea of the relation between Whitman's poetry, especially 'Song of Myself,' and American experience." Authors include Edward Dowden, John Jay Chapman, George Santayana, and Randall Jarrell. Excerpts lay groundwork for evaluating both the intrinsic merit of the poems and their utility "as an index of the quality of American consciousness generally." Brief list of suggestions for further reading.

Matthiessen. F. O. " Whitman." In his *American Renaissance: Art and Expression in the Age of Emerson and Whitman*. New York: Oxford University Press, 1941.
This critical classic views Whitman's work as an extension of Samuel Taylor Coleridge's notion of organic form. Explores Whitman's analogies between poetry and oratory, opera, and the ocean to discover the organizing principles of *Leaves of Grass* as well as individual poems. Whitman's innovations in rhythm are explained through the later theory and practice of Gerard Manley Hopkins, and Whitman's descriptions of landscape are discussed in terms of genre painting.

Metzger, Charles R. *Thoreau and Whitman: A Study of Their Esthetics*. Seattle: University of Washington Press, 1961.
These writers subscribed to "related versions of the same transcendentalist tradition." Their religious views influenced their esthetic positions. They are more practical, less theoretical, than Emerson. Like Emerson, they favor architectural examples in discussing esthetic issues. Both were conscious of the role of art in personal salvation as well as the salvation of others. Differences are more superficial than essential.

Middlebrook, Diane Wood. *Walt Whitman and Wallace Stevens*. Ithaca, N.Y.: Cornell University Press, 1974.
Despite extreme dissimilarities in poetic form, these two major figures are connected by a similar "mythology of the imagination"—the desire to project a mythic self invented for the purposes of powerful expression. Not an influence study, but an examination of Whitman's legacy of "a conception of the unfailing sufficiency of the mind's creative relation to reality." Both men sought a "spiritual centrality within American culture."

Miller, Edwin Haviland. *Walt Whitman's Poetry: A Psychological Journey*. New York: New York University Press, 1969.
Considers Whitman's lyrical self-examination as having "its origins in unconscious and infantile sources." Finds that "the tensions in his poems are . . . psychic, and the external world is of little importance." Searches for the meaning of the "inner drama" whose tensions seek resolution and release.

Observes "orgiastic rhythms" and images that reveal Whitman's concern with the violence of sexuality. Questions the traditions that ascribe a serenity to the man and his work. "Singing the Phallus" is Whitman's agenda, but behind the bravado is a frustrated, lonely individual.

——————— , ed. *The Artistic Legacy of Walt Whitman*. New York: New York University Press, 1970.
This volume, a tribute to noted Whitman scholar Gay Wilson Allen, includes an essay on Allen's contribution to the field plus a series of essays on the connections between Whitman's poetry and other branches of American art. Ned Rorem's "Words Without Song," Robert Duncan's "Changing Perceptions in Reading Whitman," and Max Kozloff's "Walt Whitman in American Art" are among the selections. See also the editor's "The Radical Vision of Whitman and Pollack." Illustrated.

——————— . *A Century of Whitman Criticism*. Bloomington: Indiana University Press, 1969.
An exciting mixture of standard and eccentric views of Whitman's poetry beginning with the earliest appraisals. Includes European views, explications, and source studies. Unusual inclusions are comments by Henry Miller, Muriel Rukeyser, Kenneth Burke, and Gustav Bychowski. Extensive chapter notes.

Miller, James E., Jr. *Walt Whitman*. Boston: Twayne, 1962.
An introductory overview of Whitman's life and art, intending "to provide as many entrances as possible to Whitman's poetry." Each chapter initiates a separate approach; topics include the democratic impulse, the development and the structural coherence of *Leaves of Grass*, the major individual poems, the recurring images, diction, and the bardic voice. The chapter on "The Individual Leaves" contains brief explications of many poems. Synthesizes major critical perspectives.

Miller, James E., Jr., Karl Shapiro, and Bernice Slote. *Start with the Sun: Studies in the Whitman Tradition*. Lincoln: University of Nebraska Press, 1960.
A collaborative mosaic of essays on Whitman and creation, Whitman and D. H. Lawrence, Whitman and Hart Crane, Whitman and Dylan Thomas, and finally the extent and magnitude of Whitman's influence on modern literature. A celebration of the unorthodox features of Whitman's vision and technique that attends to the dark undercurrents as well as to the healing, sun-lit aspects of the Whitman tradition. The plan of the book makes it a critical echo of *Leaves of Grass*.

Mitchell, Roger. "A Prosody for Whitman?" *PMLA* 84 (October, 1969): 1606-1612.
"The key to the scansion of Whitman's poetry is the caesura." Whitman breaks

his lines into grammatical unites for rhetorical emphasis, but these groupings also have prosodic significance. The relationship of groups to lines corresponds to the development of an idea, description, or action. Many passages have the "crude outline of a rhythmic parabola." Whitman's prosody is complex but usually symmetrical, and it is always functional. Mitchell illustrates his discoveries by scanning and commenting on representative passages.

More, Paul Elmer. "Walt Whitman." In *Paul Elmer More's Shelburne Essays on American Literature*, edited by Daniel Aaron. New York: Harcourt, Brace & World, 1963.
More puts passages from Whitman alongside passages from Arnold, Tennyson, and Browning to make the case that Whitman holds his own among the century's greats. Notices that Whitman's rhythms are often not as "lawless as he himself and others have supposed." Whitman often writes in a hexametric cadence dominated by the dactylic foot. Argues that Whitman's early disciples praised the lesser features of his work, delaying the true appreciation of his achievement.

Mottram, Eric. "Law and the Open Road: Whitman's 'America.' " In *Nineteenth-Century American Poetry*, edited by A. Robert Lee. Totowa, N.J.: Barnes & Noble, 1985.
"Within the impositions of competitiveness and civil war, possessive individualism and the interlocking systems of class, racial and financial power in the United States, Whitman's creative energy is directed as much as can be towards keeping the options of freedom open." Mottram points out Whitman's awareness of the limiting conditions while stressing the means by which he built a symbolic America that offered the possibility of a new human type. References to political and social thinkers.

Murphy, Francis, ed. *Walt Whitman*. Middlesex, England: Penguin, 1969.
Responses to Whitman grouped in three sections: "Contemporaneous Criticism," "The Developing Debate," and "Modern Views." Most the major critics are represented in this judicious and generous sampling. Includes comments by such poets as Randall Jarrell, William Carlos Williams, and T. S. Eliot. A broad spectrum of Whitman's work is treated.

Pearce, Roy Harvey, ed. *Whitman: A Collection of Critical Essays*. Englewood Cliffs, N.J.:, Prentice-Hall, 1962.
Groups contributions to Whitman criticism into four categories: "The Open Road," "The Integrity of *Leaves of Grass*," "The Poet in His Art," and "Democratic Vistas." The early selections by Ezra Pound and D. H. Lawrence, fellow trailblazers, stand out. Fine discussions also of Whitman as a phenomenon of American culture. Many periodical essays not elsewhere collected.

Perry, Bliss. *Walt Whitman: His Life and Work*. Cambridge, 1906. Reprint. New York: AMS Press, 1969.
An early attempt to win an enlarged public for Whitman, first published in 1906, this appreciation makes lively use of notebooks and letters. Creates a Walt Whitman legend rather than a life. Useful in explaining how one must experience large portions of the poems to discover the patterns and rhythms. Whitman wrote on a large scale, and microscopic critic tools will yield nothing. Likens Whitman's work to the prose poems of Ruskin and Carlyle. Anecdotal and familiar in tone.

Rajasekharaiah, T. R. *The Roots of Whitman's Grass*. Rutherford, N.J.: Fairleigh Dickinson University Press, 1970.
The most comprehensive of the many attempts to discover the bases of Whitman's Oriental outlook, this work surveys all the books and articles on Indian philosophy that would have been available to Whitman in the New York City libraries, especially the Astor. Attempts to go beyond affinities and make claims for influence and sources based on commonalities of imagery and style. The miracle of Whitman's sudden transformation may be in his response to this body of knowledge.

Reynolds, David S. "Whitman's Poetic Humor." In his *Beneath the American Renaissance*. New York: Alfred A. Knopf, 1988.
Whitman labeled himself a humorist, and so did Emerson in his first reaction to *Leaves of Grass*. Whitman reshaped the "Subversive Style of dark humor," playfully reproducing its concerns with abrupt shifts in image, time, and place. He changed the experimental devices of popular humor for the better, restoring their power "by investing them with new philosophical and psychological depth." The sordid aspects of popular humor, its essential nihilism, were turned into celebration.

——————— . "Whitman's Transfigured Sensationalism." In his *Beneath the American Renaissance*. New York: Alfred A. Knopf, 1988.
"Far from being a lonely rebel against his culture, he was a broad-ranging observer who made every effort to assimilate his culture's sensational themes and to reproduce them deliberately in sanitizing, transfiguring poetry." Leading up to *Leaves of Grass*, Whitman was part of a world of sensationalistic city journalism which depended on the exposé format and often used concrete catalogs of modern experience. Sexual themes that had been either repressed or trivialized would be transfigured "by ridding them of both guilt and prurience."

Rosenblatt, Jon. "Whitman's Body, Whitman's Language." In *Walt Whitman Here and Now*, edited by Joann P. Krieg. Westport, Conn.: Greenwood Press, 1985.

Argues that in the 1850's, Whitman established "an equivalence between language and body that takes romantic organicism one step beyond its previous limits": He went beyond the use of analogy between body and poetry to claim an identity. "This identity then becomes the basis for Whitman's poetic strategy in which the poet, the poem, and the reader are linked together as one being through the spiritual-physical presence of language." Suggests that the late decline in Whitman's poetry may have been the result of his growing mistrust of the body during the 1860's and 1870's.

Rubin, Joseph Jay. *The Historic Whitman*. University Park: Pennsylvania State University Press, 1973.
Records the several careers of Whitman's youth and early adulthood up to the first publication of *Leaves of Grass*. Rich detail on the Suffolk County fishing community of Whitman's childhood, his various editorships and journalistic endeavors, and his work as a political partisan. Rubin addresses the wide range of interests and experiences out of which Whitman's poetry would emerge.

Rupp, Richard H., ed. *Critics on Whitman*. Coral Gables, Fla.: University of Miami Press, 1972.
Rupp groups selections under these headings: "A Poet to Poets," "The Design of the Book," "Approaches to Whitman," "The Poem Itself" (which is a convenient gathering of explications), and "Evaluations." An eclectic mix of responses gathered from both books and periodicals. Provides a brief introduction, a list of important dates, and a selected bibliography for further study.

Salska, Agnieszka. *Walt Whitman and Emily Dickinson: Poetry of the Central Consciousness*. Philadelphia: University of Pennsylvania Press, 1985.
This comparative study is subdivided into chapters on such topics as American literary individualism, the self as persona, and language. For Whitman, the inspiring moment is generally located in the future; for Dickinson, in the past. For Whitman, this moment clarifies; for Dickinson, it energizes. Each writer carries out certain aspects of Emerson's agenda for poetry.

Schyberg, Frederik. *Walt Whitman*. Translated by Evie Allison Allen. New York: AMS Press, 1966.
Schyberg's work, first published in Copenhagen in 1933, sees Whitman's mysticism "rooted in unappeased sex urges." The unity and harmony Whitman hoped for or thought he found existed neither in his own personal life nor in America at large. Whitman's problems reflected America's problems. Provides a vivid portrait of Whitman at thirty-six ending the long period of gestation that culminated in *Leaves of Grass*. Traces the phases of *Leaves of Grass* and examines Whitman's place in world literature.

Shephard, Esther. *Walt Whitman's Pose*. New York: Harcourt, Brace, 1938.
One of the earliest attempts to separate Whitman the man from Whitman the
created voice, this study works hard at reducing complex literary issues to
plain talk, but does not always succeed. Whitman was the poet of his own
personality, but this personality was also the product of his art. Shephard
explores Whitman's use of the word "master" and gives careful readings of
many individual poems. Discussed the ways in which Whitman's pose changes
in succeeding editions of *Leaves of Grass*.

Shucard, Alan. "Walt Whitman". In his *American Poetry: From the Puritans
Through Walt Whitman*. Boston: Twayne, 1988.
Provides an overview of Whitman's childhood and early career as a newspaper
writer and editor. Observes in Whitman's short fiction some of the psychological dynamics of the mature poems. Stresses Whitman's urban consciousness
and his thoroughgoing democratic sensibility. Traces his development as a poet
and explores the "twoness" of Whitman: He can sink to the depths of popular
taste and rise to the greatest and most original poetic achievement. Explores
the Emerson legacy in "Song of Myself" and then estimates Whitman's own
legacy.

Smuts, Jan Christian. *Walt Whitman: A Study in the Evolution of Personality*.
Detroit: Wayne State University Press, 1973.
Written in 1895, this study applies "a new conception of personality" which
treats its development like that of "any other organism." Whitman chosen as a
severe test of the theory. Biographically faulty, Smuts's work establishes the
uniquely democratic context of Whitman's personality. Applies evolutionary
theory to personality study: "the property of developing from within, from
itself, and of reorganizing all nutritive material according to its own inner
requirements." Sections on naturalism, emotionalism, applied spiritualism,
and religious spiritualism.

Snyder, John. *The Dear Love of Man: Tragic and Lyric Communion in Walt Whitman*. The Hague, Netherlands: Mouton, 1975.
Depicts Whitman as not only a poet of joyful communion but also a "brooding
tragedian" who sees men fundamentally as "lonely, inviolably alienated individuals." Notes a shift in the course of Whitman's career from a lyric sensibility toward the tragic mode; suggests that the impact of the Civil War and
of Whitman's own aging spurred this shift. Whitman wanted to get America to
see itself tragically, to move beyond the "political and moral suicide
. . . infecting its literature."

Spencer, Benjamin T. "A Half Century of Whitman." In his *The Quest for Na-
tionality*. Syracuse, N.Y.: Syracuse University Press, 1957.

Whitman was the focal point of democratic and national ideology for fifty years. Spencer reviews Whitman's early work as journalist and editor, particularly his toil for the Democratic Party. Explores Whitman's conscious search for the means to define and create a national literature. His subject— the country, the states, the land, the people—was to Whitman in itself a poem. Whitman captured the national culture in its own voice; he converted ideology into sensibility.

Stovall, Floyd. *The Foreground of Leaves of Grass*. Charlottesville: University Press of Virginia, 1974.
Looks to Whitman's family life, his journalistic enterprises, and his readings and clippings to find the materials later transformed. Illuminating chapters on Whitman's responses to stage drama, to opera, to phrenology, and to history. European influences considered, as well as Whitman's near-contemporaries among the British poets. Explores Whitman's interest in literary theory.

Symonds, John Addington. *Walt Whitman*. Reprint. New York: Benjamin Blom, 1967.
This 1893 study helped introduce the broad lines of Whitman's life as well as the unique features of his work to British readers. The discussion provides a context of writers familiar to that audience. Symonds' earlier role as an advocate of Whitman's genius is remembered in this anecdotal and often autobiographical work. Details Whitman's enthusiasm on the subjects of America, self, sex, and "the people." Stresses that Whitman's work "is peculiarly rich in subjects indicated for the sculptor or painter."

Tanner, James T. F. *Walt Whitman: A Supplementary Bibliography: 1961-1967*. Kent, Ohio: Kent State University Press, 1968.
This list has two parts. The first is a chronological ordering of earlier bibliographies. The second includes criticism, biography, and reviews in alphabetical order by author. The supplement updates Evie Allison Allen's "Check List" cited above.

——————. "Walt Whitman and the New Morality: Contemporary Reconsideration." In *Walt Whitman Here and Now*, edited by Joann P. Krieg. Westport, Conn.: Greenwood Press, 1985.
Discusses the relevance of Whitman's vision to contemporary America. Speculates that Whitman would not have been shocked by our political scandals, and he would no doubt have been pleased by our less inhibited attitudes toward sexuality. He would have appreciated our attempts to liberate minorities and to liberate language from sexist usages. He would see America as continuing to strive for the ideas announced in his poems. Whitman's blend of common sense and passion is a useful model for our own situation.

Templin, Lawrence. "The Quaker Influence on Walt Whitman." *American Litera-*
ture 42 (May, 1970): 165-180.
   Presents "the facts of Whitman's relationship to Quakerism" as they inform
   his outlook and writing. There are similarities between the Quaker preparation
   for and expectation of spiritual illumination and Whitman's own dependence
   on inspiration. The humanitarian streak in Whitman may be a Quaker inheri-
   tance. The Whitman paradox of a sense of community achieved through individual intuition parallels the Quaker community's dependence on the individual's Inner Light. Specific influence of Elias Hicks explored.

Thomas, M. Wynn. *The Lunar Light of Whitman's Poetry*. Cambridge, Mass.:
   Harvard University Press, 1987.
   Sees the poems as reflections of "a historically specific period of social crisis."
   Poetry helped Whitman adapt his ideals to a changing environment. The crisis
   of the Civil War was a turning point in his ability to modify his ideals without
   abandoning them. After this event, his poetry could not catch up with or
   effectively express his radically changed impression of America's destiny. His
   best late poetry dwelt in the past. A series of linked essays rather than a
   systematic argument.

Tichi, Cecelia. "Walt Whitman, the Literatus of the New Earth." In her *Environ-*
   mental Reform in American Literature from the Puritans Through Whitman.
   New Haven, Conn.: Yale University Press, 1979.
   This study of how "the ideology of environment reform" is reflected in American literature begins with the Puritan notion of a divinely directed mission.
   Whitman's poems effect a transformation in language and in the individual
   which promotes environmental reform. In Whitman, such reform is not part of
   a social program, but the consequence of the capacity for renewal in each of
   us. By avoiding polemics, Whitman makes his vision more affecting. "The
   Song of the Redwood Tree" is the central poem in this treatment.

Waggoner, Hyatt H. "Walt Whitman: Signing for Soul and Body." In his *American*
   Poets from the Puritans to the Present. Boston: Houghton Mifflin, 1968.
   Begins with Emerson's reactions to Whitman and then considers Whitman's
   use of the confessional mode. Suggests that Whitman realized himself most
   fully by fulfilling Emerson's notion of what a poet should be. In some ways,
   Whitman was the truer Transcendentalist because "he was never tempted to
   obliterate the actual to get at the real." Stresses such undervalued poems as
   "To Think in Time" and "There Was a Child Went Forth."

Wallace, Ronald. "Walt Whitman: Stucco'd with Quadrupeds and Birds All Over."
   In his *God Be with the Clown: Humor in American Poetry*. Columbia: University of Missouri Press, 1984.

Whitman's discussion of the "Great Poet" has many parallels with George Meredith's description of the "Comic Spirit." The notion of equality links these works. Whitman's own humor comes from a "robust and rhapsodic rowdiness." The Kentuckian or backwoodsman is the prototype for Whitman's narrator, who offers the humor of outrageous claims. "Whitman satirizes people who evade life." Detailed discussion of "Song of Myself" as a comic poem.

Waskow, Howard J. *Whitman: Explorations in Form.* Chicago: University of Chicago Press, 1966.
Defines "Whitman's formal range by demonstrating how each of his forms works." Addresses the conflicting approaches to Whitman as dialectician and organicist. Formal categories developed are combinations of traditional ones that Whitman blended and remade. "Bi-polar unity," "narrative," and "mono-drama" are the essential formal concepts, though not exhaustive or comprehensive ones. Extensive references to the formal conventions that Whitman inherits and subverts. Focus is on function.

Weirick, Bruce. "Walt Whitman." In his *From Whitman to Sandburg in American Poetry: A Critical Survey.* Reprint. New York: Biblo and Tannen, 1967.
First published in 1924, this survey classifies Whitman's role in American literary culture as equivalent to those of Homer, Virgil, Dante, and Shakespeare in their respective epochs. Treats Whitman's modernity, his "cosmic consciousness," his master passions, and his significance for the twentieth century. Special topics include Whitman's attitudes toward nature, toward democracy, and toward friendship. Whitman's vision of nature goes beyond the pantheism of the Romantics to embrace "this clashing chaos of reality, of struggle and survival."

Wheat, Edward M. "Whitman's 'Language Experiment' and the Making of a Therapeutic Political Epic." *Midwest Quarterly* 28 (Summer, 1987): 437-454.
Reviews Whitman's intense period of language study and the essential elements in his posthumously published *An American Primer* (1904). Whitman was aware of the connection between linguistic change and political change. His revolutionary politics required a revolution in language, a freedom from the inherited feudal English. "The tension between the lyric and the epic modes in *Leaves of Grass* corresponds to the political tension between the one and the many." Describes *Leaves of Grass* as Whitman's "text for democratic education."

Willard, Charles B. *Whitman's American Fame: The Growth of His Reputation in America After 1892.* Providence, R.I.: Brown University Press, 1950.
Explores Whitman's posthumous career as artist and cultural symbol. Com-

ments first on the early group of enthusiasts who first tried to bring attention to Whitman's achievement. Journalistic critics are treated next, followed by the academic biographers and critics. A most interesting section reviews Whitman's reputation among creative writers. The final two chapters synthesize and update "the critical evaluation" and "the general fame."

Winwar, Frances. *American Giant: Walt Whitman and His Times*. New York: Tudor, 1941.
An attractive telling of Whitman's life story against the backdrop of vigorous expansionism and the heartbreak of the Civil War. Winwar traces Whitman's busy career as journalist, his forays into prose fiction, and finally his poetic flourishing. Like many popular biographies, this one selects from available evidence to provide a novelistic character and series of actions. Walt the Colossus, one of Whitman's characteristic poses, is the character developed here.

Woodress, James, ed. *Critical Essays on Walt Whitman*. Boston: G. K. Hall, 1983.
This copious collection of previously published comment is divided into two sections. "Reviews and other Early Reactions" presents, sometimes in excerpt form, most of the significant reactions to Whitman's work during his lifetime. "Essays and Other Forms of Criticism" includes passages of anecdote, letters, and enthusiasm along with more analytical treatments of Whitman's work. Useful comments by Sidney Lanier, Gerald Manley Hopkins, Algernon Charles Swinburn, and Willa Cather. The editor's introduction surveys the direction of Whitman criticism.

Wright, James A. "The Delicacy of Walt Whitman." In *The Presence of Walt Whitman*, edited by R. W. B. Lewis. Selected Papers from the English Institute. New York: Columbia University Press, 1962.
In spite of the coarseness of his stance, the robustness of his person, and the immodest subject matter of many poems, Whitman is a poet of the greatest delicacy. Wright explores this delicacy first in Whitman's music, his tactful maneuverings "beyond the permissible variations of the iambic." He then turns to diction and finally to form. He praises Whitman's courage for daring "to subject his delicacy to the tests of the real world."

Zweig, Paul. *Walt Whitman: The Making of a Poet*. New York: Basic Books, 1984.
Zweig's focus is upon the five years leading up to the first edition of *Leaves of Grass*. He sets out to answer the question: How could an ordinary journalist turn himself into the most original of our poets in such a short period of time? Zweig notes the changes in Whitman's prose, his omnivorous reading and experimentation, and the creation of a new self that accompanied the creation of the breakthrough poems. The most vivid treatment of how Whitman took in and refashioned the aesthetic, political, and technological currents swirling around him.

Leaves of Grass

Asselineau, Roger. "Nationalism vs. Internationalism in *Leaves of Grass.*" In *Critical Essays on Walt Whitman*, edited by James Woodress. Boston: G. K. Hall, 1983.
One paradox of *Leaves of Grass* is Whitman's simultaneous celebration of America, a celebration often implicitly at the expense of the world the settlers left behind, and of internationalism, a vision of a cosmic brotherhood of all peoples. The bridging idea is that America is itself "the modern composite Nation, formed from all." Whitman's patriotism was sometimes expansionist: He imagined a pan-American country and perhaps even a supranational solidarity. In his letters, Whitman's expansionist views are more chauvinistically expressed than in the poems.

Crawley, Thomas Edward. *The Structure of Leaves of Grass*. Austin: University of Texas Press, 1970.
Attempts to separate structural issues from "biographical and sociological entanglements." Chapters elucidate "Whitman's Organic Principle," "The Christ Symbol," and then the major sections of the work itself. Final chapter traces the evolution of succeeding editions. Sees the unified spirit of *Leaves of Grass* in "the thematic development of recurring symbols applied at once to the personal and national themes." Sees the revisions and additions to the seventh edition (1881) resulting from Whitman's concerns about overall pattern.

Hindus, Milton, ed. *"Leaves of Grass" One Hundred Years After*. Stanford, Calif.: Stanford University Press, 1955.
Essays by William Carlos Williams (a brief and generalized appreciation), Richard Chase, Leslie Fiedler, Kenneth Burke, and others. John Middleton Murry assesses Whitman as democracy's poet-prophet. David Daiches explores Whitman's need for and use of the catalog technique. Other topics include free verse, epic and lyric aspects, and images of Whitman. Hindus' introduction provides an overview of the major approaches to and evaluations of *Leaves of Grass*.

Hoople, Robin P. " 'Chants Democratic and Native American': A Neglected Sequence in the Growth of *Leaves of Grass.*" *American Literature* 42 (May, 1970): 181-196.
Contends that few critics have paid proper attention to these poems as a sequence. Sees their appearance in the 1860 edition of *Leaves of Grass* as part of Whitman's "attempt to bring about an evangelical conversion of the heretics of democracy." Constituting one-fifth of the book, " 'Chants Democratic' has the richest and most carefully wrought internal structure of all the poem

clusters" in this edition. Hoople examines the cycle, discovering subordinate sequences and claiming that these poems are Whitman's most immediate expression of the tensions in his political surroundings.

Kennedy, William Sloane. *The Fight of a Book for the World.* Reprint. Folcroft, Pa.: Folcroft Library Editions, 1974.
Part 1 is a narrative of "the reception of *Leaves of Grass* by the world" from its first appearance down to the 1920's. Kennedy records almost every significant comment about the book. Part 2 is a study of how *Leaves of Grass* took shape and was modified in successive editions. Kennedy straightens out the titles and dates of the many poems and provides analyses of several. Part 3 contains bibliographical material. First published in 1926.

Kinnaird, John. "*Leaves of Grass* and the American Paradox." In *Whitman: A Collection of Critical Essays*, edited by Roy Harvey Pearce. Englewood Cliffs, N.J.: Prentice-Hall, 1962.
Whitman's duality—as child and man, individual soul and collective voice, male and female—creates a series of paradoxes in his work. Such troubled questions about identity stand unresolved in his poems and were celebrated "*because* they were insoluble." The Whitman of Manhattan and the Whitman who sings of wilderness are difficult to reconcile. Whitman's vision of America is a prophetic one, often at odds with the values in evidence before him.

Lewis, R. W. B. *The American Adam: Innocence, Tragedy, and Tradition in the Nineteenth Century*, 41-53. Chicago: University of Chicago Press, 1955.
Observes that in *Leaves of Grass* Whitman issues no complaints about the weight of the past; indeed, he hardly acknowledges a past. Only the ongoing and the present concern Whitman in this "Yankee Genesis," the account of the creation of a new world "with a happy ending for Adam." The first phase of the work identifies the self as a new kind of person born into freedom and forever innocent. The second phase brings the world in being. The God-like nature of the poet allows him to project "a world of order and meaning and identity."

_____ . "Walt Whitman: Always Going Out and Coming In." In *American Poetry to 1914*, edited by Harold Bloom. New York: Chelsea House, 1987.
Charges that Whitman's own editing and reshuffling of his poems created misleading groupings. Revisions and deleted passages worked with these packages to obscure the authentic poet and replace him with "a synthetic entity that was more posture than poet." Lewis systematically reviews the key changes in successive editions of *Leaves of Grass*, noting the increase in "oratory and rant" and the fashioning of "the good gray poet" image.

Marki, Ivan. *The Trial of the Poet: An Interpretation of the First Edition of Leaves of Grass*. New York: Columbia University Press, 1976.
Makes a claim for the special strength and purity of form of the first edition. Provides a detailed interpretation centered on the "common triplicate process" by which Whitman advances his works. This process involves a vaguely Hegelian dialectic as well as triads of imagery: "the basic formula of Whitman's processes of consciousness consists of elemental impulses of self-assertion invariably followed by self-denying reactions of compulsive force." This process sustains and renews itself.

Miller, James E., Jr. *A Critical Guide to 'Leaves of Grass.'* Chicago: University of Chicago Press, 1957.
This two-part study first examines a number of the major poems, concerning itself with the dramatic structure of each. The individual poems are likened to plays, each having a protagonist and an unfolding action. The second part views the panorama of *Leaves of Grass* as a whole, tracing its structural evolutions. Miller considers the structure of themes, the structures of time and space, and the structure of personality. Explores the kinship of *Leaves of Grass* to epic literature.

Pollack, Georgiana. "The Relationship of Music to *Leaves of Grass*." *College English* 15 (March, 1954): 384-394.
Examines the relationship between the style of *Leaves of Grass* and "recitative"—the rhetorical element of opera. The accentual regularity of Whitman's lines is like a musical measure that allows counterpointing by the rush or relaxation of natural speech inflection. The parenthetical aside, various kinds of repetition, and the enfolding of variously sized expressive units all borrow from or parallel the devices of recitative as it interacts with the musical score.

Renner, Dennis K. "Tradition for a Time of Crisis: Whitman's Prophetic Stance." In *Poetic Prophesy in Western Literature*, edited by Jan Wojcik and Raymond-Jean Frontain. Madison, N.J.: Fairleigh Dickinson University Press, 1984.
Points out how biblical prophetic devices are used to draw parallels between ancient Israel facing the crisis of exile and America facing the crisis of the Civil War. In *Leaves of Grass*, Whitman assumes the stance of the Hebrew prophets to meet a similar crisis of national unity.

"Cavalry Crossing a Ford"

Thomas, M. Wynn. *The Lunar Light of Whitman's Poetry*, 210-211. Cambridge, Mass.: Harvard University Press, 1987.

The poem "is an attractive little visual set piece, a design composed exclusively of contrasting colors and attitudes, allowed to stand as an unqualified record of brave color and pageantry." This is one of a handful of poems in which Whitman lets his aesthetic perception dominate over any deeper spiritual concerns. The pain and tragedy of the war is shut out. Thomas contrasts the poem to a companion prose piece in which Whitman's harrowing awareness of war's pain and suffering is expressed.

"Crossing Brooklyn Ferry"

Anderson, Quentin. "The World in the Body." In his *The Imperial Self*. New York: Alfred A. Knopf, 1971.
  Whitman is at once transformed by the scene, a transformer of the scene, a part of the scene, a ferry passenger, and a representative of mankind. In the poem, active and passive elements combine. Whitman announces and joins "a procession of life" in which the expressive sunset, the nearby urban communities, the hills and the harbor are figured in a dynamic, mutual embrace. Whitman's determination to absorb all reveals a need to coopt all, to reign supreme. This stance is at odds with his democratic agenda.

Carlisle, E. Fred. *The Uncertain Self: Whitman's Drama of Identity*, 59-67. East Lansing: Michigan State University Press, 1973.
  Sees the poem as a dialogue between the poet and others, a sharing of experience from action to meditation. The technique asks that poet and reader identify with one another. The meaning of the shared experience lies with this common identity and not beyond it. "Meaning arises only in the lived moment—in the sphere of the interhuman where the poet discovers the essential 'we' unfolding in existence and in the poem." Dramatizes not life but living.

Donoghue, Denis. "Whitman." In his *Reading America: Essays on American Literature*, 87-93. New York: Alfred A. Knopf, 1987.
  Considers this poem "the best of Whitman," a work in which his great delicacy and decorum are in control: The man and his style are one. "Whitman's favourite subject is movement, process, becoming: no wonder he loved bridges and ferries, which kept things moving while defining relationships, one thing with another." All that Whitman celebrates—water, clouds, people—must be translated into personal terms and put into personal relationship with the chanting voice. Whitman's perceptions are remade into the poem's cadences.

Miller, Edwin Haviland. *Walt Whitman's Poetry: A Psychological Journey*, 199-208. New York: New York University Press, 1969.

A hymn to the "joy of the sensuous body," a "hedonistic statement of faith," the poem is "deeply concerned with the devitalization of the body and the senses in the era of the machine." The poem's repetitions, though annoying, help express the theme of eternal recurrence. "Crossing Brooklyn Ferry" becomes "part of the flux it describes." The relationship of body and soul parallels that of mother to fetus: "The child emerges from the fertilized womb, and the soul is the summation of the eroticized body."

Thomas, M. Wynn. *The Lunar Light of Whitman's Poetry*, 92-116. Cambridge, Mass.: Harvard University Press, 1987.
Compares the technique of poem to American paintings of the period, especially to the use of light in the "luminist" school. This "limpid quality" of light may be "indigenous to the United States." Finds correlatives in word-painting for the Emersonian light of the soul. Light is related to inner and social vision. Considers the significance of stillness versus movement and the importance of the ferry as a "focal point of modern, democratic life." The diffuse light, the sky and water, help Whitman spiritualize the materialism of the city.

"I Sing the Body Electric"

Aspiz, Harold. *Walt Whitman and the Body Beautiful*, 67-69; 221-222. Urbana: University of Illinois Press, 1980.
Daring in its Victorian context, the poem celebrates the body "as the repository of generations yet unborn and as the domicile and complement of the soul." Based, in part, on Whitman's study of plates in an anatomy book and on his interest in body language. Asserts the traditional bond between physical health and spirituality. Electricity figures as an attractor, a source of energy, and a mysterious sublime element. The female carries the negative charge, her magnetism symbolic of sexuality and maternalism.

Miller, James E., Jr. *A Critical Guide to 'Leaves of Grass,'* 40-45. Chicago: University of Chicago Press, 1957.
Notes that this poem dominates the "Children of Adam" section since the body is the central fact in the poet's argument. The soul's origin is in the body, whose divinity must be accepted. Physical nearness is a kind of fulfillment in itself. Not only the body's sensuality is celebrated, but also its innocence and naturalness. The poem's imagery blends the scientific with the Edenic to suggest "that the primitive ideal may be realized in a complex, scientific society."

"A Noiseless Patient Spider"

Miller, James E., Jr. *A Critical Guide to 'Leaves of Grass,'* 153-155. Chicago: University of Chicago Press, 1957.
  The central device is the vivid dramatization of a single image. Whitman makes a specific symbolic application, linking the spider's working to that of the soul. The poem "is a brilliant affirmation of the need for spiritual love" in which Whitman "demonstrates in a very subtle and complex sense the path between reality, his soul, and the reader's soul and reveals his yearning for the 'gossamer' connection." Whitman built upon an earlier manuscript in which the spider was briefly mentioned, characteristically finding in this concrete image the proper starting point for a poem.

"Out of the Cradle Endlessly Rocking"

Canby, Henry Seidel. "Unifying Style in 'Out of the Cradle.'" In *Out of the Cradle Endlessly Rocking*, edited by Dominick P. Consolo. Columbus, Ohio: Charles E. Merrill, 1971.
  Examines Whitman's "harmonizing expression" achieved by "perpendicular alliteration" (initial sounds from line to line), interior alliteration, present participle endings, and initial trochaic meters. The poem's structure is like that "of a good essay" as well as the pattern of opera. Whitman's syntax imitates oratorical patterns. Considers Whitman's method largely intuitive, success or failure dependent upon inspiration.

Consolo, Dominick P., ed. *Out of the Cradle Endlessly Rocking*. Columbus, Ohio: Charles E. Merrill, 1971.
  A casebook designed to give the range of approaches to and interpretations of this major poem. The excerpts are all taken from previously published books or articles. Consolo's introduction discusses this poem as a key to Whitman's own concept of poetry and of his characteristic role or stance. Sees all of Whitman's work reflecting the same view of the creative process elaborated here. Early and late versions of the poem are included for comparison.

Fussell, Paul, Jr. "Whitman's Curious Warble: Reminiscence and Reconciliation." In *The Presence of Walt Whitman*, edited by R. W. B. Lewis. Selected Papers from the English Institute. New York: Columbia University Press, 1962.
  Classifies the poem as an "American Shore Ode," a genre defined as "a lyric of some length and philosophic density spoken (usually at a specific place) on an American beach; its theme tends to compass the relationship of the wholeness and flux of the sea to the discreetness and fixity of land objects." Fussell provides a brilliant structural and stylistic analysis, focusing on elements of stasis, flow, balance, and cyclical action.

Gutman, Stanley T. "Conflations in Walt Whitman's 'Out of the Cradle." *American Imago* 44 (Summer, 1987): 149-158.

Whitman conflates three stages of his persona's development so that it is not always clear which stage is being referred to. The first stage involves "the loss of the oceanic security of his mother's womb"; the second, his sexual awakening at the age of twelve; the third, a questioning of worth and vocation upon the death of his father. Whitman reproduces "the manner in which the psyche transforms present conflicts in the light of past conflicts" and vice versa. Memory is reshaped to serve present needs.

Miller, Edwin Haviland. *Walt Whitman's Poetry: A Psychological Journey*, 175-186. New York: New York University Press, 1969.

An introspective meditation on the sources and purposes of Whitman's art, this poem's unconventional form resonates in the psychic depths of memory, tapping even the state of infantile trauma. Recapturing the young boy's awakening is a way of allegorizing his later awakening as an artist. As the boy leaves the womb of the world, so the artist leaves the protection of fettered vision. His sharpened senses transform him, though there are corresponding losses. The acknowledgment of death is both cause for grief and means to liberation. Also in Consolo.

Spitzer, Leo. "*Explication de Texte* Applied to Walt Whitman's Poem 'Out of the Cradle Endlessly Rocking.'" In *Out of the Cradle Endlessly Rocking*, edited by Dominick P. Consolo. Columbus, Ohio: Charles E. Merrill, 1971.

The theme of world harmony is expressed in a triad of interrelated voices: those of the bird, the sea, and the poet. Spitzer relates the Platonic and Pythagorean notion of the music of the spheres, tracing ways in which other poets have used music or song as a correlative for heavenly or cosmic harmony. Examines the poem's three-part structure and epic style as well as the swelling sentences that egoistically make the reader wait for the subject. Explores Whitman's manipulation of tonal change.

Walcutt, Charles C. "Whitman's 'Out of the Cradle Endlessly Rocking.' " In *Out of the Cradle Endlessly Rocking*, edited by Dominick P. Consolo. Columbus, Ohio: Charles E. Merrill, 1971.

Assumes that poetry originates in "childhood memory, mature passion, and philosophical speculation," all of which are present in this poem. The particular object of love must be absent for love to be transcendent and for the contemplation of universals. Death suggests unity of being, the ultimate awareness, which can be approached through "a single intense vision." Death returns separateness to oneness, as "separate individuals are returned to the unity of material being."

Whicher, Stephen E. "Whitman's 'Out of the Cradle Endlessly Rocking.' " In *Out of the Cradle Endlessly Rocking*, edited by Dominick P. Consolo. Columbus, Ohio: Charles E. Merrill, 1971.

The poem achieves "a reconciliation of opposites." Love and death, polar principles of affirmation and negation, are brought into harmony by a ripple of associated images and connotations. The poem does not argue that the problem of life is resolved by death, but that death itself is "solved." Throughout, the literal senses of key words are translated into their opposites. The poem's appeal is not to reason, but to the emotions.

"Passage to India"

Bickman, Martin. "Voyages of the Mind's Return." In his *The Unsounded Centre: Jungian Studies in American Romanticism*. Chapel Hill: University of North Carolina Press, 1980.

Compares Whitman's poem with Poe's *Eureka* and Emerson's "Plato," finding in all three an underlying scheme of unity-division-reintegration. This pattern aligns with Carl G. Jung's view of the development of consciousness. India—or Asia—is not so much a fixed destination as it is "a realm of beginnings, completions, and yet new beginnings." The land is addressed more like an ocean, the destination still a passageway. As the single speaker is transformed into the entire race, so is mankind's psychic history repeated in each individual.

Carlisle, E. Fred. *The Uncertain Self: Whitman's Drama of Identity*, 170-175. East Lansing: Michigan State University Press, 1973.

"Whitman's transcendence of history and his discovery of the mythic significance of technological communication return him to the . . . historical, cultural, and mythic source of his life." He seeks a communal past that is both literary and historical. It is a realm temporally and spiritually removed from the present. The closing euphoria of the poem does not lessen the problematic nature of death and spirit for Whitman. His confidence in immortality is not unwavering.

Coffman, Stanley K., Jr. "The Motion of the Circle." In *Whitman the Poet*, edited by John C. Broderick. Belmont, Calif.: Wadsworth, 1962.

The poem's theme is that "knowledge leads inevitably to faith." The imagery suggests a central nature that radiates "outward through forms of increasing complexity and widening extent." Images of motion are various and contradictory, leaving a composite impression of a "dialectical union or merging of opposites." Overall impression is of "ever-recurring circles of spirit manifesting itself and returning to its source."

Miller, Edwin Haviland. *Walt Whitman's Poetry: A Psychological Journey*, 212-222. New York: New York University Press, 1969.

Views the poem as "the swan song of a poet in retreat both in his art and his subject matter." Though because of its length and late composition "Passage to India" is often seen as the culmination of Whitman's mystical outlook, it is really a patchwork of earlier material insufficiently fused. It is too cerebral, too schematic, without the impulsive energy of Whitman's best work. The poem's subdued eroticism may reveal "Whitman's loss of confidence in the sensuous life and the withering of his artistic powers"; it also shows the poet resolving his psychic conflict with his father.

Miller, James E., Jr. *A Critical Guide to 'Leaves of Grass,'* 120-129. Chicago: University of Chicago Press, 1957.

Whitman's essential subject is the relationship between time and space on the one hand, and these with death. The poem has three sections each on the spanning of the earth (space), time and history, and death and the soul's journey. Whitman's final destination lies outside measurement, but the journey must go through and transcend extension and duration. The passage—the Suez Canal—links not only continents but also cultures, histories, and visions of human destiny. Also in Rupp.

"Scented Herbage of My Breast"

Miller, Edwin Haviland. *Walt Whitman's Poetry: A Psychological Journey*, 151-153. New York: New York University Press, 1969.

This poem examines the problem of appearance and illusion in a complex, daring way. One level carries a variation on the theme of art's permanence in a changing world. "As nature blooms and dies only to renew itself, so artistic 'blossoms' confer immortality upon the poet." The poem also identifies the poetic act with the sexual act as genital imagery replaces the conventional symbolism of heart and breast. The speaker's supine position is "the posture of love and death."

"The Sleepers"

Black, Stephen A. *Whitman's Journey into Chaos: A Psychoanalytic Study of the Creative Process*, 125-137. Princeton, N.J.: Princeton University Press.

At the poem's core are "infantile sexual fantasies" in which the poet "becomes the infant tyrant identifying with those who might in reality tyrannize him." Fearing rejection, the poet's unconscious does not seek homosexual love, but rather the autoerotic release that corresponds to the "infantile sense of oneness." Like many Whitman poems, this one describes a process of regression, a fleeing of adult choices, symbolized by the images of nursing. The sleepers' beauty is associated with the peace of the dead, now freed from desire and tension.

Eva Mary, Sister. "Shades of Darkness in 'The Sleepers.'" In *Critics on Whitman*, edited by Richard H. Rupp. Coral Gables, Fla.: University of Miami Press, 1972.
Examines the degrees of darkness imaged in the poem and their connections to psychological states and states of awareness. Darkness is associated with earth, death, sexual identity, the womb, old age, claustrophobic and expansive notions of what lies beyond death, and fulfillment. The ultimate, complete darkness, without gradation or shading, encompasses all. "As one moves through the layers of darkness in 'The Sleepers,' one participates in the confusion of the dream world."

Hutchinson, George B. *The Ecstatic Whitman: Literary Shamanism and the Crisis of Union*, 59-67. Columbus: Ohio State University Press, 1986.
As elsewhere in *Leaves of Grass*, "the protagonist performs the functions of healer and prophet. The first section of the poem indicates his curative intentions and that he is troubled by the suffering of others; the last two sections represent the accomplishment of his curing as well as a religious vision." Hutchinson likens the experience of the poem to a "shamanic seance" in which the seer "at the threshold of descent" is overheard by an attentive listener (the reader).

Marki, Ivan. *The Trial of the Poet: An Interpretation of the First Edition of Leaves of Grass*, 235-239. New York: Columbia University Press, 1976.
One movement of the poem is progressive, "from nightfall to dawn, from confusion to reassurance, from fear to trust." There is, simultaneously, a more important cyclical pattern. Together, they indicate "elementary unconscious tensions . . . of [Whitman's] erotic impulses and inhibitions." Under the protection of the dream motif, the persona of "The Sleepers" confronts Whitman's fears most directly. This reading absorbs insights from many other critics.

Miller, James E., Jr. *A Critical Guide to 'Leaves of Grass,'* 130-141. Chicago: University of Chicago Press, 1957.
Divides the poem into two sections of identification, two that relate death with ocean imagery, two that focus on time and love, and two that assert union. "The effect of night and sleep— or submergence in the mystical state of the spiritual world —is twofold: there is a leveling and there is a healing." Miller praises Whitman's ability to reproduce and juxtapose psychic states ranging from confusion to unobstructed vision. An underrated poem in which Whitman creates innovations in dramatic technique.

Reynolds, Michael S. "Whitman's Early Prose and 'The Sleepers.'" *American Literature* 41 (November, 1969): 406-414.

The key elements of this poem are the dream journey, the conscious structure, and the stream-of-consciousness technique. Whitman's mastery of these elements is only a surprise if we ignore the fact that he experimented with such vehicles in his earlier prose. Whitman's journalistic pieces "From the Desk of a Schoolmaster" and "Dreams" show him experimenting with the dream motif and with the observation of dreamers. Some of the content of the poem parallels passages in Emerson's comments on Swedenborg.

Zweig, Paul. *Walt Whitman: The Making of a Poet*, 245-247. New York: Basic Books, 1984.

Calls this poem the "dark twin" of "Song of Myself," in which the poet's restlessness, his search for new strengths and for change, takes him symbolically through the healing and generative power of darkness. The theme of release in darkness is a favored nineteenth century motif: The way down is the way up. Darkness itself undergoes change in the poem; "it is a nightmare, a spiritual medicine, a resolver of conflict." Emphasizes Whitman's "variable voice" in this, one of his finest poems.

"Song of Myself"

Beaver, Joseph. *Walt Whitman—Poet of Science*, 108-118. Reprint. New York: Octagon Books, 1974.

Traces Whitman's incorporation of a concept of "continuous and uninterrupted" evolution. Whitman understood the scale of evolutionary time, the stages of the chemical, geological, and organic processes that formed the earth and then generated life, the primitive life forms, and then the ascent of man. The poem also reveals Whitman's grasp of the yet unnamed process of "natural selection." The persona clearly sees himself as carrying the evolutionary process within and as being an incarnation of the latest stage of the selection process.

Blasing, Mutlu Konuk. "Walt Whitman, a Kosmos, of Manhattan the Sun." In her *The Art of Life: Studies in American Autobiographical Literature*. Austin: University of Texas Press, 1977.

This poem demonstrates how "autobiographical writing necessarily involves a splitting or doubling of the self." Yet Whitman redefines self-consciousness so that his poem enters a self-transcending mode. Whitman's stance sidesteps the Romantic problem of subjectivity: The hero incorporates all that he sees or experiences. To behold anything is necessarily to behold a part of himself. Whitman denies narrative progression while addressing evolutionary progression. Poetic form replaces personality.

Chase, Richard. "One's Self I Sing." In *Critics on Whitman*, edited by Richard H. Rupp. Coral Gables, Fla.: University of Miami Press, 1972.
Explores the poem's "comic spirit" and tone. "Whitman's comic poetry deflates pretensions and chides moral rigidity by opposing to them a diverse, vital, indeterminate reality." The protagonist celebrates the process of his own becoming and self-exploration. That the personality is not yet fully formed or fixed (in this way like America) is the cause of exultation. Relates poem to other major works of nineteenth century American literature. Excerpted from Chase's *Walt Whitman Reconsidered* (above).

Cowley, Malcolm. "An Analysis of 'Song of Myself.'" In *Critical Essays on Whitman*, edited by James Woodress. Boston: G. K. Hall, 1983.
Considers this Whitman's greatest poem and also "one of the great poems of modern times." Argues that the version in the first edition of *Leaves of Grass* is the purest; later, Whitman corrupted his own style and concealed the original meaning. Notes affinities with prophetic works by Christopher Smart, William Blake, Rimbaud, and Nietzsche. The psychological structure of the poem is coherent; it works like a musical progression, a rhapsody. Whitman achieves an independent, profound, discovery of the outlook of Eastern mysticism, and his presentation has more philosophical rigor than it is usually accorded.

Crawley, Thomas Edward. *The Structure of Leaves of Grass*, 90-95. Austin: University of Texas Press, 1970.
Describes "Song of Myself" as the "nuclear poem" of *Leaves of Grass* that creates "the great composite democratic individual," a version of Whitman himself that is held as paradigmatic. The poem stands in relation to the rest of *Leaves of Grass* as the Old Testament stands to the New. It holds the prophecy that the other "leaves" fulfill. Christ-figure developed through allusions to death and resurrection, the Second Coming, and a descent into Hell. The persona is also Christlike in offering comfort, aid, and challenge to others.

Frederickson, Robert S. "Public Onanism: Whitman's Song of Himself." *Modern Language Quarterly* 46 (June, 1985): 143- 160.
Discusses the psychological implications of Whitman's "public performance of what most of us would do only in private." Connects this exhibitionistic impulse to the issues of alienated identity and narcissistic unity that "merges self with experience." Concludes that Whitman's narcissism actually shuts the reader out, making the desired consummation impossible.

Gatta, John, Jr. "Whitman's Re-Vision of Emersonian Ecstasy in 'Song of Myself.'" In *Walt Whitman Here and Now*, edited by Joann P. Krieg. Westport, Conn.: Greenwood Press, 1985.

Argues that "Emerson's account of enthusiastic transport as a 'transparent eyeball' in chapter 1 of *Nature* has been dramatically reimagined in Whitman's equally famous record of sublime self-realization in section 5 of 'Song of Myself.' " Gatta points out parallels in setting, expectation, and the ecstatic moment in both works. Whitman's version of the wedding between the individual and the universal adds sexual and bodily accent to the more abstract treatment in Emerson. Emerson never overwhelms his disciple; Whitman feels free to extend and even correct his poetic father.

Kepner, Diane. "From Spears to Leaves: Walt Whitman's Theory of Nature in 'Song of Myself.' " *American Literature* 51 (May, 1979): 179-204.
Whitman's thought in this poem has an underlying consistency. He presents a theory of nature that can by understood by "arriving at the meaning of key words which he uses in various contexts." Whitman's nature reconciles things and thoughts, materialism and spiritualism. The universal is to be perceived in each particular. The visible, material world can "show us what is permanent and changeless about ourselves."

Levine, Herbert J. "Union and Disunion in 'Song of Myself.' " *American Literature* 59 (October, 1987): 570-589.
Whitman's poem reflects the political issues of the 1850's and particularly the rhetoric of political discourse. Figures of union, disunion, and reunion anticipate "the painful trajectory of American destiny in the era of the Civil War." The poem establishes "a federated model of personal destiny" that undergoes dismemberment and reformulation.

Miller, James E., Jr., ed. *Whitman's "Song of Myself"—Origin, Growth, Meaning*. New York: Dodd, Mead, 1964.
Miller provides, on facing pages, the 1855 and 1892 versions of the poem as well as early notebook versions. Six essays consider the nature of the poem's structure, style, tone, philosophy, genre, and vision. A final section suggests approaches and questions for further study. A comprehensive casebook that brings together outstanding materials.

Pearce, Roy Harvey. "The Long View: An American Epic." In his *The Continuity of American Poetry*. Princeton: Princeton University Press, 1961.
Discusses the poem as part of a continuum of epic attempts in American poetry going back to Joel Barlow's *Columbiad* (1801), with which Pearce makes comparisons and contrasts. Sees Whitman consciously looking for the poetic qualities that would serve modern society as the traditional epic served past societies. The essence of the poem is growth and movement, "the motion of the protagonist's sensibility." This meditative poem is a work "of ordering, not of order."

Scholnick, Robert J. " 'The Password Primeval': Whitman's Use of Science in 'Song of Myself.' " *Studies in the American Renaissance* (1986): 385-425.

In the preface to the 1855 *Leaves of Grass*, Whitman uses sexual imagery to describe "a harmonious and productive coming together of poet and scientist." Whitman made use of the scientific concepts expounded by Edward Livingston Youmans (1821-1887). Scholnick reviews the relationship between the two men, summarizes Youman's career, and then shows how Youman's thinking on evolution and related matters informs Whitman's poem. He also shows how Youman's ideas on the relationship between mind and matter influenced Whitman.

Steele, Jeffrey. "Song of Myself: A Field of Potential Being." In his *The Representation of the Self in the American Renaissance*. Chapel Hill: University of North Carolina Press, 1987.

Searches for an approach that responds in a balanced fashion to both the poem's "psychological rhythm and its rhetorical power." "Song of Myself" is "an audacious work of self-dramatization." The persona's claims are an "act that constitutes the being of its audience." The poem is a "psychological ritual" that expands the reader's sense of the world and creates the possibility of Emersonian self-reliance. Steele reviews much of the major criticism along the way.

Warren, James Perrin. "The 'Real Grammar': Deverbal Style in 'Song of Myself.' " *American Literature* 56 (March, 1984): 1- 16.

Whitman achieves a poetic diction both elliptic and idiomatic by employing "deverbal nouns" — words that are identical to their verbal base. Whitman's technique is counter to the evolution of the English language. The characteristic vitality of his work is a consequence of giving dynamism to otherwise static (noun) formulations. Examples of this diction include "urge," "breed," and "hope."

Zweig, Paul. *Walt Whitman: The Making of a Poet*, 227-275. New York: Basic Books, 1984.

Sees the poem as, in part, the record of Whitman's struggle to become himself and the record of its own creation. Finds sources in Whitman's earlier prose and in his notebooks. Examines the balancing of themes and images that, without any narrative skeleton, constitutes the unity of the work. Suggest resemblances between "Song of Myself" and the classic nineteenth century novel. This poem, which anchors and dominates the rest of *Leaves of Grass*, is an "engine of self-making." Brilliant analysis of the creative process.

"Song of the Open Road"

Waskow, Howard J. *Whitman: Explorations in Form*, 187-202. Chicago: University of Chicago Press, 1966.

Suggests that in this work, the poet had to resolve two problems: what to do on the road and how to relate to burdensome readers. The poem must move from the physical to the symbolic plane so that the particularity of the journey won't be confining. Whitman is less a guide than a model. Thus, his readers needn't come along with him. They are encouraged to follow paths of their own discerning, just as the poet is doing. Speaker and reader encourage each other in a vital communication that can only take place in the cleansing and border-less outdoors.

"Starting from Paumanok"

Miller, James E., Jr. *A Critical Guide to 'Leaves of Grass,'* 55. Chicago: University of Chicago Press, 1957.
The distinctive quality of Whitman's poetry arises from a subtle attention to sound and rhythm beneath an immediate sense of wild abandonment. "The total impression, then, is one of primitive ritual—of rites of abandonment instinct with form." The list of Indian names is a supreme instance of Whit-man's musicality, the sounds calling up "echoes of the primal world" as the poet sings the natural glory of the continent.

"There Was a Child Went Forth"

Cavitch, David. *My Soul and I: The Inner Life of Walt Whitman*, 32-35; 37-42. Boston: Beacon Press, 1985.
The poem asserts "that every childhood experience went into making the person who now remembers as he writes." Another poem of the poet's becom-ing, this work treats the growth of his separate identity, an identity distanced from parents because of a sense of an unapproachable father and general parental neglect. Images of developing sexuality are focused on a lonely, confused sensibility whose outlet is masturbation. "When the tide of sexual feeling overwhelms him, Whitman becomes both the lover and the loved."

Miller, Edwin Haviland. *Walt Whitman's Poetry: A Psychological Journey*, 24-40. New York: New York University Press, 1969. Also in Woodress.
This "diagnosis of the emergent self" traces the stages of consciousness from the perception of an edenic landscape through the noisy complexities of so-ciety. Whitman understands the necessity of the narcissistic stage, the disil-lusionments of maturation, and the complex role of family in forming the personality. Whitman's own loneliness and his antidote of fantasy are taken as universal. "Whitman's fear of personal involvement is part of the hidden or 'indirect' meaning" of this poem which "records the failure of basic relationships."

Waggoner, Hyatt H. "Walt Whitman: Signing for Soul and Body." In his *American Poets from the Puritans to the Present*, 170-174. Boston: Houghton Mifflin, 1968.
Sees the poem as epitomizing Whitman's philosophic stance: "The poem moves toward and through the birth of consciousness, with the alienation this brings, and beyond conscious rationality to reunion and reintegration." Waggoner resists psychoanalytic explanations that protect the reader from confronting the challenges of Whitman's text. Whether or not the relationship with the mother lies behind certain formulations, the poem has important things to say about achieved innocence, the illumination that depends on darkness, and the relationship of the individual to nature.

"To a Locomotive in Winter"

Miller, Edwin Haviland. *Walt Whitman's Poetry: A Psychological Journey*, 211-212. New York: New York University Press, 1969.
Argues that Whitman's technique belies his assertions. While insisting that the locomotive is an "emblem of motion and power," he ends up making a kind of toy out of it by prettifying and trivializing. The effectiveness of the passages that celebrate the "Fierce-throated beauty" pay little attention to the mechanical marvel itself, but rather reveal Whitman's unconscious fascination with the locomotive as a sexual symbol. Whitman's taming of the locomotive is the consequence of his unstated fears.

"When Lilacs Last in the Dooryard Bloom'd"

Adams, Richard P. " 'Lilacs' As Pastoral Elegy." In *Critics on Whitman*, edited by Richard H. Rupp. Coral Gables, Fla.: University of Miami Press, 1972.
A systematic study of how Whitman uses the conventions of pastoral elegy. Finds seven of seventeen conventional devices used, including the announcement of the death, nature's sympathetic mourning, the placing of flowers on the coffin, the irony of spring's renewal, the funeral procession, the eulogy for the deceased, and the movement toward reconciliation. No references in poem to mythology or to the literally pastoral elements. Compared to nineteenth century British precedents.

Black, Stephen A. *Whitman's Journey into Chaos: A Psychoanalytic Study of the Creative Process*, 234-244. Princeton, N.J.: Princeton University Press.
" 'Lilacs' signals capitulation in the search for sexual identity begun a decade before." Lincoln, the father figure, is addressed with imagery of feminine connotation. Whitman has discovered that he can not repress the parts of himself identified with his mother. The poem is fraught with "terrifying fantasies"

barely transformed and hidden. The call to death is a resignation, a sign of Whitman's physical and psychological weariness, his inability to integrate the conscious and unconscious worlds. Whitman is an accomplice in his own "symbolic castration."

Brown, Calvin S. "The Musical Development of Symbols in Whitman." In *Interpretations of American Literature*, edited by Charles Feidelson, Jr., and Paul Brodtkorb, Jr. New York: Oxford University Press, 1959. (Excerpted from Brown's *Music and Literature*. Athens: University of Georgia Press, 1948.)
While considering Whitman to be "practically a musical illiterate," Brown finds nevertheless that "in a few poems of medium length he attained a firm structure and real poetic distinction by a treatment of symbols closely parallel to the musical development of themes." Brown demonstrates how this musical development works in "When Lilacs Last in the Dooryard Bloom'd," arguing that this use of symbols gives the poem, for all its particularities, the universality of music.

Faner, Robert D. *Walt Whitman and Opera*, 154-159. Philadelphia: University of Pennsylvania Press, 1951.
The poem is in sonata form. Its introduction presents the key images which are then treated as a composer treats musical themes. Exposition, development, recapitulation, and coda are the stages of sonata form that the poem follows. Whether or not Whitman knew these terms or consciously applied sonata structure, his experience of music allowed him to translate these movements into verbal art. Faner discounts the comparisons of this poem's structure to rondo form.

Feidelson, Charles, Jr., "Symbolism in 'When Lilacs Last in the Dooryard Bloom'd.'" *In Critics on Whitman*, edited by Richard H. Rupp. Coral Gables, Fla.: University of Miami Press, 1972.
The true subject is neither Lincoln nor the poet, but rather the poetic process. Symbols work "like characters in a drama." The lilac stands for spring and thus the process of rebirth. Death is represented by the coffin's journey and by the drooping star. The thrush's song is likened to the speaker's thoughts and feelings as expressed in poetry. The trinity of symbols gives this poem more stability than is found in Whitman's other long poems.

Matthiessen, F. O. "Whitman." In his *American Renaissance*, 618-624. New York: Oxford University Press, 1941.
A masterful appreciation of the genesis and major strengths of one of Whitman's best-managed poems. Matthiessen notes that Lincoln is never described, that Whitman handles his subject "by thematic use of three primary symbols . . . which are repeated with the most subtle ordonnance that he ever

managed." Whitman's blending of the different senses is a successful "act of pioneering" that helped "the modern sensibility feel at home in the natural world." Whitman shows here more that elsewhere a genuine capacity for suffering the world's tragic evils.

Waskow, Howard J. *Whitman: Explorations in Form*, 222-242. Chicago: University of Chicago Press, 1966.
Examines the "pauses, turnings, and radical shifts" that require reader participation. Aside from orchestrating key images, Whitman here orchestrates moods associated with the images singly or in combination. Traces psychic shifts generated by the fragmented narrative. The reader is required to become involved in the quest for order. We perform "a mental rearrangement of the 'twisted' elements into more regular patterns," approximating as we do so the patterns of Whitman's own imagination.

FREDERICK GODDARD TUCKERMAN
(1821-1873)

General Studies

Boswell, Jeanetta. "Frederick Goddard Tuckerman." In her *Spokesmen for the Minority: A Bibliography of Sidney Lanier, William Vaughn Moody, Frederick Goddard Tuckerman, and Jones Very, with Selective Annotations*. Metuchen, N.J.: Scarecrow Press, 1987.
This is a bibliography of secondary materials. See full entry in "General Treatments of the Period."

Bynner, Witter. Introduction to *The Sonnets of Frederick Goddard Tuckerman*, edited by Bynner. New York: Alfred A. Knopf, 1931.
Bynner's long essay was the first important step in the rediscovery of Tuckerman. Tuckerman's poetry expressed the myriad contradictions of existence, of life and death, of joy and grief. Tuckerman senses and shares the cyclical polarity of experience, and he writes of these not as phenomena intellectually observed, but as emotional and spiritual truths that life has confirmed. Bynner claims that these sonnets "rank with the noblest in the language and dignify America."

Cady, Edwin H. "Frederick Goddard Tuckerman." In *Essays on American Literature in Honor of Jay B. Hubbell*, edited by Clarence Gohdes. Durham, N.C.: Duke University Press, 1967.
After reviewing Tuckerman's reputation among his contemporaries, his fall to obscurity, and his slight comeback in the twentieth century, Cady assesses Tuckerman's achievement. Tuckerman's true distinction is found in his sonnet sequence. "The sources here of poetic power are four: the implied drama of the *persona*, the speaking voice, the figure observed or observing, sometimes the 'I' of the sonnets; the diction; the beautifully controlled tonalities; the often superb imagery."

Donoghue, Denis. "Frederick Goddard Tuckerman." In his *Connoisseurs of Chaos: Ideas of Order in Modern American Poetry*. 2d ed. New York: Columbia University Press, 1984.
Using Whitman as a foil, Donoghue describes Tuckerman's world as "a private realm of worry and silence." Like Whitman, Tuckerman assumed that his work relied upon his own resources. His sonnets present a closed system, a triangle of man, nature, and God. Tuckerman's poems place an observer at a point within the triangle from where he looks over the scene. Donoghue presents careful readings of a number of poems, stressing the dominant mood of despair.

England, Eugene. "Tuckerman and Tennyson: Two Friends on Either Side of the Atlantic." *New England Quarterly* 57 (June, 1984): 225-239.

A careful use of letters and other documents establishes the nature of Tuckerman's visit to Tennyson and their ongoing relationship. Tuckerman was one of the few people to get Tennyson to discuss his own work, and these discussions influenced Tuckerman, who noted Tennyson's remarks in copies of his poems. Tuckerman's anti-Romanticism may be partly explained by Tennyson's influence, as may his outlook as a dedicated apprentice to his art. Tuckerman's work shows a "nominalist sense of flux and of unrecoverable loss through time."

Golden, Samuel A. *Frederick Goddard Tuckerman*. New York: Twayne, 1966.

This compact book reviews the life and works in a clear, thorough, and sympathetic manner. Tuckerman's sonnets "move inexorably from despair to tragedy to optimism." He never creates a distance between himself as author and a persona: the poems are thus strictly autobiographical—personal records of inner conflict. Golden describes Tuckerman's attention to craft, his characteristic manner, the sequencing of the sonnets, and his major themes. Separate chapter on "The Cricket." Chronology and selected bibliography.

Howe, Irving. "A Neglected American Poet." In his *Celebrations and Attacks*. New York: Horizon Press, 1979.

"In the sonnets and 'The Cricket' Tuckerman writes out of a hard sense of human limitation: he does not confuse himself with the cosmos, the trees, or the spiritual aether." His poems, though occasionally marked by weak syntax and archaisms, are notable for their common-sense realism. His observation of nature and his presentation of moral and psychological issues have the power of felt, pondered experience. Unlike his more illustrious contemporaries, Tuckerman does not use his poems to mount the platform or to utter prophecies.

Seed, David. "Alone with God and Nature: The Poetry of Jones Very and Frederick Goddard Tuckerman." In *Nineteenth-Century American Poetry*, edited by A. Robert Lee. Totowa, N.J.: Barnes & Noble, 1985.

In Very's Poems, "isolation defines man's relationship to God"; in Tuckerman, "it becomes a liability since his poems are all the more secular." The essay places these recently rediscovered poets into the traditional categories of belief and poetic manner, though neither fits very well. "Very's sonnets show the egotism latent in Transcendentalism turning itself inside out." Tuckerman's self-analysis is strikingly modern in its refusal of religious props.

Winters, Yvor. Foreword to *The Complete Poems of Frederick Goddard Tuckerman*, edited by N. Scott Momaday. New York: Oxford University Press, 1965.

Ranks Tuckerman with Dickinson and Very as "one of the three most remark-able American poets of the nineteenth century." All three were relatively isolated, and each is different from the others. Tuckerman's sensibility is not that of New England Romanticism but more like "the gentler French symbol-ism" of Verlaine. Winters develops parallels between Tuckerman's sonnets and works by Rimbaud, Baudelaire, and Valery. "The Cricket," Winters says, "is the greatest poem in English of the century."

"The Cricket"

Golden, Samuel A. "The Cricket: 'The Shadow grows.' " In his *Frederick Goddard Tuckerman*. New York: Twayne, 1966.
In this dream poem, the poet takes a long, retrospective view of his life in an uncharacteristically public voice. "Essentially, it is a happy poem in which freedom and escape from the external world are achieved by a complete surrender to forces that Tuckerman had hitherto been unable to understand or to conquer." The irregular form of the poem announces Tuckerman's "eman-cipation from formal and technical problems of composition and . . . from any sort of restraint." The poem's rich sonic texture and colorful imagery are remarkable. "The Cricket" is to be read in conjunction with the sonnets. It is Tuckerman's affirmation of self-worth.

Winters, Foreword to *The Complete Poems of Frederick Goddard Tuckerman*, edited by N. Scott Momaday. New York: Oxford University Press, 1965.
Winters provides a structural analysis of this poem, which belongs in the "great ode" tradition of works by Dryden, Keats, and Tennyson. The cricket becomes "a symbol for non-human nature and for the primitive and sub-human in human nature and has been used to create a deep longing for these qualities and for death." Winters praises Tuckerman's ability to conduct the poem's argument through imagery, not relying on interpretive assertions. The first four stanzas present various aspects of the cricket which are drawn to-gether in the final and finest stanza.

EMILY DICKINSON
(1830-1886)

General Studies

Allen, Mary. "Concise Creatures: Emily Dickinson." In her *Animals in American Literature*. Urbana: University of Illinois Press, 1983.
"Dickinson's affinity for small animals is that of one unacclaimed artist for another." She attends to what is undomesticated and to the individual rather than the group. Often, "animals shock through the unorthodoxy of their existence as seen by anthropomorphic man." Dickinson favors the conventionally undesirable—those that threaten even when they do not harm—because they awaken emotion. Thus, she can put them in the service of her art, which aims at emotional awakening.

Anderson, Charles R. *Emily Dickinson's Poetry: Stairway of Surprise*. New York: Holt, Rinehart and Winston, 1960.
Deduces from Dickinson's poems a theory of art concerned with wit, word-play, and the tension of circumference and center. Treats poems in thematic groups, such as "The Outer World," "The Inner World," and "The Other Paradise." Appreciates Dickinson's adventurousness and grants her a clear vision of her purposes as an artist. Considers her work an attempt to find her place in the universe.

Anderson, Peggy. "The Bride of the White Election: A New Look at Biblical Influence on Emily Dickinson." In *Nineteenth-Century Woman Writers of the English-Speaking World*, edited by Rhoda B. Nathan. New York: Greenwood Press, 1986.
Argues against the general fashion that Dickinson's poems of doubt are the ones to be taken seriously. Examines those poems that exhibit traditional Christian faith. Taking the Bible, not Puritanism, as criterion, Dickinson's faith seems relatively orthodox. Too many recent scholars know far too little about the Bible and thus miss the degree and nature of Dickinson's references and reactions to it. Earlier scholarship was more reliable on this matter. Even poems of doubt need to be explored "within a Christian context."

Barker, Wendy. *Lunacy of Light: Emily Dickinson and the Experience of Metaphor*. Carbondale: Southern Illinois University Press, 1987.
"Repeatedly in Dickinson's writing, images of sun dazzle only to abandon, beckon only to burn, while images of darkness . . . frequently provide quiet refuge from the often-frightening and obliterating rays of the sun." Sunlight represents deity, male energy, and male power. Dickinson's images individual-

ize "the metaphoric valuings of the Judeo-Christian tradition." Her "extensive pattern of light/dark imagery comprises an encoded statement of female poetics."

Baym, Nina. "God, Father, and Lover in Emily Dickinson's Poetry." In *Puritan Influences in American Literature*, edited by Emory Elliot. Urbana: University of Illinois Press, 1979.
"Her use of the child's voice is intricately connected to expressions of relations between the child and the male parent, between the sexes, and between the self and God." Often, the father figure is one who withholds or is ungenerous. The mask of the child enables Dickinson to speak unpleasant truths while avoiding the consequences of such speech. These poems reflect the end of the Puritan tradition and of a certain kind of family.

Benfy, Christopher E. G. *Emily Dickinson and the Problem of Others*. Amherst: University of Massachusetts Press, 1984.
Examines the strands of American thought enveloped and refined in Dickinson's poetry. Considers strategies of the lyric tradition that work to shut out the world beyond the poet's mind, Dickinson's consciousness of the blocking process, and her engagement with the dichotomy of expressing and withholding— the special ways in which her poetry "makes room for relations of reciprocity between the human being and the world." Focuses on poems not often anthologized.

Benvenuto, Richard. "Words Within Words: Dickinson's Use of the Dictionary." *ESQ* 29 (1st Quarter, 1983): 46-55.
Dickinson's dictionary was an 1844 reprint of Webster's *American Dictionary of the English Language* first published in 1841. Benvenuto suggests the ways that Dickinson used the dictionary: checking etymologies, collateral words, and synonyms. He then imagines Dickinson's journey through the dictionary during the composition of "A narrow Fellow in the Grass" and a few other poems. One can get closer to Dickinson's intentions by consulting the very dictionary she used when making her choices, especially when meanings, usages, and overtones have undergone change.

Bickman, Martin. "Kora in Heaven: Emily Dickinson." In his *The Unsounded Centre: Jungian Studies in American Romanticism*. Chapel Hill: University of North Carolina Press, 1980.
Dickinson's poems equate death and love in accord with "the realities of psychic experience" as defined by Jung. She often taps the myth of Persephone, a myth of ambivalence that locates the heroine both in and out of the mortal world. Flower and water imagery have a mythic suggestiveness supporting the Persephone equation. The images of death, sacred marriage, and re-

birth are symbolic enactments of the psychic drama of the "mind moving toward individuation."

Bingham, Millicent Todd. *Ancestor's Brocades*. Reprint. New York: Dover, 1967.
Tells the story of the editing and publication of Dickinson's letters and poems. Bingham was the daughter of Mabel Loomis Todd, one of Dickinson's first editors, from whom Bingham learned much of the story. She traces the early growth of interest in Dickinson's art through the hard work of the dedicated partisans who enabled those writings to reach a public. Charmingly anecdotal and filled with intriguing personal and legal issues. First published 1945.

Blackmur, R. P. "Emily Dickinson: Notes on Prejudice and Fact." In his *Language and Gesture*. New York: Harcourt, Brace, 1952. Also in Blake and Wells.
After clearing away various prejudices that have clouded assessments of Dickinson, Blackmur explores the limitations of her art. Granting her an aptitude for language and penetrating insights, Blackmur argues that "the private and eccentric nature of her relation to the business of poetry" made success or failure accidental. She rarely found a way to control "the means of objective expression." Much of her work is "fragmentary indicative notation," not finished poetry.

Blake, Caesar R. and Carlton F. Wells, eds. *The Recognition of Emily Dickinson*. Ann Arbor: University of Michigan Press, 1964.
A collection of critical responses in three chronological groupings: 1890 to 1900, 1901 to 1930, and 1931 to the early 1960's. One of the richest samplings available, this compilation traces the process by which Dickinson's work became part of the literary canon. The editors provide brief introductions to each study indicating the importance of the contribution to the building of Dickinson's status. A blend of book chapters, periodical essays, introductions, and reactions to criticism.

Blasing, Mutlu Konuk. "Emily Dickinson's Untitled Discourse." In her *American Poetry: The Rhetoric of Its Forms*. New Haven, Conn.: Yale University Press, 1987.
Dickinson mistrusts the symbolic systems legislated by a patriarchal culture. Her semantic quibbles, syntactical breaks, and other defiant stances mark a resistance to the authorized masculine models of perception and valuation. She dissects language to fashion a new, radical tool, and she uses the sanctioned models only with a subversive irony. Blasing's analysis rests on partial explications of poems not often anthologized.

Bloom, Harold, ed. *Emily Dickinson: Modern Critical Views*. New York: Chelsea House, 1985.

Selections from eight readily available books give a balanced overview of the present state of Dickinson criticism. Represented are Albert Gelpi, David Porter, Sharon Cameron, Charles R. Anderson, and others. Includes a chronology, a bibliography, and an introduction by Bloom that is more accurately a separate essay on Dickinson's originality. Convenient to consult if the excerpted titles are not otherwise available.

Bogan Louise. "A Mystical Poet." In *Emily Dickinson: Three Views*. Amherst, Mass.: Amherst College Press, 1960.
Reviews the tradition of mystical poetry in England, and particularly the relationship between mysticism and the Romantic spirit. Dickinson's unorthodox religious feelings ran deep within her. She fought against the dogma of guilt and gloom. Bogan sees parallels to William Blake and Emily Brontë. The openness and inclusiveness in her work are the result of seclusiveness in life. Greatly concerned with the haunting of the self.

Boruch, Marianne. "Dickinson Descending." *Georgia Review* 50 (Winter, 1986): 863-877.
Explores the reasons behind critics' need to mix endless homage with endless gossip about Dickinson. We are unable to let go of her, yet her work is an example of purposeful incompleteness. "The strain and silence in Dickinson's best work suggests something not finally and perfectly etched, but willfully incomplete, broken off—sometimes violently." Dickinson is eternally withholding, from herself and from the audience that hungers for more of her. Boruch feels that there are dangers in this hunger.

Brashear, Lucy. "Emily Dickinson's Dramatic Monologues." *ATQ*, no. 56 (March, 1985): 65-76.
By combining drama and lyric, Dickinson evokes a single dramatic encounter as it appears to the speaker, and from this one-sided conversation emerges a sudden insight or revelation. Sometimes the central character is a divided self—both speaker and audience. Some monologues address an anthropomorphic God or Death. Others address casual acquaintances or a lover. The dramatic love poems form the largest group; Dickinson recognized that this genre allowed for the exposure of emotional tension.

Budick, E. Miller. *Emily Dickinson and the Life of Language*. Baton Rouge: Louisiana State University Press, 1985.
In her social withdrawal, Dickinson entered the world of words in an attempt "to understand the phenomenon that is consciousness itself." Dickinson explored the symbolic vitality and the symbolic liabilities of language, creating a poetry that is "a paradoxical condemnation and celebration of symbolic perception and symbolic language." Thus, Dickinson's poetry is fundamentally

about language itself. Dickinson rebelled against the traditional New England symbolism.

Burbick, Joan. "Emily Dickinson and the Economics of Desire." *American Literature* 58 (October, 1986): 361-378.
Dickinson's world is reflected in her poems. Her outlook includes "the determined desire for social order and class stability, emerging from the Protestant vision of industrial capitalism." Many poems articulate the costs of desire in economic terms. The regulation of emotion creates a sexual impoverishment: both desire and restraint have their price.

Bzowski, Frances. "'Half-Child—Half Heroine': Emily Dickinson's Use of Traditional Female Archetypes." *ESQ* 29 (3rd Quarter, 1983): 154-169.
Dickinson uses "central female images which defy the sexual and civil power of the male." In this practice, she is close to the sentimental writers of her day. Images of "the nun-like Bride of Christ and . . . the young woman who dies just before sexual consummation" arise from the collective female unconscious, but Dickinson and some of her contemporaries adapted these types to a vision of an "unconquerable female principle"—"a triumph of femaleness."

Cameron, Sharon. *Lyric Time: Dickinson and the Limits of Genre*. Baltimore: Johns Hopkins University Press, 1979.
Argues "that the temporal problems in Dickinson's poems are frequently exaggerations of those generic features shared by all lyrics." Focuses on the extreme temporal dislocations, developing an "unabashedly theoretical" discussion of temporal structure in lyric poetry. Sees Dickinson's poems as striking "a balance between the stasis-making representation of subject and object . . . and the serial and sequential transformations" represented by Whitman and other American lyric poets.

Capps, Jack L. *Emily Dickinson's Reading, 1836-1886*. Cambridge, Mass.: Harvard University Press, 1966.
Against the image of Dickinson's stubborn independence, this careful survey of Dickinson's reading helps reshape our understanding of her methods and her meanings. Dickinson's own comments on her reading are followed by a chapter on her use of the King James Bible and then by chapters on readings grouped by literary periods. Capps's comments reveal how knowledge of allusions and sources illuminates the poems themselves. Stresses the degree to which the vicarious experience of reading was important to the reclusive Dickinson.

Clendenning, Sheila T. *Emily Dickinson: A Bibliography 1850-1966*. Kent, Ohio: Kent State University Press, 1968.

Includes almost one thousand entries cataloguing (1) editions of Dickinson's writings, (2) first or early printing of individual poems, (3) books and sections of books, (4) bibliographies and bibliographical discussions, (5) unpublished dissertations and selected theses, (6) essays and parts of essays in periodicals, and (7) review articles. A guide to research into the life and work of Dickinson treating both primary and secondary sources.

Cody, John. *After Great Pain: The Inner Life of Emily Dickinson*. Cambridge, Mass.: Harvard University Press, 1971.
A psychoanalytic reading based on the "assumption that early in Emily Dickinson's life she experienced what she interpreted as a cruel rejection by her mother." Considers the recurrence of certain symbols (sun, sea, moon, bee) as affording the same kind of evidence that free association would offer a psychoanalyst working with a patient—especially as these same symbols occur in Dickinson's letters. A study of personality, not intellect or achievement.

Davis, Thomas M. "Emily Dickinson and the Right Way to Tripoli." In *Artful Thunder: Versions of the Romantic Tradition in Honor of Howard P. Vincent*, edited by Robert J. DeMott and Sanford E. Marovitz. Kent, Ohio: Kent University Press, 1975.
Dickinson's early poetry reveals a traditional response to nature that later becomes complicated by an awareness of nature's ambiguity: It is both God's work and corrupted. Nature's revelatory message depends upon the redeemed mind's way of receiving. Nature has meaning, but the defining quality of poetic acts may be compromised by a lack of faith. In her late poems, Dickinson forsakes the ego's quest for meaning: She accepts that which she cannot know.

—————— , ed. *Fourteen by Emily Dickinson*. Chicago: Scott, Foresman, 1964.
Davis has selected fourteen of Dickinson's best-known poems and gathered for each a collection of from three to eight critical commentaries. In most cases, the critical materials are chosen to show critics engaged with one another's arguments. The poems and commentaries are followed by a series of study questions and theme topics. Bibliography contains a listing of "Analyses of Single Poems." Critics represented include John Ciardi, Allen Tate, Yvor Winters, and Charles R. Anderson.

Dickie, Margaret. "Dickinson's Discontinuous Self." *American Literature* 60 (December, 1988): 537-553.
Dickinson's "chief means of revolt" is in choosing "the publicly degraded lyric form." The lyric, in the nineteenth century, was essentially a woman's form, a form unfit for the great enterprise of celebrating America's grandness.

The precariousness of the form coincided with the precariousness of female identity. Dickinson's subversive use of the lyric reveals a self that is discontinuous, profligate, and excessive—and thus revolutionary.

Diehl, Joanne Feit. *Dickinson and the Romantic Imagination*. Princeton, N.J.: Princeton University Press, 1981.
Finds Dickinson to be an inheritor and subverter of Romantic tradition. Acknowledging Dickinson's eccentricity, Diehl asserts the importance of contexualizing her achievement. The major chapters measure Dickinson's poems and aesthetic against those of Wordsworth, Keats, Shelley, and Emerson. The significance of Dickinson's feminine sensibility in this subversion is given careful attention. Dickinson's poems are responses to the poetic tradition that formed her and a remaking of the given, conventional self through an art that negates in order to create.

Diggory, Terence. "Armored Women, Naked Men: Dickinson, Whitman, and Their Successors." In *Shakespeare's Sisters: Feminist Essays on Woman Poets*, edited by Sandra M. Gilbert and Susan Gubar. Bloomington: University of Indiana Press, 1979.
Diggory examines representative passages from Dickinson and Whitman to point out distinctions between "male and female traditions in American poetry that have their roots in these two great contemporaries." Armor and its function of concealment are treated with repugnance by Whitman but are highly valued by Dickinson. "Dickinson and Whitman agreed that any utterance could be a disclosure of identity, but they disagreed about the desirability of the disclosure." Diggory follows this dichotomy in the works of Robert Frost and Sylvia Plath.

Donoghue, Denis. *Emily Dickinson*. Minneapolis: University of Minnesota Press, 1969.
A pamphlet overview of Dickinson's life and work that emphasizes her relationships with men, the pattern of her daily life, and her tendency to pursue trains of thought that most of us try to avoid. Considers her "special area of feeling" to be "preappointed pain, how we choose it, the consequences of the choice." Urbane yet accessible. Selected bibliography.

_____ . "Emily Dickinson." In his *Reading America: Essays on American Literature*. New York: Alfred A. Knopf, 1987.
The first section offers a congenial survey of major schools of thought on Dickinson's outlook and achievement. The second section stresses Dickinson's "slant" or oblique way of approaching her subjects, her tendency to render the spiritual forces that concern her in allegorical or "statuesque" terms so that she can step aside from them. From such a distance, she could manipulate a drama

of these internal forces, never letting her mind be completely possessed by the enormity of her subject. Dickinson's strategies allow her to remain in control.

Duchac, Joseph. *The Poems of Emily Dickinson: An Annotated Guide to Commentary Published in English, 1890-1977*. Boston: G. K. Hall, 1979.
This invaluable reference work "cites all commentary on individual poems," even the briefest. Arranged alphabetically by first lines, the citations include thumbnail descriptions, usually single sentences, capturing the essence of the commentary. Includes books and periodicals, but not dissertations or microform materials. The place to go after exhausting citations in the present bibliography.

Duncan, Douglas. *Emily Dickinson*. Edinburgh, Scotland: Oliver and Boyd, 1965.
This compact presentation of the life and works stresses the individual voice and the linkage between biographical and critical interest in her poems. One chapter stresses the formal and technical features, another the tension between involvement and detachment. Dickinson was at once "the participator and the commentator." Praises her ability to argue in verse, to create moods, to handle narrative. Includes survey of critical history.

Eberwein, Jane Donahue. *Dickinson: Strategies of Limitation*. Amherst: University of Massachusetts Press, 1985.
Explores "limitation" as a guiding principle of Dickinson's life and art. Considers how a narrow compass of responsibility and ambition allows for maximum control over one's life. The esthetics of Dickinson's poetry correspond to this behavior. Dickinson's "sensitivity to processes of size" reveals an essential paradox regarding the virtue of smallness, with its implicit promise of growth, over existent magnitude, which holds no such promise.

——————. "Emily Dickinson and the Calvinist Sacramental Tradition." *ESQ* 33 (2nd Quarter, 1987): 67-81.
The religious vocabulary of Dickinson's poems often includes diction associated with Christian sacraments. Eberwein examines this diction "within the specific context of Calvinist sacramental theology as understood by nineteenth-century Congregational communities," and then attempts "to read the words as [Dickinson] would have recognized them" in pursuit of the poet's religious outlook. Of course, Dickinson adjusted these symbols to her personal vision.

Elam, Helen Regueiro. "Dickinson and the Haunting of the Self." In *The American Sublime*, edited by Mary Arensberg. Albany: State University of New York Press, 1986.
"Dickinson is haunted by this otherness which poetry tries to heal and which it reveals." The abyss within, its empty horror, is the theme in many of her

poems. Consciousness that includes such an awareness is never totally fulfilling. The sense of being outside nature, outside life, beside one's own self is a
characteristic of sublime terror. The quest for self-sufficiency ends in isolation.

Erkkila, Betsy. "Dickinson and Rich: Toward a Theory of Female Poetic Influence."
    American Literature 56 (December 1984): 541-559.
    Explores possible paradigms for a female literary tradition through "the
    mother-daughter myth of Demeter and Kore," which is described as "a pattern
    of female union, separation, return, and renewal." Female poets reach a "uni-
    fied sense of self and power" by returning to matrilineal sources. Adrienne
    Rich's response to Dickinson—a "re-conceiving" of Dickinson rather than a
    rejection—illustrates this dynamic. (See Rich below.)

Ferlazzo, Paul J. *Emily Dickinson*. Boston: Twayne, 1976.
    A succinct, clear introduction to the life and work with traditional subsections
    on faith, mortality, love, and nature. Most interesting is the chapter called
    "The Struggle for Sanity," which reviews the prominent psychoanalytic discus-
    sions and illustrates the stages of Dickinson's purported breakdown through
    partial explications of key poems. Contains a separate chapter on Dickinson's
    letters. A good place to begin.

——————— , ed. *Critical Essays on Emily Dickinson*. Boston: G. K. Hall, 1984.
    This most comprehensive collection begins with the earliest responses to
    Dickinson's work and represents just about every significant contributor to
    Dickinson studies. Ferlazzo's introduction reviews the history of Dickinson
    scholarship with sections on bibliography, editions and manuscripts, biogra-
    phy, and criticism. A particularly generous sampling of recent critical ap-
    proaches, but also useful for late nineteenth century reactions.

Finch, A. R. C. "Dickinson and Patriarchal Meter: A Theory of Metrical Codes."
    PMLA 102 (March, 1987): 166-176.
    Most of Dickinson's work uses the hymn stanza that alternates iambic tetrame-
    ter with iambic trimeter. Only rarely does she use the dominant standard of
    iambic pentameter. "An analysis of Dickinson's iambic pentameter involves
    determining both the ways the words comment on the meter and the relation
    between the meaning of these lines and that of other lines in the poem."
    Dickinson uses iambic pentameter "as a signifying code" accompanying shifts
    in perspective and emotion. The code relates to gender issues.

Ford, Thomas W. *Heaven Beguiles the Tired: Death in the Poetry of Emily Dickin-
    son*. University: University of Alabama Press, 1968.
    Considers the existential character of Dickinson's death poetry, arguing that
    "her preoccupation with doubt, time, despair, and the separation of man from

nature" anticipates the currents of existential thought. Ford does not see Dickinson as having a systematic view of death, but rather a consuming interest that "was the most important single factor in shaping the contours of her poetry." Poems reveal a personal tension that is neither morbid nor Romantic.

Franklin, R. W. *The Editing of Emily Dickinson: A Reconsideration.* Madison: University of Wisconsin Press, 1967.
Traces the history of editing the manuscripts, emphasizing the problems in dealing with Dickinson's unorthodox punctuation and variant versions. Using Thomas H. Johnson's variorum edition as a starting point, Franklin discusses the work yet to be done. Printing of necessity misrepresents manuscripts. Dickinson's handwriting makes the distinction between small and large letters difficult. Discovering authorial intention for incomplete poems is a special problem, as Dickinson left alternative versions in her drafts.

Gelpi, Albert. "Emily Dickinson and the Deerslayer: The Dilemma of the Woman Poet in America." In *Shakespeare's Sisters: Feminist Essays on Woman Poets*, edited by Sandra M. Gilbert and Susan Gubar. Bloomington: University of Indiana Press, 1979.
Compares the psychosexual implications of Dickinson's poems to those of Cooper's *The Deerslayer*. The ritual of proving one's manhood by spilling blood is adopted by Dickinson in "My Life had stood—a Loaded Gun." She participates "in the killing of the doe without a murmur of pity or regret; she wants the independence of will and the power of mind which her allegiance with the woodsmen makes possible." In other poems, Dickinson uses phallic images to appropriate male privileges.

_____ . "Emily Dickinson's Word: Presence as Absence, Absence as Presence." *American Poetry* 4 (Winter, 1987): 41- 50.
Dickinson's poems "demonstrate both the continuities and discontinuities between Romanticism and Modernism." She uses language to validate her isolation rather than making it a line of communication with others. Language, "her sole companion," is an expression of the consciousness that "originates in loss," and it is also a substitute for experience. No one makes the fact of absence more real than Dickinson; language itself becomes the strongest presence.

Glenn, Eunice. "Emily Dickinson's Poetry: A Revaluation." *Sewanee Review* 51 (Autumn, 1943): 574-588.
Argues against the romantic criticism that had been fatal to the appraisal of Dickinson's achievement. "Emily Dickinson has been put in her place, the wrong place, and kept there." The tendency to quote short passages out of context, rather than to examine whole poems, has also had negative effects.

Glenn provides analyses of several poems, showing what makes each successful. Glenn discusses compression, striking metaphorical power, control over
tone, use of paradox, and the ways in which the various elements interact "to
produce an effect of reconciliation."

Griffith, Clark. *The Long Shadow: Emily Dickinson's Tragic Poetry*. Princeton, N.J.:
Princeton University Press, 1964.
Argues that Dickinson's tragic vision is profound, and that the typical anthol-
ogy pieces of whimsy and chipperness are trivial and unrepresentative. Indeed,
Griffith finds Dickinson's lighter poems unconvincing, almost insincere. De-
tailed discussions of relatively few poems illustrate the rigor and complexity of
Dickinson's thought and the deep resonances of her tragic sensibility.

Higgins, David. *Portrait of Emily Dickinson: The Poet and Her Prose*. New
Brunswick, N.J.: Rutgers University Press, 1967.
Examines the rewards and limitations of "society-by-mail" for the nineteenth
century in general and Dickinson in particular. Many of the poet's workshop
scraps of language were turned into either poetry or prose (letters). Dickinson's approach to either form was much the same, and so her letters and poems
illuminate one another. Many letters were revised or pieced together from
earlier fragments. Like the poems, the letters served to promote Dickinson's
sense of self. Higgins finds the letter-poems of special interest.

Homans, Margaret. "Emily Dickinson." In her *Woman Writers and Poetic Identity*.
Princeton, N.J.: Princeton University Press, 1980. Also in Bloom.
Dickinson is openly conscious of "the difficulties of being a woman and a
poet." Her expressive power springs "from her particular way of understanding
her femininity" and her ability to put problems of identity behind her."
Dickinson's Puritan ancestor's transmitted a myth of Eve in which "Eve's
words are secondary and stray from truth." Careful readings of the letters and
poems show the ironic means by which Dickinson refused to let her words be
either masculine or subordinate.

Howe, Susan. *My Emily Dickinson*. Berkeley, Calif.: North Atlantic Books, 1985.
An imaginative and highly personalized exploration of the ways in which
Dickinson's sex, class, education, and inherited traits were recalculated within
her self-imposed exile to produce a unique poetry. Part 1 raises issues of
identity, memory, and intellectual conscience. Part 2 defines Dickinson's response to Calvinist tradition, largely through comparisons to the life and work
of Jonathan Edwards. Part 3 concerns itself with the stance of "triumphant
negation" and with the dramatic element in Dickinson's work. Howe also
examines Dickinson's relationship with Thomas Wentworth Higginson.

Johnson, Greg. *Emily Dickinson: Perception and the Poet's Quest*. University: University of Alabama Press, 1985.
Traces the emphasis Dickinson places upon perception as an instrument of poetic quest. Visual perception is "the fulcrum of all experience that matters and the only reliable guide toward a more comprehensive and synthetic vision." Presents the biographical factors relevant to Dickinson's insistence on perception's centrality. Perception—ways of seeing—is the ultimate subject of her work. Many poems that deal with seeing or aesthetics are explicated.

Johnson, Thomas H. *Emily Dickinson: An Interpretive Biography*. Reprint. New York: Atheneum, 1967.
Dickinson lived in three worlds: a world of friendship, a world of nature, and a world of spirit. Her poetry reflects these arenas of identity, sometimes separately and sometimes in combination. Discusses the development of Dickinson's interest in professional technique, examining her experimentation with off-rhyme, metrical inversion, and punctuation. An excellent guide through the poems as well as through the circumstances that produced them.

Juhasz, Suzanne. *The Undiscovered Continent: Emily Dickinson and the Space of the Mind*. Bloomington: Indiana University Press, 1983.
Examines Dickinson's way of looking at the mind as a place in which to live and also what kind of living went on there. Dickinson creates a special poetic language to address mental experience. Three kinds of intense mental experience—pain, delight, and eternity—are explored in terms of the language constructs that enact them. The implications of Dickinson's "choice of solitude" are examined. Living in the mind is discussed as a particular condition of women.

―――――――― , ed. *Feminist Critics Read Emily Dickinson*. Bloomington: Indiana University Press, 1983.
Nine essays that examine imagery and language as it reflects or reveals gender dynamics in nineteenth century American society. Some essays explore how Dickinson's poetic diction defines her sense of herself as a poet. Others are concerned with archetypal imagery. Contributions by Sandra M. Gilbert, Margaret Homans, Cristanne Miller, and others. Bibliography by Sherri Hallgren. Juhasz's introduction gives a brief overview of psychoanalytic and feminist contributions to Dickinson studies.

Kazin, Alfred. "Wrecked, Solitary, Here: Dickinson's Room of Her Own." In his *An American Procession*. New York: Alfred A. Knopf, 1984.
Contrasts Thoreau's idealization of experience with Dickinson's inner realism. For her, words not simply the transcription of experience; rather, "they often invented it." She focused not on the seasonal cycle, but on the human cycle of

moods. A great scrutinizer of the mind's shadings and of emotion itself. "The voice of her poetry is peculiarly immediate, exclamatory, anguished, and antic in its concern." Concentration is Dickinson's hallmark trait. For her, death is a much more substantial problem than the Transcendentalists made of it.

Kher, Inder Nath. *The Landscape of Absence: Emily Dickinson's Poetry*. New Haven, Conn.: Yale University Press, 1974.
Explores the "metaphoric-metamorphic structures of her art" in an attempt to grasp her overall poetic vision. Dickinson's poetry is "one long poem of multidimensional reality," each unit representing a phase of the whole as well as the whole in small. Dickinson creates a personal mythology that pierces the material world in order to apprehend the spiritual. Detailed examination of "the aesthetics of terror" and the central metaphor of contending with absences.

Keller, Karl. *The Only Kangaroo Among the Beauty: Emily Dickinson and America*. Baltimore: Johns Hopkins University Press, 1979.
In separate chapters, draws connections between Dickinson and Anne Bradstreet, Edward Taylor, Jonathan Edwards, Harriet Beecher Stowe, Nathaniel Hawthorne, Walt Whitman, and others. Difficult to confront directly, Dickinson becomes indirectly knowable as defined by these affinities. Keller's secondary concern is to define Puritan esthetics by examining Dickinson's work alongside of these other writers. Robert Frost is an inheritor of this aesthetic.

Leder, Sharon, with Andrea Abbot. *The Language of Exclusion: The Poetry of Emily Dickinson and Christina Rossetti*. New York: Greenwood Press, 1987.
Focuses on "the shared historical experience of these two most 'private' poets . . . [to] reveal their public significance." The "spinster/recluse model" is inadequate for examining their work. The poems of Dickinson and Rossetti "expand our vision of Victorian society" because both women were rooted in and concerned with contemporary history. As reformers of language, they took initiatives toward "reforming the public realm."

Leyda, Jay. *The Years and Hours of Emily Dickinson*. 2 vols. Reprint. New York: Archon Books, 1970.
First published in 1960, this book "presents the materials without attempting to build them into a comprehensive structure." A chronology of documents transcribed and extracted from manuscript and printed sources from which readers can make their own biographical interpretations. Includes letters, newspaper items, diary entries.

Lindberg-Seyersted, Brita. *The Voice of the Poet: Aspects of Style in the Poetry of Emily Dickinson*. Cambridge, Mass.: Harvard University Press, 1968.

This investigation employs linguistic research to uncover three special areas of language habits. Colloquialness involves how speech rhythms are "counter-pointed to a metrical scheme . . . in syntactical structures." Slantness is a technique of indirection or suggestion. Privateness relates to the most idiosyncratic aspects of Dickinson's style. Detailed statistical analyses of the poet's linguistic tendencies.

Loving, Jerome. *Emily Dickinson: The Poet on the Second Story*. Cambridge: Cambridge University Press, 1986.
"This book is about Dickinson's success in appreciating failure." Begins near the end of her life, and—through documents and readings of the poems—works to demonstrate "that the seeming dissonance in her words and images in really resonance." Examines the impact on Dickinson of her brother Austin's extramarital affair with regard to her own problem of commitment to a lover. Close, psychoanalytical readings of many poems.

Lowenberg, Carlton. *Emily Dickinson's Textbooks*. Lafayette, Calif.: privately printed, 1986.
An annotated bibliography of the textbooks available in New England during the 1840's. Forms of language, systems of logic, precepts of moral and religious instruction, and a detailed knowledge of then-current science all first became available to Dickinson through such textbooks. Draws from those in use at the Amherst Academy and the Mount Holyoke Female Seminary. While some are known to have been used by Dickinson, others represent the types likely to have been part of her schooling. A fascinating glimpse at the poet's formal education.

Lucas, Dolores Dyer. *Emily Dickinson and Riddle*. Dekalb: Northern Illinois University Press, 1969.
Applies a review of the history, psychology, and formal traditions of the riddle to Dickinson's poetry. "Deliberately obscure, having an element of conscious deception, a riddle never really unites, nor does it sever cleanly either." This ambiguous aspect of the riddle, its nature as transition, is the feature particularly applicable to Dickinson's work. Her personifications are especially ambiguous. Riddles would have formed a significant part of Dickinson's early reading. They were a popular technique in Bible study.

MacLeish, Archibald. "The Private World." In *Emily Dickinson: Three Views*. Amherst, Mass.: Amherst College Press, 1960.
Observes a sharp contrast between the regular ticking of the familiar hymnal beat and the "density of sense" in Dickinson. Her imagery joins the sensory with the invisible so that we do not so much see it as contemplate it. The abrupt shifts between the abstract and the concrete provide a peculiar power.

Form less vital to understanding her work than emotion, order, and voice. "The tone and timbre of the speaking voice" carry the dramatic distinctiveness of Dickinson's poetry.

McNeil, Helen. *Emily Dickinson*. New York: Pantheon, 1986.
McNeil assesses the grounds for and the meaning of Dickinson's belated recognition. She argues that not only was Dickinson's reclusiveness a strategy for asking forbidden questions, but that the absence of a readership during her lifetime gave her poetry its unique freedom and stature. Dickinson's isolation allowed her to avoid the sanctioned sentimental model for women. Her symbolic silence registered as a social affront. Dickinson's metaphors work like metonymy; "that is, as if the signifier and signified were at the same level of figuration."

Miller, Cristanne. *Emily Dickinson: A Poet's Grammar*. Cambridge, Mass.: Harvard University Press, 1987.
Examines the effects of and reasons for Dickinson's "elliptically compressed, disjunctive, at times ungrammatical" uses of language. The tension between her urgent desire to move her readers and her riddling style is a source of her power. She was responding to the amazing power in language, its conventional uses in her time, and "her sense of herself as a woman and a poet." Sections on grammatical features, sources of diction, and readings of particular poems.

Miller, Ruth. *The Poetry of Emily Dickinson*. Middletown, Conn: Wesleyan University Press, 1968.
Extremely useful chapters on Dickinson's poetic manner, her work habits, and on the fascicles. Miller employs graphs of the fascicles to reinforce her analysis of Dickinson's organizing principles. She perceives a similar narrative process working through each one. Also, she shows how each poem "modulates an image of a preceding poem." Two appendices further clarify the unity of the fascicles, and another appendix documents Dickinson's reading.

Morris, Timothy. "The Development of Dickinson's Style." *American Literature* 60 (March, 1988): 26-41.
Argues against the view that Dickinson's poetry reached stylistic maturity almost immediately. One of her achievements was to remake the hymn quatrain into a "more purely literary" instrument. Another achievement was to develop, in her "late manner," a way of responding to, adapting, and reworking her earlier texts. Morris diagrams Dickinson's changing tendencies in using rhyme and enjambment to show modifications of stanza form.

_____ . "The Free-Rhyming Poetry of Emerson and Dickinson." *Essays in Literature* 12 (Fall, 1985): 225-240.

Dickinson's short-lined poems in irregular meter are the ones that most show her formal debt to Emerson. These poems, which use asymmetrical rhyme schemes, are modeled on poems like Emerson's "Merlin I" and "Merlin II." Emerson's poems assert and represent an aesthetic stance to which Dickinson's are a response. Morris examines the issue of poetic form as raised by Emerson's poems and then explores Dickinson's reaction in poems 160, 473, and 257. Both writers foreshadowed twentieth-century practice.

Mossberg, Barbara A. C. *Emily Dickinson: When a Daughter Is a Writer*. Bloomington: Indiana University Press, 1982.
This feminist approach to Dickinson's life and work views the poems as responses to being a woman in a patriarchal society. The poetry is understood as the creative result of Dickinson's dual role as rebellious daughter and dutiful one. Considers the absence of references to Dickinson's mother as key evidence for the poet's quest "to establish an independent identity." Focuses on themes and techniques of abnegation, denial, and diminution. A clear and comprehensive application of feminist theory.

Mudge, Jean McClure. *Emily Dickinson and the Image of Home*. Amherst: University of Massachusetts Press, 1975.
Assuming that the impressions of childhood and adolescence are of lasting importance, Mudge places Dickinson in that early physical environment, the place in which her sensitivity to space was formed. "Emily Dickinson's image of house or home, touching the poet's tangible and intangible worlds at once, is perhaps the most penetrating and complex figure she employs." The recurrence of such images defines Dickinson's inner landscape, her "spatial inscape."

Munk, Linda. "Emily Dickinson's Religious Wordplay." *ESQ* 32 (4th Quarter, 1986): 232-252.
Dickinson may be using "religious puns to discredit religious decorum by pointing to startling relations in what she considers to be the real order of things." Munk explores substitution and other strategies to illustrate Dickinson's response to Emerson's pronouncements on the rhetoric of religion. Wordplay helps redeem corruptions in language; it is "one way back to the garden of primary meanings." Dickinson's wordplay is cleansing both linguistically and spiritually.

Myerson, Joel. *Emily Dickinson: A Descriptive Bibliography*. Pittsburgh: University of Pittsburgh Press, 1984.
Lists and briefly describes all printings of all editions through 1982. Also covers miscellaneous collections of her writings, all first appearances of indi-

vidual works in books or pamphlets, and all American and English first periodical appearances. The "Index to Poems" provides the printing history of each poem. Myerson's introduction considers bibliographical problems.

Oates, Joyce Carol. "Soul at White Heat: The Romance of Emily Dickinson's Poetry." *Critical Inquiry* 13 (Summer, 1987): 806-824.
Though Dickinson's poetic voice is always recognizable, there is "a tone of the purest anonymity" that invites us to think of her as speaking of our condition as well as hers. Taken together, her poems form "a romance of epic proportions" in which the object of the quest is "to realize the soul." The poems, on one level, are about the creation of a self capable of creating them. One receives from her work "a heightened sense of the mind's unchartered possibilities." Many individual poems examined.

Oberhaus, Dorothy Huff. " 'Tender Pioneer': Emily Dickinson's Poems on the Life of Christ." *American Literature* 59 (October, 1987): 341-358.
Dickinson wrote poems on the life of Jesus Christ throughout her career. "When read together as a group allowing each to illuminate the others, these meditations on Jesus' birth, life, Crucifixion, and Resurrection form something like a nineteenth-century American Gospel." Some of these poems tap the metaphysical tradition while others stress the Gospel's contemporary relevance. Christ is represented in many roles but always in an intensely personal way.

Patterson, Rebecca. *Emily Dickinson's Imagery*. Amherst: University of Massachusetts Press, 1979.
In Dickinson's "unconscious symbolism" as well as in her conscious manipulation of traditional images and symbols, Patterson finds a highly charged erotic poetry, homosexual in orientation. Demonstrates the prevalence of oral, orgasmic, and voyeuristic motifs. Treats in separate chapters jewel imagery and color imagery, with special attention to the characteristic uses of the colors in the poet's "palette." A massing of evidence to illuminate the masculine element in Dickinson's character.

_____ . *The Riddle of Emily Dickinson*. Boston: Houghton Mifflin, 1951.
Concerned less with biography than with "establishing the identity of the person about whom she wrote her poems," Patterson nevertheless promotes a theory that Dickinson's relationship with Kate Scott Anthon contributed to her breakdown as well as to the fruitful recovery that produced many of the poems. Explores the resonances of Dickinson's social impotence with the motif of power in her writing. Considers the meaning of Dickinson's intense concentration on the moment of death. Much material on Kate Anthon and many short quotations from the poems.

Philip, Jim. "Valley News: Emily Dickinson at Home and Beyond." In *Nineteenth-Century American Poetry*, edited by A. Robert Lee. Totowa, N.J.: Barnes & Noble Books, 1985.

Examines poems that reveal Dickinson's mixed attitude toward home, domestic duties, the lively college community of Amherst, and the surrounding Connecticut Valley. Dickinson's "investigative power" into states of mind works through natural and household imagery, making her worldly and otherworldly at the same time. Follows "movements of challenge and advance" in Dickinson's work in the context of her isolation. A compact yet far-ranging treatment.

Phillips, Elizabeth. *Emily Dickinson: Personae and Performance*. University Park: Pennsylvania State University Press, 1988.

This character study hopes to set aside the myth of the tragic heroine whose withdrawal from the world was caused by "the trauma of disappointment in love." Dickinson was fairly self-satisfied. Writing for pleasure, she could write as she pleased—choosing her readers for her own benefit. Her life included many active roles—child, daughter, sister, friend, homemaker—and these experiences naturally inform her work. The poems are self-conscious literary performances, histrionic more than autobiographical.

Pickard, John B. *Emily Dickinson: An Introduction*. New York: Holt, Rinehart and Winston, 1967.

A compact treatment that considers the reasons for and consequences of Dickinson's relatively private career as a poet. Pickard finds clues in the nature of Dickinson's New England background and family relationships. Treats poems and poetic topics in broad categories: "A Poet's Mind," "A Poet's Practice," "Nature," "Social Scene and Love," "Pain and Death," and "Immortality." Notes that few American poets have enjoyed the combination of critical and popular success that awaited Dickinson.

Pollack, Vivian R. *Dickinson: The Anxiety of Gender*. Ithaca, N.Y.: Cornell University Press, 1984.

Sees the obvious identity-crisis motif in Dickinson's work as specifically a problem of sexual identity. Dickinson questions whether the sources of her despair are her own failings or the world's imperfection. Some poems bridge this dichotomy of blame, though most maintain it. Pollack finds in the poems a conscious manifestation of "permanently arrested development." Indebted to feminist critics as well as to Sewall and Cody.

Porter, David T. *The Art of Emily Dickinson's Early Poetry*. Cambridge, Mass.: Harvard University Press, 1966.

Examines the "developmental period" in Dickinson's career with attention to stylistic habits. Argues that Dickinson's mannerisms are not gratuitous or spontaneous but purposeful. The book is organized around Dickinson's handling of metrics, rhyme, imagery, diction, and voice. Porter attends to the techniques of fragmentation and probes the thematic implications of those techniques. A fine primer on poetic craft.

——————— . *Dickinson: The Modern Idiom*. Cambridge, Mass.: Harvard University Press, 1981.
Dickinson's "awareness of her apartness," expressed in many of her poems, was an awareness of artistic and emotional need that had no "enabling authority and direction" from the literary traditions she inherited. Dickinson had to make her own way, find her own conventions and diction in order to release her particular vision. Porter examines her writing methods, tools, and worksheets in order to discover what the unauthorized printed versions of her poems do not reveal. He also defines Dickinson's art by establishing what she did *not* do as a poet. Chapters on her relationship to modernism.

Reynolds, David S. "The American Woman's Renaissance and Emily Dickinson." In his *Beneath the American Renaissance*. New York: Alfred A. Knopf, 1988.
Puts Dickinson's achievement in the context of feminine agitation and the "social and literary flowering . . . in women's culture." Asserts that an "ironic, stylized genre" expressive of women's misery had already been established by the time Dickinson began writing her "elliptical poems." After reviewing this literature (primarily novels), Reynolds argues that Dickinson's feminist critics have missed "the cultural forces that liberated her" in their search for all the evidence of repression.

Rich, Adrienne. "Vesuvius at Home: The Power of Emily Dickinson." In *Shakespeare's Sisters: Feminist Essays on Woman Poets*, edited by Sandra M. Gilbert and Susan Gubar. Bloomington: University of Indiana Press, 1979.
Rich searches for a Dickinson whose strength she can tap: "I have come to imagine her as somehow too strong for her environment, a figure of powerful will, someone whose personal dimensions would be felt in a household." Rich examines, through the poems, the poet's relationship to her own power and the risk to feminine identity inherent in projecting that power. She insists that Dickinson had a clear sense of who she was, and the she was the first to go beyond "the conventions of womanly feeling."

Robinson, John. *Emily Dickinson: Looking to Canaan*. Boston: Faber & Faber, 1986.
This student guide, prepared for British readers, explores the heritage of Puritan New England as it formed Dickinson's outlook. Describes the theatrical nature of Dickinson's poems and the ways in which her techniques of irony

questioned the Calvinist assumptions of her upbringing. Dickinson's poems record a struggle with God while her ceremonial language encounters and challenges the world. A highly personalized essay with constant use of the first-person pronoun.

Rosenbaum, S. P. *A Concordance to the Poems of Emily Dickinson*. Ithaca, N.Y.: Cornell University Press, 1964.
This index to the words—and thus the images and ideas—of Dickinson's poems enables the student to discover constant or shifting meanings, characteristic traits in diction, habits of word combining, frequencies of occurrence, and whatever else the critical imagination can find with such a tool. Each listed word is followed by contextual passages and reference to the poem in which the passage appears. Based on Thomas Johnson's edition of *The Poems of Emily Dickinson*.

Rosenthall, M. L., and Sally Gall. "American Originals II: Emily Dickinson's Fascicles." In their *The Modern Poetic Sequence: The Genius of Modern Poetry*. New York: Oxford University Press, 1983.
This study treats the poetic sequence as the major genre in modern English language poetry, a way out of the limitations of the lyric. Dickinson's work is a precursor of this genre. Dickinson arranged many of her poems into little manuscript booklets (called "fascicles") in which themes are orchestrated by the interaction of units in a carefully planned order. Readers should appreciate her art in these larger structures as well as in the individual units.

Rupp, Richard H., ed. *Critics on Emily Dickinson*. Coral Gables, Fla.: University of Miami Press, 1972.
A collection of representative excerpts from major critical traditions and approaches to Dickinson's work. Most of the selections survive being plucked from longer articles or book-length studies. Includes a section of explications and another of brief evaluations. The explications most often stress diction and prosodic technique. Though the best-known poems are not treated, these are useful samples of how to explicate poems, focusing on key elements in Dickinson's work.

St. Armand, Barton Levi. *Emily Dickinson and Her Culture: The Soul's Society*. Cambridge, England: Cambridge University Press, 1984.
Describes the changing society to which Dickinson's imagination responded. Discusses the place of keepsakes, scrapbooks, commonplace books, emblem books, portfolio verses, and popular journalism as they affect the character of the poet's work. Explores the psychology of assemblage and collecting; also discusses the typology and technique of landscape painting and their parallels in Dickinson's poems.

Salska, Agnieszka. *Walt Whitman and Emily Dickinson: Poetry of the Central Consciousness*. Philadelphia: University of Pennsylvania Press, 1985.
This comparative study is subdivided into chapters on such topics as American literary individualism, the self as persona, and language. For Whitman, the inspiring moment is generally located in the future; for Dickinson, in the past. For Whitman, this moment clarifies; for Dickinson, it energizes. Each writer carries out certain aspects of Emerson's agenda for poetry.

Sewall, Richard B. "Emily Dickinson." In *Voices and Visions: The Poet in America*, edited by Helen Vendler. New York: Random House, 1987.
Sewall develops a rich context of family circumstances and regional religious culture within which to examine Dickinson's achievement. Her withdrawal into her art never loses contact with the rhythms of Protestant hymns. However, Sewall sees Dickinson less as a religious poet and more "as an explorer, or experimenter, of the spirit, trying out on her own pulses . . . mood after mood, passion after passion, 'ideas-as-lived,' felt on the pulse and in the bloodstream." She gives us not advice but a special rendering of "what it feels like to be alive."

——————— . *The Life of Emily Dickinson*. 2 vols. New York: Farrar, Straus & Giroux, 1974.
This is the definitive life, an attempt at re-creating a sense of Dickinson's inner and outer world by weighing all of the available evidence. Sewall's opening chapter discusses the special problems of Dickinson biography. Volume 1 is almost entirely given over to background—the culture of Puritan New England. Volume 2 begins with the day of Dickinson's birth. Excellent treatment of education and friendships. Illustrated. Poetry used to capture Dickinson's moods at key moments in her life.

——————— , ed. *Emily Dickinson: A Collection of Critical Essays*. Englewood Cliffs, N.J.: Prentice-Hall, 1963.
A solid overview, through selections, of the history of Dickinson studies from Conrad Aiken, Allan Tate, and Yvor Winters up until the early 1960's. Throughout, Sewall depends on critics who are also poets, giving the collection a poet's sensibility. John Crowe Ransom and Richard Wilbur are other contributors. A chronology of important dates is included. Many essays attest the importance of Thomas H. Johnson's edition of the poems.

Sherwood, William R. *Circumference and Circumstance: Stages in the Mind and Art of Emily Dickinson*. New York: Columbia University Press, 1968.
Attempts to show, through reading the poems in their proper order (a procedure made possible be recent scholarly editing), "a development of mind." Distinguishes four major periods in the development of Dickinson's views.

Discusses Dickinson's "fascination with the mechanics of perception," her argument with Transcendentalism, and her indifference to political issues. Many individual poems are discussed at length.

Shurr, William H. *The Marriage of Emily Dickinson: A Study of the Fascicles.* Lexington: University Press of Kentucky, 1983.
Dickinson's "fascicles" are manuscript booklets which the poet herself put together. These gatherings must be assumed to have purposeful designs. The reconstruction of the fascicles by R. W. Franklin allows us to explore the ways in which Dickinson saw relationships among her poems. Shurr explores problems in chronology, Dickinson's habits in grouping poems, and the concatenation of themes and metaphors. He discovers in the work the story of Dickinson's passionate relationship with the Reverend Charles Wadsworth.

Simons, Louise. "Emily Dickinson's Willed Paradise: In Defeat of Adam and Repeal." *American Imago* 42 (Summer, 1985): 165- 182.
Though Dickinson's poems are referential, they are not especially mimetic; "the world created by the poems provides an alternative to the actuality of existence in the social world of Amherst, Massachusetts, in the third quarter of the nineteenth century." Simons explores the causes for and nature of this "privatized world . . . that Dickinson creates as a habitat for this ego" according to the methodology of Freudian ego psychology.

Smith, Lorrie. "Some See God and Live: Dickinson's Later Mysticism." *ATQ*, n.s. 1 (December, 1987): 301-310.
Poem 1733 is one instance of the manner in which, in her later work, "Dickinson relinquished the desire for visible proof of God's grace by imagining revelation as a reciprocal act of human and divine will." Amalgamating Old and New Testament allusions, Dickinson's poem is the culmination "of her long process of questioning and, more importantly, writing about the significance of Christian faith in her own life." Dickinson's identification with Moses is significant here and in three earlier poems.

Stocks, Kenneth. *Emily Dickinson and the Modern Consciousness.* New York: St. Martin's Press, 1988.
An attempt "to place Emily Dickinson in her representative role in the mainstream tradition of our literature" without denying her unique outlook and style. Stocks sees Dickinson as a significant precursor of the modernist movement. Her work reflected not the "prevailing fashions" but rather the "real underlying currents" of her era. Dickinson is especially accessible today because her work speaks of alienated beings without the traditional anchors of faith or fulfilled relationships.

Stonum, Gary Lee. "Emily Dickinson's Calculated Sublime." In *The American Sublime*, edited Mary Arensberg. Albany: State University of New York Press, 1986.
The hundreds of poems that employ mathematical terms and ideas seem purposely to address the challenge of the sublime. Dickinson's poetry "courts the romantic sublime" through images of counting and measuring that suggest the need to control something immeasurable. Though the poet aspires to the power of the sublime, her attempt at imaginative possession through computation is peculiar. Mathematics has its own mysticism and language, both of which are part of Dickinson's deliberately unromantic approach.

Taggart, Genevieve. *The Life and Mind of Emily Dickinson*. Reprint. New York: Cooper Square Publishers, 1967.
An attempt to make sense of the letters and poems as primary sources for biography. Taggart opts for an emphasis on the inner life, allowing the poems to serve as guides even though many of them were not dated when this book was written (first published in 1930) was written. The relationship with Higginson is center stage. Interesting discussions of Dickinson's use of legal vocabulary and sonic devices as well as of her habits of revision.

Thomas, Heather Kirk. "Emily Dickinson's 'Renunciation' and Anorexia Nervosa." *American Literature* 60 (May, 1988): 205- 225.
Claims that Dickinson's poetry displays "patterns of starvation and renunciation typical of female victims of anorexia nervosa." Evidence from her life and letters supports the contention that she suffered from this syndrome. Thomas traces the development of Dickinson's symptoms, especially the rejection of food and the adoption—in certain poems—of the little-boy persona. The anorexic "conquers her nourishers" and gains power by deprivation.

Thomas, Owen. "Father and Daughter: Edward and Emily Dickinson." *American Literature* 40 (January, 1969): 510-523.
Attempts to assess "the nature and extent" of Edward Dickinson's influence on his daughter and the importance of this influence to an understanding of her poetry. After reviewing the scanty biographical evidence, Thomas divides Dickinson's poetic career into four periods, each corresponding to a distinct phase of the intensity of her father's influence. Edward is viewed as a source of strength. His "deep and pervasive" influence is related, tenuously, to passages from his daughter's poems.

Thota, Anand Rao. *Emily Dickinson: The Metaphysical Tradition*. Atlantic Highlands, N.J.: Humanities Press, 1982.
Although Dickinson had immediate choices and models in the American genteel tradition, the English Victorian tradition, and the fading English Romantic

tradition, her poetry is more akin to that of the seventeenth century. Her sensibility is with the modes of thought and manner of a John Donne, whose work was being discovered when she began to write. Dickinson is "a poet of antithesis," as was Donne and his followers. Thota surveys the poems to illustrate these affinities.

Todd, John Emerson. *Emily Dickinson's Use of the Persona.* The Hague, Netherlands: Mouton, 1973.
The "I" in Dickinson's poetry is rarely autobiographical, but rather a created character. Dickinson assumes "a variety of dramatic poses to express different moods" and to create fresh renditions of her experience and reading. She could be a proud queen, a child, a meek bride, a dying invalid, a barefoot boy. Todd explores the poems under several persona groupings. Treatment of schizoid persona particularly interesting.

Waggoner, Hyatt H. "Proud Ephemeral." In his *American Poets from the Puritans to the Present Day.* Boston: Houghton Mifflin, 1968.
Comparisons with the Puritans or with Emerson can lead us to forget that Dickinson was firmly rooted in her own time. Nevertheless, Emerson's thinking gave her a religious alternative and shaped her sense of the poet's role. The imagery and style of Emerson's essay, "Circles," and its accompanying poem find echoes in Dickinson's work. Though inconsistent on matters of faith, her thinking shows a consistent pattern of growth which Waggoner develops in detail and connects to the later thought of William James.

Walker, Cheryl. "Tradition and the Individual Talent." In her *The Nightingale's Burden: Woman Poets and American Culture Before 1900.* Bloomington: Indiana University Press, 1982.
Develops insights into the characteristic stances and situations of American woman poets by comparison and contrast. Dickinson's foil is Helen Hunt Jackson: "Although personally rebellious, Jackson was not a renegade as a poet. Dickinson . . . was personally conservative and poetically heterodox." One of Dickinson's major contributions was to allow woman poets to "take their work seriously." Jackson is only of historical interest; Dickinson steps out of time. She is no mere "poetess," but a genuine poet.

Wallace, Ronald. "Emily Dickinson: A Day! Help! Help! Another Day!" In his *God Be with the Clowns: Humor in American Poetry.* Columbia: University of Missouri Press, 1984.
Dickinson's "tendency toward effervescence and exuberant stand-up comedy provoked her to write a number of playful light-verse poems with no ostensible purpose other than good fun." Humor also lies in her self-deprecating stance, her adoption of a Yankee persona, and her playing the child's role. In some

poems, the comedy is defensive; in others, it is sharply satiric. Petulance and paradox are key sources of humor.

Ward, Theodora. *The Capsule of the Mind: Chapters in the Life of Emily Dickinson*. Cambridge, Mass.: Harvard University Press, 1961.
Six essays grouped into two sequences explore the inner life of the young Dickinson, the crisis of self, emotional currents after 1865, and the major friendships with Josiah Gilbert Holland, Elizabeth Chapin Holland, Samuel Bowles, and T. W. Higginson. Ward's concern is with the poems that map Dickinson's emotional turmoil, especially when the images and symbols suggest psychological dimensions not susceptible to Dickinson's characteristic control.

Watts, Emily Stipes. "Refinement and Achievement." In her *The Poetry of American Women from 1632 to 1845*. Austin: University of Texas Press, 1977.
This chapter puts Dickinson's work in a valuable perspective. The connections between her poems and those of her relatively obscure predecessors and contemporaries reveal that claims made for the uniqueness of Dickinson's special concerns and practices apply to other writers as well. Dickinson's achievement is greater, but her ambitions and general aesthetic demeanor have much in common with other woman writers. Watts demonstrates Dickinson's awareness of these other writers.

Weisbuch, Robert. *Emily Dickinson's Poetry*. Chicago: University of Chicago Press, 1975.
Traces Dickinson's "compound vision" and its polarities of power and vulnerability, creation and negation, possibility and denial. Sees the poems as a series of internal debates that pose alternatives and occasionally unite or transcend them. Finds in Dickinson's work "the need to distinguish two antithetical modes of thought" and to raise the symbolic mode above common sense. Considers Dickinson's "anti-allegory" manner and her two distinct typologies of death.

Weissman, Judith. " 'Transport's Working Classes': Sanity, Sex, and Solidarity in Dickinson's Late Poetry." *Midwest Quarterly* 29 (Summer, 1988): 407-424.
The poems Dickinson wrote after 1864 have been universally dismissed, perhaps because they do not conveniently support fashionable critical approaches. "The last poems are as unusual in form, image, expression, as the poems of the 1860s." They are less restless, less volcanic poems, and they show a Dickinson who had found not only hope but also faith and charity. They are Dickinson's last and relatively tranquil words on issues treated in agonized fashion earlier in her life.

Wells, Henry W. *Introduction to Emily Dickinson*. Reprint. New York: Hendricks House, 1959.
Provides a biography of the poet's spiritual life, a setting of Dickinson's work into its framing literary history, and finally a close reading of her poems. This latter section stresses the epigrammatic qualities of Dickinson's verse as well as those works in the "lighter vein" and the "lyric spirit." Final sections discuss imagery, structure, and diction. Dickinson's meticulous weighing of words and her syllabic miserliness are hallmarks of her unique achievement. First published in 1947.

Wilbur, Richard. "Sumptuous Destitution." In *Emily Dickinson: Three Views*. Amherst, Mass.: Amherst College Press, 1960.
The external details of nature that Dickinson could record so brilliantly, her pleasure in surface accuracy, did not please her as much as accuracy regarding inner experience. She was deprived of a steady faith, of love, and of literary recognition. She became a "congregation of one" whose appetites both worldly and spiritual became magnified. The soul's infinite hunger is a connecting theme in her poetry. In a way, "she *was* dead," but in her poetry she came to a private mastery of life.

Wilson, Suzanne M. "Structural Patterns in the Poetry of Emily Dickinson." *American Literature* 35 (March, 1963): 53-59.
"The major structural plan or ordering of logical elements conforms to that most commonly found in the sermon and consists of three parts: statement or introduction of topic, elaboration, and conclusion." The introductory statement is most often presented in a figure of speech. Sometimes the statement-and-elaboration sequence is repeated a number of times before a conclusion is reached. In some poems, the conclusion is implicit rather than explicit. This fundamental pattern suggests a conscious shaping rather than an instinctive method of composition.

Winters, Yvor. "Emily Dickinson and the Limits of Judgment." In his *In Defense of Reason*. Reprint. Denver: Alan Swallow, 1961.
Grants that Dickinson's poetic genius is of "the highest order," but finds that even her best poems share characteristics of her very worst. Her most commonly praised poems are her worst. Dickinson's struggle with mystical traditions generated most of her significant work. She meets major moral and philosophical questions with "directness, dignity, and power." She is capable of brilliant technique that allows her to plunge into obscure areas and illuminate them. Judges that only Melville is a greater writer among Americans; Dickinson is "one of the greatest lyric poets of all time." First published in 1947.

Wolff, Cynthia Griffin. *Emily Dickinson*. New York: Alfred A. Knopf, 1986.
   A readable, novelistic treatment that straddles scholarly and popular biographical modes. Wolff makes convenient grouping of poems for analysis and shows both how the poems interact with one another and how they respond to particular cultural issues of Dickinson's era. The issues include personal voice, religious wrestling, love, and the expressiveness of divinity in the world. Many poems are skillfully explicated. Thorough, unobtrusive scholarship.

Wolosky, Shira. *Emily Dickinson: A Voice of War*. New Haven, Conn.: Yale University Press, 1984.
   Argues that Dickinson's verse, though the critical tradition is otherwise, "registers issues and events outside of her private sphere." The poems engage the external world aggressively and profoundly. Dickinson's characteristic sensibility is not one of fear, but one of ferocity. The metaphor of warfare or battle is a unifying one. The "historical trauma" of the Civil War is fully registered, as is cultural and personal "metaphysical conflict."

_____ . "Rhetoric or Not: Hymnal Tropes in Emily Dickinson and Isaac Watts." *New England Quarterly* 61 (June, 1988): 214- 232.
   Earlier comparisons of these two writers considered formal parallels and Dickinson's parodic stance toward Watts. The relationship, however, also involves matters of doctrine and rhetoric. Dickinson's verse raises questions regarding "the relationship between hymnal figures and the truths they are meant to convey." The poet "restructures hymnal modes and tropes she borrows from Watts . . . to subvert his doctrinal assertions." Often, Dickinson goes on "to subvert her own subversions."

Wylder, Edith. *The Last Face: Emily Dickinson's Manuscripts*. Albuquerque: University of New Mexico Press, 1971.
   Argues for the purposeful, rhetorical use of a notational system in the manuscript poems, including rhetorical uses of punctuation. Dickinson employed the symbols of nineteenth century elocutionists as keys to oral interpretation. Wylder reviews the art of elocution, especially inflection and rhetorical pause, and then shows how Dickinson's notation indicates the oral dimension of the poems. Treats habits of capitalization as marking primary metrical stresses.

"I taste a liquor never brewed" (214)

Anderson, Charles. *Emily Dickinson's Poetry: Stairway of Surprise*, 73-76. New York: Holt, Rinehart and Winston, 1960.
   Dickinson borrows the device of hyperbolic fantasy from tall tale humor in a "cosmic spree" that could be a parody of Emerson's "Bacchus." The parallels

with "Bacchus" include close echoes of language up to a climactic point, and then a sudden veering away to an opposite conclusion that seems to deny the mystical basis of Emerson's aesthetic. The scene in which the sun becomes a celestial lamppost "may well be a comic version of spiritual intoxication as set forth in the Book of Revelations."

Juhasz, Suzanne. *The Undiscovered Continent: Emily Dickinson and the Space of the Mind*, 106-108. Bloomington: Indiana University Press, 1983.
The poem is a "celebration of delight" allowing fantasy free reign. Dickinson finds that the mind's reality, its power, can oppose and transcend ordinary reality. The temporality of earthly (summer) delights renders them imperfect; ideal delight is the mind's province. Intoxication in this poem is finally an act of playful imagination, of mental power. Here, delight can last.

Ward, Theodora. *The Capsule of the Mind: Chapters in the Life of Emily Dickinson*, 51-52. Cambridge, Mass.: Harvard University Press, 1961.
The dreamy, intoxicated state expressed here is one that must be understood by the speaker as transient. No doubt written to express the stimulation of love, the poem's expansive feeling is so exaggerated as to be doomed to come into conflict with reality. If the poet's ecstatic state is a response to her love for a married man, then the hints of limitation, of impossible excess, reveal a subtle awareness of forthcoming disaster.

"Wild Nights — Wild Nights!" (249)

Cody, John. *After Great Pain: The Inner Life of Emily Dickinson*, 385-386. Cambridge, Mass.: Harvard University Press, 1971.
Argues that the poem is "a good example of heightened erotic stimulation" and a clear refutation to any view of Dickinson that finds her "devoid of erotic stirrings." The direct longing in this poem confirms the less direct evidence found in those poems that reveal sexual dread, a dread that would be inconsistent with "indifference to sexual encounter." It does not take a malignant reader to find the erotic core of fantasy expressed in this poem.

Miller, Ruth. *The Poetry of Emily Dickinson*, 90-96. Middletown, Conn.: Wesleyan University Press, 1968.
The imagery can point to a longing for Jesus as well as to a longing for union with a particular man—or with any man. Miller stresses the poem's maritime references, seeing "flexible strands of navigation metaphors" that link this poem with more than twenty others that use water imagery similarly. "Wild" need have no erotic connotation, but may rather describe weather conditions. Dickinson may have based the poem on the engraving for emblem 11 in her father's copy of Quarle's *Divine Emblems*.

Todd, John Emerson. *Emily Dickinson's Use of the Persona*, 36-37. The Hague, Netherlands: Mouton, 1973.

Dickinson here adopts a male persona, a longing lover, to project a vision of "unrestrained sexual passion." We need not understand the poem as an auto-biographical effusion from a reclusive spinster. The persona here employed by an act of imagination speaks aggressively and economically. The middle stanza "interposes the complementary state of peace and motionlessness suggesting the fulfillment of the sexual act." Such a reading does not deny the possibility of the speaker's desire for spiritual union with God.

"There's a certain Slant of light," (258)

Anderson, Charles R. *Emily Dickinson's Poetry: Stairway of Surprise*, 215-218. New York: Holt, Rinehart and Winston, 1960. Also in Rupp.

Not a nature poem, but an evocation of despair. The winter light is "as uncertain of source and indirect in impact as the feeling of despair often is." Dickinson makes the abstract feeling concrete by "converting light waves to sound waves" that affect the entire body. The clash of the colloquial word "Heft" with the grandness of "Cathedral Tunes" conveys the discordant, oppressive mood. This kind of paradoxical clash is made more succinctly in the phrase "Heavenly Hurt," suggesting both ecstasy and disappointment.

Cameron, Sharon. *Lyric Time: Dickinson and the Limits of Genre*, 100-103. Baltimore: Johns Hopkins University Press, 1979.

The poem is about how meanings fuse with one another. The world generates transformations that it cannot then alter. Light's indirectness changes our understanding of what we see without fundamentally changing the thing itself. Only at a great distance is light itself beheld, and at its moment of disappearance when it reveals death. Death is "the straightening of premonition into fact, figure into fulfillment."

Kher, Inder Nath. *The Landscape of Absence: Emily Dickinson's Poetry*, 80-81. New Haven, Conn.: Yale University Press, 1974.

The distance on the look of death could mean either "the unseeing gaze of the dead," or that "death is its own perceiving organ," or that distance is "the pause between life and death." By living in the awareness and consciousness of death, one "lives more intensely and freely." The poem is not an outcry of negative despair, for "death as pure negation is not the finale of Dickinson's poetic world." By living in despair one can experience freedom from despair.

Pollack, Vivian R. *Dickinson: The Anxiety of Gender*, 218-221. Ithaca, N.Y.: Cornell University Press, 1984.

The poem may express a sense of frustration, a feeling of threat accompanying spiritual illumination. Consciousness weighs the speaker down, though the brief glimpse of design offers fleeting hope. The primary mood of despair cannot be communicated. Blankness has no translation. The past, when apprehended in this mood, this light, becomes unusable, as does any notion of connection to the future. The frozen self can only, barely, recognize itself.

St. Armand, Barton Levi. *Emily Dickinson and Her Culture: The Soul's Society*, 239-241. Cambridge: Cambridge University Press, 1984.
The light here "acts as both penetrating spear and murderous blunt instrument," thus Dickinson undergoes a sort of crucifixion without hope of resurrection. She is passive, numb, unable to find a path to feeling or meaning. There are no telling contrasts delivered by this mood or this light. Dickinson "has fixed exactly in her art the specific spiritual state of particular natural phenomena at a precise moment in time." This method is in accord with the esthetics of Romanticism.

Winters, Yvor. "Emily Dickinson and the Limits of Judgment." In his *In Defense of Reason*, 297-298. Reprint. Denver: Alan Swallow, 1961.
Dickinson performs virtuoso variations on the poulter's measure base that is her favorite metrical norm. "The final stanza is a triumphant resolution of the three preceding: the first and third lines, like the second and fourth, are metrically identical." Winters' detailed prosodic analysis shows how "the elaborate structure of this poem results in the balanced hesitations and rapid resolutions which one hears in reading it. This is metrical artistry at about as high a level as one is likely to find it."

"I felt a Funeral, in my Brain," (280)

Anderson, Charles R. *Emily Dickinson's Poetry: Stairway of Surprise*, 208-209. New York: Holt, Rinehart and Winston, 1960.
Spiritual death is made concrete in terms of physical death. The narrative of the burial rites imparts a dramatic energy to the material. The contrast between sounds and soundlessness juxtaposes an unbearable world of sensation against a numbed or trancelike state beyond sensation, yet the bells associated with heaven also intrude upon this silence. To read the poem as a fantasy of imagined death is to misread this projection of a "duality of consciousness."

Budick, E. Miller. *Emily Dickinson and the Life of Language*, 205-211. Baton Rouge: Louisiana State University Press, 1985.
The poem considers the limits of reason and of a symbolism that assumes a universe consisting of parallel layers of meaning. The material and spiritual worlds are not necessarily related in ways accessible to logic and reason. The

narrator's perception begins to grow when the "Plank in Reason" breaks; now she can plunge down "through the bottom of her false analogies" into a new realm of symbolic relationships where knowing can be complete. The movement is from a spatial concept to a "then" which is actually "the negation of a temporal one."

Griffith, Clark. *The Long Shadow: Emily Dickinson's Tragic Poetry*, 245-250. Princeton, N.J.: Princeton University Press, 1964.
Dickinson uses a symbolic structure derived from details of a funeral service to record "the breakup of rational powers" and the "triumph of lunacy." The treading feet and the drumlike beating of the service suggest "some intolerable pressure" causing the normal "configurations of sense" to break up. The loss of reason is addressed in the last two stanzas as the entrance into another world, a mockery of celestial peace and silence figured grotesquely by the surreal symbol of an enormous ear. Related to the techniques of modern symbolist poetry.

Phillips, Elizabeth. *Emily Dickinson: Personae and Performance*, 46-54. University Park: Pennsylvania State University Press, 1988.
Rather than making this poem a step in Dickinson's "psychobiography," we might see it as one of a group of responses to the Civil War. It projects Dickinson's "sympathetic and imaginative participation with those she loved in the rites for the ruddy-faced boy they had all finished knowing." Phillips collects evidence from the letters to support her case. Dickinson deserves more credit as an inventor of representative voices rather than as a confessional poet near mental collapse.

"The Soul selects her own Society—" (303)

Budick, E. Miller. *Emily Dickinson and the Life of Language*, 138-143. Baton Rouge: Louisiana State University Press, 1985.
The poem demonstrates "the way in which elements of both Puritanism and Emersonianism share certain fundamental misperceptions about the self. The poem's diction links psychology, sociology, and theology to an anterior problem of the nature of human perception. It is both an attack on Puritan-Transcendentalist snobbery and an exposure of the negative consequences of a particular dogma. The prideful piety of the elect, "because it images itself in the likeness of God, excludes God from the society of self."

Griffith, Clark. *The Long Shadow: Emily Dickinson's Tragic Poetry*, 210-212. Princeton, N.J.: Princeton University Press, 1964.
The subject of the poem is "the spiritualization of the total self." The regal

Soul—a queen of sorts—rules over every other feature of the speaker's being, but her aloof, condescending self-assurance is only apparent. The Soul is so isolated that she is deeply vulnerable to the intrusion of impurity of any kind: "she occupies a cloister that is fearfully liable to invasion." The poem leaves us with a question: When "the valves of her attention have shut out life, what is left for her to focus upon?"

Luscher, Robert M. "An Emersonian Context of Dickinson's 'The Soul Selects her own Society.' " *ESQ* 30 (2nd Quarter, 1984): 111-116.
In this poem, Dickinson may be adapting the concept of selection elaborated in Emerson's neglected essay, "Spiritual Laws," which provides a rationale for "the soul's selective solitude." The poem neither applauds nor condemns the soul's reclusiveness. The soul's exclusions reflect its individual nature, and the selection process is an education and a form of nourishment. Those shut out perhaps "beckon in the wrong manner and at the wrong portals." The process of selective concentration "defines and defends the act of poetic creation."

Wolosky, Shira. *Emily Dickinson: A Voice of War*, 128-129. New Haven, Conn.: Yale University Press, 1984.
The poem may reflect the electoral process Dickinson observed when her father ran for public office. "One" is only herself, a soul that has "withdrawn into its own center." The processional majesty of the process is undercut by the outcome, as within that exclusionary center the soul finds neither "the divine whole" nor "the infinite world" but only itself. One of many instances of "the self as an entrapping circle."

"After great pain, a formal feeling comes—" (341)

Brooks, Cleanth and Robert Penn Warren. *Understanding Poetry*. 1st ed. New York: Henry Holt, 1938. Also in Rupp.
The capitalization of "He" refers to Christ, thus the first stanza's question has to do with whether the speaker is experiencing Christ's pain (on the cross) through confusions of time and dissolution of sensibility. The "Quartz contentment" conveys the associations we make with stone, such as hardness, but escapes the cliché and introduces new associations: The speaker's contentment is "crystalized . . . out of the pain." Quartz participates in the imagery of numbness through visual likeness to ice.

Cameron, Sharon. *Lyric Time: Dickinson and the Limits of Genre*, 167-169. Baltimore: Johns Hopkins University Press, 1979.
The movement of the poem is toward progressive clarity made possible by "a self standing outside of the otherness that possesses it." The parts of the body

are discussed as if they belonged to someone else. In the second stanza, "death is only an analogy for the body that has lost its spirit, for the vacancy of will." The sequence of "Wood," "stone," and "Lead" is one of "progressive hardening" undercut by the final image of "Snow" with its "susceptibility to transformation." The poem is about letting go of feeling, not of life.

Griffith, Clark. *The Long Shadow: Emily Dickinson's Tragic Poetry*, 242-244. Princeton, N.J.: Princeton University Press, 1964.
The emotion described involves exhaustion on the other side of passion—a point beyond "further need of restraint or control." Perception of time is lost, as is spatial awareness. Dickinson describes "an emotion which is, paradoxically, the absolute absence of emotion." The persona's suffering has dehumanized her, left her performing "automatic gestures" in a "barely conscious coma." We see a rigor mortis of the inner self.

Sherwood, William R. *Circumference and Circumstance: Stages in the Mind and Art of Emily Dickinson*, 111-115. New York: Columbia University Press, 1968.
Because the process of recovery requires "participation in structured and repetitive action," the poem works through images of motion and form held in tension with those of immobility and dissolution. Any meaningless routine will help restore the "shattered sensibility," even the "formal imitation" of death demands a focused awareness that is, paradoxically, regenerative. The "Quartz contentment" involves "the absence both of tension and hope." A complex lyric meditation on perception concludes the poem.

"I heard a Fly buzz—when I died—" (465)

Ford, Thomas W. *Heaven Beguiles the Tired: Death in the Poetry of Emily Dickinson*, 112-114. Tuscaloosa: University of Alabama Press, 1968.
Dickinson connects stillness with death and emphasizes it by contrasting it with noise. Stillness between claps of thunder is intensified, and the phrase "Heaves of Storm" allows the connotation of "dying throes." This stillness is also suffocating. Death's approach is regal—an "Onset"—as is usual in her poems. The synesthesia of the blue buzz may suggest how the senses of a dying person become confused. Blue is the color of the fly.

Griffith, Clark. *The Long Shadow: Emily Dickinson's Tragic Poetry*, 134-137. Princeton, N.J.: Princeton University Press, 1964.
If we consider the fly as a "feeder upon carrion," we can conclude that as death approaches the speaker has a terrible vision "that stink and corruption are death's only legacies." Rather than the expected Sign of Beatitude from the King, there is only the buzzing of a loathsome insect. However, if the vitality

of the buzzing fly represents life, then perhaps life is the "ugly annoyance" from which the speaker is ready to depart.

Miller, Ruth. *The Poetry of Emily Dickinson*, 32-34. Middletown, Conn.: Wesleyan University Press, 1968.
A useful review of the ways in which this poem has been interpreted, these pages show how perplexing and provocative Dickinson's art can be. Includes comment by Gerhard Friedrich, Caroline Hogue, Charles Anderson, and John Ciardi. Miller then goes on to discuss why it is that Dickinson's work encourages such divergent responses.

Weisbuch, Robert. *Emily Dickinson's Poetry*, 99-102. Chicago: University of Chicago Press, 1975.
Sees this much-discussed poem as one of those in which Dickinson forces "her otherworldly imagination to admit earthly realities." The persona is faced with uncertainty about the supernatural. The failure of vision is not only an imagining of death's approach, but a failure of the imagination itself. The focus of attention on what is outside the speaker is a "frantic externalizing" of inner experience and doubt. The fly may be a representation of this doubt.

"Mine—by the Right of the White Election!" (528)

Eberwein, Jane Donahue. "Emily Dickinson and the Calvinist Sacramental Tradition." *ESQ* 33 (2nd Quarter, 1987): 67-81.
The phrase "Royal Seal" refers to those sacraments that reflect the covenantal dynamic. "A bargain has been struck for the speaker with God. The contract committing her soul to him has been sealed by Christ through his atonement." The word "seal" is also used by Calvinist theologians in discussing baptism, which they believed extended "a symbolic promise to the children of church members" of future cleansing, grace, and redemption. Calvin's discussion of the prince's seal illuminates Dickinson's meaning here and in other poems.

Pollack, Vivian R. *Dickinson: The Anxiety of Gender*, 174-176. Ithaca, N.Y.: Cornell University Press, 1984.
The concern with legalistic terms distances the emotional experience of marriage even while the speaker attempts to legitimize it. The speaker is wildly egotistical, becoming more and more expansive and godlike "in an empty universe." The speaker may be asserting her marriage to God or her right to it. It is also possible that the speaker is God, or an arrogant usurper of God's position.

"I like to see it lap the Miles" (585)

Leder, Sharon, with Andrea Abbot. *The Language of Exclusion: The Poetry of Emily Dickinson and Christina Rossetti*, 145-146. New York: Greenwood Press, 1987.
Dickinson's father brought the railroad to Amherst. She equated him and the train with power, a power she questioned in various ways. She did not attend the ceremonies for the completion of the rail line, but rather watched them from a distance, unnoticed. The poetic commemoration describes "the on-slaught of the train's presence on her countryside." In this scene, people are absent—irrelevant. This intrusion on the landscape alters space and time. There is a fear of power about to go out of control, "a sense of displacement and accommodation."

Todd, John Emerson. *Emily Dickinson's Use of the Persona*, 11-12. The Hague, Netherlands: Mouton, 1973.
Dickinson's use of the "little child" persona here is the source of wit and humor. The child's innocence allows comparisons unavailable to the adult mind. The poem may be read, then, as a satire on progress, reducing the economic and technological significances of this newest kind of transportation to the cartoon horse of childhood whimsy. Such a reduction or reimagining of the train raises questions about its ultimate importance. Dickinson uses this persona on many occasions.

Wright, Nathalia. "Emily Dickinson's Boanerges and Thoreau's Atropos: Locomotives on the Same Line?" *Modern Language Notes* 52 (February, 1957): 101-103.
Argues that Dickinson's development of the "iron horse" metaphor may be indebted to a passage in the "Sounds" chapter of *Walden*. Both treatments of the locomotive appeal chiefly to the sense of hearing; and "both trains traverse mountains and valleys and pass beside shanties." Dickinson's simile "neigh like Boanerges" seems a transformation of Thoreau's "snort like thunder." Wright presents other "imagistic similarities."

"I cannot live with You—" (640)

Cameron, Sharon. *Lyric Time: Dickinson and the Limits of Genre*, 78-82. Baltimore: Johns Hopkins University Press, 1979.
Finds that "the poem is structured as a list of criteria that would make union impossible," though stanzas 2 and 3 digress from this pattern. Union is prohibited, ironically, because it has already occurred. The injunction is against its repetition. Key passages "are rich with the pride of acknowledged sexuality," and this attitude compromises the conventional supremacy of Paradise. Contends that "the excess of pleasure" is what drives the lovers apart.

Ferlazzo, Paul J. *Emily Dickinson*, 69-70. Boston: Twayne, 1976.

Dickinson's longest poem "considers in turn life, death, resurrection, and judgment; and she concludes that in every condition their love cannot be allowed to flourish." Discusses the image of the sexton locking up the porcelain in terms of Dickinson's Puritan Amherst setting. The speaker's "idolatrous love would prevent her from acknowledging her true saviors." Self-denial is the only possibility.

Glenn, Eunice. "Emily Dickinson's Poetry: A Revaluation." *Sewanee Review* 51 (Autumn, 1943): 574-588.

On pages 582-584, Glenn compares Dickinson's poem with Andrew Marvell's "The Definition of Love." Both works are extremely complex in tone. "There is an emphasis on sensuality and also regard for discipline, which comes out in the references to orthodox religious conceptions." However, "the sensibility of the poet and her reaction to the situation, as the poem shows, cannot be contained in the measuring cup of discipline." The shocking figure of speech "your face would put out Jesus" is adroitly extended through the three stanzas that follow it. Both Dickinson and Marvell explore the idea of impossibility.

"Because I could not stop for Death—" (712)

Anderson, Charles R. *Emily Dickinson's Poetry: Stairway of Surprise*, 241-246. New York: Holt, Rinehart and Winston, 1960.

The natural terror of riding toward death is subdued by the civility of the driver. The tonally flat review of youth, maturity, and age, along with the framing references to morning and evening, suggests the indifference of life to death's constant presence. The poem rhythmically slows to approach the grave. Then, at the threshold, a fleeting sensory image of the "Horses Heads" stands out against the fading of all other impressions.

Cameron, Sharon. *Lyric Time: Dickinson and the Limits of Genre*, 127-131. Baltimore: Johns Hopkins University Press, 1979.

The poem cannot be reduced to a tidy allegory, though it has some of allegory's characteristics. "The ride with death, though it espouses to reveal a future that is past, in fact casts both past and future in the indeterminate present of the last stanza." The speaker cannot "arrive at a fixed conception" and thus the poem, the quest, is resolved only with rhetorical bravado. The poem shifts from being an "assertion of knowledge" to being a "confession of . . . failure."

Griffith, Clark. *The Long Shadow: Emily Dickinson's Tragic Poetry*, 127-134. Princeton, N.J.: Princeton University Press, 1964.
Sees the poem as one of a number of imaginative constructions of Dickinson's own death. "Immortality," the third figure in the chariot, is a kind of chaperon who "keeps the relationship beyond reproach, ensures that the journey will have a respectable ending." But if Death is not a courtly gentlemen, rather a malevolent deceiver, than Immortality is "party to a wicked fraud." The poem's power resides in a tension of ambiguities: Is the woman escorted to a death that opens upon the great hereafter, or is she cruelly "raped of life?" Griffith finds this ambivalence uncharacteristic.

Johnson, Thomas H. *Emily Dickinson: An Interpretive Biography*. Reprint. New York: Atheneum, 1967.
The diminishing concreteness of the last two stanzas accompanies the movement to the grave. Time and seasonal change have already stopped; now motion ceases as well. The absoluteness of this cessation is connected to the timelessness of eternity. Even Death, the forceful companion in the early stanzas, has lost significance: having served his purpose, he is left behind. Excerpted in Rupp.

McNeil, Helen. *Emily Dickinson*, 129-131. New York: Pantheon, 1986.
"Although the coach is moving, it moves in a register that has stopped in relation to daily time. Here, the move from the house is a move out of time, and the uncanny house is the house of death, which resembles a fine mansion, but isn't." The obscenity that is death itself is realized by the speaker's sexual humiliation in finding her clothing transparent. The poem relocates the protagonist from one house to another, and yet the status of the house remains ambiguous, functioning as "a hedge against dualism."

Pickard, John B. *Emily Dickinson: An Introduction*, 52-55. New York: Holt, Rinehart and Winston, 1967.
Instead of a fearful journey, this treatment of death's invitation presents a restful trip. The politeness of the overture masks the fact that the speaker has no choice. Immortality, present at the outset, is barely acknowledged as the terms of the journey seem familiar. Tensions in life are indicated by words like "strove." The country outing shifts, in rhythm and image, to another dimension. Death's courtesy is a deception that hides his terrifying purpose and ultimate power, clarified at the end.

Pollack, Vivian R. *Dickinson: The Anxiety of Gender*, 190-193. Ithaca, N.Y.: Cornell University Press, 1984.
Dickinson's persona repels "thought and emotion," easily accepting Death's invitation—though not seeking it—because she feels no pressure to choose

Miller, Cristanne. *Emily Dickinson: A Poet's Grammar*, 122-126. Cambridge, Mass.: Harvard University Press, 1987.

The poem "is an adolescent fantasy about coming of age that breaks down before what should be its happy conclusion—powerful adulthood—revealing the flaw in its initial fiction but perhaps also the extreme limitation the speaker feels in her life choices." Miller demonstrates how "Dickinson's compression, parataxis, textual variants, and densely compact metaphor" affect the poem's meanings. The speaker "has too much power to touch others without destroying their lives and not enough to control her own."

Porter, David T. *Dickinson: The Modern Idiom*, 209-218. Cambridge, Mass.: Harvard University Press, 1981.

Expresses the dilemma of instrument and purpose. The poet's life and the loaded gun represent language itself, with the clear implication that language has destructive power. However, language does not die. This power needs authority, sanction, direction. Dickinson faced a crushing sense of purposelessness, an enormous loneliness, paradoxically coupled with a certainty of power. The world offers no answer, thus the poem enacts a turning away from the world.

Weisbuch, Robert. *Emily Dickinson's Poetry*, 25-39. Chicago: University of Chicago Press, 1975.

"The poem presents one resolution of a debate which Dickinson's poetry continually carries on with itself. Is it better to maintain an independence, however limited in power, or to gain power by ceding oneself to a greater?" The poem proceeds by a series of interlocking explicit and suggested analogies; it is not reducible to one-for-one correspondences. Weisbuch's long analysis tests his theory of "analogical scenelessness as an interpretive method." Identifying the greater power is a subordinate issue. Ambiguities are not signs of weakness in Dickinson's art but of strength.

Wolff, Cynthia Griffin. *Emily Dickinson*, 442-446. New York: Alfred A. Knopf, 1986.

Relates the riddling nature of this poem (and others) to biblical paradoxes, particularly that of deliverance from (and through) death into eternal life. Connects the poem to Trinitarian theology that found New Testament narratives of Christ's coming as the specific fulfillment of Old Testament prophecies. Examines the paradoxical duality of Christ as mortal and as God, as well as the complex relationship between God and death in our culture. Questions whether the poem is fully successful.

Wolosky, Shira. *Emily Dickinson: A Voice of War*, 92-95. New Haven, Conn.: Yale University Press, 1984.

Stresses the literal level of the poem. Written in a time of warfare, the poem

between this world and the next or between love and death. She i:
incurious about herself and the past, but alert to the journey. She see
writing "her own obituary" as she enters into this "death-marria
formula anticipates a revelation, but none is forthcoming. The quest
an "anti-quest."

Wolff, Cynthia Griffin. *Emily Dickinson*, 274-276. New York: Alfred A
1986.

Relates the poem to the "specter of genteel carnality" as manife.
seduction novel, one of the first fictional forms to become popular in ,
The structure parallels the typical seduction plot, blending it eerily
"bride-of-Christ" tradition in religious literature. The yoking of tl
narrative traditions creates a probing parody, a questioning of the lat
tion which Dickinson finds grotesque. She makes her point by alignin
a form of cheap romance.

"My Life had stood — a Loaded Gun — " (754)

Cody, John. *After Great Pain: The Inner Life of Emily Dickinson*,
Cambridge, Mass.: Harvard University Press, 1971.

The poem expresses not so much the sublimation of love as the sublim
rage. Dickinson looks back from a convalescent perspective on the de
symptoms connected with emerging "masculine identifications" an
viously repressed bisexual impulses." The poem's "He" is identified
the Loaded Gun is the "illusory female phallus." The Pillow repres
comfort of maternal nurturing. A detailed, difficult, but provocative a

Dobson, Joanne A. "Oh, Susie, it is dangerous." In *Feminist Critics Rea*
Dickinson, edited by Suzanne Juhasz, 85-86. Bloomington: Indiana Un
Press, 1983.

"The powerful emotional effect of the masculine figure in [Dick]
poems, its intangibility, its godlike qualities, her fascination with it a
fear of it, and its tendency to exist in an absolute space and time
suggest the personal and internal makeup of the animus, with its energy
autonomous existence in the timeless, spaceless realm of the unconsciou

Loving, Jerome. *Emily Dickinson: The Poet on the Second Story*, 45-47. Cam
England: Cambridge University Press, 1986.

Man lacks the power to change (or die) on his own. He waits upon God
Yet this situation does not create an adversary relationship. God's fina
allows our individual beauty to "explode into the truth of the genera
Still, the particular life is more important than the general or univers
because the particular is all potential ("Loaded Gun") while the general
depletion, the spent consequence, of that potential.

reflects the popular belief that "war is a manifestation of divine power, and man, God's instrument in waging it." The concluding stanza asserts the paradox of divinity who has power over life and death but cannot die. Thus, the poem's speaker is God, and the poem examines "divine power in conjunction with human agency." Sees in the poem's rhetoric a parody of psalmic tropes such as those found in the work of Isaac Watts.

"A narrow Fellow in the Grass" (986)

Anderson, Charles R. *Emily Dickinson's Poetry: Stairway of Surprise*, 120-121. New York: Holt, Rinehart and Winston, 1960.
The first four stanzas have a calm, literal level that focuses on the snake's elusiveness and its alien nature. This suddenness of appearing and vanishing is the attribute that makes the snake so different, a difference highlighted by the comfortable, familiar tone. The absence of punctuation in the last six lines speeds up those lines and adds to the power of the image. The magical disappearance causes terror and leads to the association with evil—a sense of being suddenly emptied out of human warmth and feeling.

Johnson, Greg. *Emily Dickinson's Poetry: Perception and the Poet's Quest*, 35-37. Tuscaloosa: University of Alabama Press, 1985.
The essence of the snake is its ability to elude perception. Its presence is inferred by the disturbance of the grass. The actual sighting of the snake is rendered in the passive voice, indicating that the viewer can hardly take credit for this "chance occurrence of an instant." The snake's deceptiveness and evanescence, its resistance to perception, make it terrifying. The poem's final phrase presents "a brutally physical realization of the emptiness of her perception."

Pickard, John B. *Emily Dickinson: An Introduction*, 63-64. New York: Holt, Rinehart and Winston, 1967.
"A series of artistic progressions develop the snake image into a symbol of the unknown." The initial treatment is playful, though there are disturbing undercurrents regarding the snake's inability to hide. Then we see the snake's fondness for desolate places. Finally, we encounter an inner emptiness in the speaker's reaction. The poem contrasts "nature's surface beauty" with the "hidden terror" that fascinates the beholder.

SIDNEY LANIER
(1842-1881)

General Studies

Beaver, Joseph. "Lanier's Use of Science for Poetic Imagery." *American Literature* 24 (January, 1953): 520-533.

Beaver examines and assesses the verbal and figurative uses of science in Lanier's poems. In a number of poems, Lanier uses chemical terms in a way that shows fairly technical chemical knowledge. Photosynthesis and the properties of light are described in "Corn." Other figures are based on how compounds are formed and how matter decomposes. Astronomical concepts, geological references, and even botanical conceits can be found in Lanier's work. Like many of his contemporaries, Lanier did not shun science but absorbed its findings into his vision and poetic imagination.

Boswell, Jeanetta. "Sidney Lanier." In her *Spokesmen for the Minority: A Bibliography of Sidney Lanier, William Vaughn Moody, Frederick Goddard Tuckerman, and Jones Very, with Selective Annotations*. Metuchen, N.J.: Scarecrow Press, 1987.

This is a bibliography of secondary sources. See the full entry in "General Treatments of the Period."

De Bellis, Jack. *Sidney Lanier*. New York: Twayne, 1972.

Argues that Lanier left an enduring body of work in spite of splitting his energies between music and writing. Lanier's contributions to modern symbolist techniques are significant, as is his ability to handle ideas through paradox and irony. Traces the stages of Lanier's development as a poet, illustrating both his ties to Southern traditions and the elements that transcend those traditions. Examines the influence of Lanier's reading and gives detailed analyses of the major poems.

_____ . *Sidney Lanier, Henry Timrod, and Paul Hamilton Hayne: A Reference Guide*. Boston: G. K. Hall, 1978.

In this resource guide to three nineteenth century Southern poets, each section has a brief introduction to the life and critical reputation followed by bibliographical listings. De Bellis attempts to include all writings about the author and his works likely to be of use to scholars, though newspaper articles and theses are generally excluded. Entries are briefly annotated, and the listings on each poet are indexed by author, title, subject, and the poet's own works.

England, Kenneth. "Sidney Lanier in C Major." In *Reality and Myth: Essays in Memory of Richard Croom Beatty*, edited by William W. Walker and Robert L.

Welker. Nashville, Tenn.: Vanderbilt University Press, 1964.
Examines contradictions in Lanier's ideas about the South, especially between those expressed in his prose and those in his poetry. In the poems, he shows a fondness for the old South: a suspicion of trade and sharp tradesmen, a selection of placenames that evoke the land and not the material civilization spread upon it, a chivalric idealization of women. His attitude toward Negroes is equivocal. Lanier was an enthusiastic amateur who gained real proficiency at nothing.

Foerster, Norman. "Lanier." In his *Nature in American Literature*. Reprint. New York: Russell & Russell, 1958.
Argues that Lanier's best poems are poems of nature; he is the only poet who has given us an adequate representation of the Southern scene. His poems reveal him to be an accurate, if not a trained, ornithologist and botanist. However, Lanier's accuracy is less important than the truth of vision and feeling in his poems. He is effective at spiritualizing nature. Many pieces begin with or include a forest rhapsody, such as the celebration of the live-oak woods in "The Marshes of Glynn."

Gabin, Jane S. *A Living Minstrelsy: The Poetry and Music of Sidney Lanier*. Macon, Ga.: Mercer University Press, 1985.
A compact critical biography most concerned with the unique qualities of Lanier's poetry and the dependence of those qualities on his musical training. Not only Lanier's theoretical grasp but also his professional experience as a musician made him the poet he was. Lanier's place in the history of American music is explored, as is the impact of the Centennial Exposition of 1876. Gabin takes a close look at Lanier's musical compositions and at the more exaggerated musicality of his late poems.

Graham, Philip, and Joseph Jones. *A Concordance to the Poems of Sidney Lanier*. Austin: University of Texas Press, 1939.
This word list provides citations with usages for all but function words in Lanier's published poems and poem drafts. The list is keyed to Mary Day Lanier's *Poems of Sidney Lanier* and H. W. Lanier's *Poem Outlines*. Poems published in periodicals but not collected by the time of this concordance are keyed to their appearance in the periodical sources. Useful for habits of diction, special contexts of appearance, and other stylistic studies.

Hollander, John. "Sidney Lanier and 'Musicality.'" In *American Poetry to 1914*, edited by Harold Bloom. New York: Chelsea House, 1987.
Hollander refines our understanding of how Lanier's notions of musical form apply to his poetry. In his most characteristic work, Lanier "continually in-

vokes literal and figurative music as a trope for universal expressiveness." His larger, embracing thematic concern links music to poetry by connecting both to the sublime. Emotional mimesis is the ideal of each art.

Lorenz, Lincoln. *The Life of Sidney Lanier*. New York: Coward- McCann, 1935.
A somewhat sentimentalized account that examines Lanier's Southern birthright and dwells on his illness and sense of exile. Lanier's persistence is rightly admired. Lorenz provides detailed discussions of many poems, though the works are most often viewed as extensions of Lanier's personality rather than as aesthetic wholes. This romantic treatment rests in part on personal reminiscences and then-unpublished letters.

Mims, Edwin. *Sidney Lanier*. Boston: Houghton Mifflin, 1905.
Primarily biographical with little critical comment, this study depends upon Lanier's own words and those of people who knew him well. Stresses Lanier's early years and his relationship with the South "in order to avoid a misconception that he was a detached figure." A final chapter assesses Lanier's achievement as critic and poet. Notes Lanier's lack of spontaneity on the one hand and the unrevised state of many works on the other. Observes the overuse of sonic devices that sometimes creates "a mere chanting of words."

Parks, Edd Winfield. "Lanier As Poet." In *Essays on American Literature in Honor of Jay B. Hubbell*, edited by Clarence Gohdes. Durham, N.C.: Duke University Press, 1967.
An abbreviated version of the argument found in Parks's book (below). Lanier overextended himself, never properly measuring his strengths or effectively marshaling his forces toward his too-lofty goals. His early poems show the "transitory influence" of Poe, Byron, Coleridge, and Keats. A mixture of the antique and the contemporary marks Lanier's vocabulary. Parks examines "Corn" and other major works in some detail, as well as some lesser-known lyrics. Lanier produced "a thin sheaf of authentic poetry" that deserves much greater recognition.

_____ . *Sidney Lanier: The Man, the Poet, the Critic*. Athens: University of Georgia Press, 1968.
An economical, forceful appraisal of the life and work based on a series of lectures. Though Lanier aimed to meet the highest standards of achievement and to win acclaim, he fell short of his goals. Too often, his poems announce their contrived nature. Others reveal his excessive didacticism or his fondness for archaic terms. Still, Lanier's successes are genuine. He is "one of our most vital and interesting minor poets." Rich intellectual dimension and effective musical structure mark his best long poems, and a small number of his lyrics are among the finest we have.

Starke, Aubrey Harrison. *Sidney Lanier: A Biographical and Critical Study*. Reprint. New York: Russell & Russell, 1964.
Originally published in 1933, this is a comprehensive account of Lanier's life as well as a detailed appraisal of his work as poet and theorist, including the ways in which Lanier's theories hampered his genius. Discusses the interaction of Lanier's work as a composer of music and of poetry; also considers the interface between his scholarship and his creative work. The story of Lanier's struggle for acceptance is told with energy and warmth. Many poems analyzed in depth. Praises Lanier's daring with metrical substitution.

Warren, Robert Penn. "The Blind Poet: Sidney Lanier." In *American Poetry to 1914*, edited by Harold Bloom. New York: Chelsea House, 1987.
Attacks Starke's biography for making exaggerated claims for Lanier and then addresses the assumptions behind Lanier's critical and poetic stances. Points out inconsistencies in Lanier's positions on nationalism, science, and social issues. If only Lanier's poetry is to save him from oblivion, he may not be saved. Lanier never learned how to make ideas function in poetry. His allegorizing becomes a mere mannerism, and his "emotionalism was a species of self-indulgence." Finds Lanier blind to all that was valuable in his own time.

Webb, Richard, and Edwin R. Coulson. *Sidney Lanier: Poet and Prosodist*. Athens: University of Georgia Press, 1941.
Two complementary essays combining good scholarship, common sense, and readability. Webb tackles the scientific spirit underlying Lanier's musical and prosodic theories and experiments, noting that this spirit did not contradict Lanier's concern with expressing emotion. Coulson treats Lanier's place in the history of American poetry, illustrating his impact on other poets and critical thinkers. A valuable, concise overview.

Weirick, Bruce. "Sidney Lanier and the South." In his *From Whitman to Sandburg in American Poetry: A Critical Survey*. Reprint. New York: Biblo and Tannen, 1967.
First published in 1924, this account stresses Lanier's courage in combatting his spiritual and physical ailments following exposure to the Civil War. Lanier was able to find true joy in the natural world and to aspire toward worthy, if unattainable, ideals. Lanier's lyricism is one in which an appreciation of nature and religious elation mingle beautifully. Weirick feels that while Lanier's vision and his achievement are admittedly narrow and limited, it is amazing that someone in his circumstances accomplished so much.

Williams, Stanley T. "Experiments in Poetry: Sidney Lanier and Emily Dickinson." In *Literary History of the United States*. Edited by Robert E. Spiller et al. 3rd ed., rev. New York: Macmillan, 1963.

Sees Lanier and Dickinson as among those poets whose works reflect a "harsh truthfulness" and the groundswell of realism accompanying the new science and the aftermath of the Civil War. Lanier's pseudoscientific analogizing between music and poetry in *The Science of English Verse* reflects this trend. Lanier was infected by the "faith-doubt psychosis" of his times, as was Dickinson. Her experiments were both less programmatic and more thoroughgoing. Both rebelled against the Victorian mode; both knew it could not contain the new American experience.

Young, Thomas Daniel. "Lanier and Shakespeare." In *Shakespeare and Southern Writers*, edited by Philip C. Kolin. Jackson: University Press of Mississippi, 1985.
Lanier's lectures on Shakespeare focus on the sonnets rather than the plays. For Lanier, "Shakespeare came out of the Anglo-Saxon tradition and . . . his works mark the climax of that tradition." Lanier tries to date the plays by shifts in Shakespeare's prosodic habits in the direction of greater freedom. While not reliable scholarship, the lectures show that Lanier had read widely and carefully from Anglo-Saxon through Elizabethan poetry. His own theories, on which his practice was in part based, grew out of his thorough acquaintance with these rich traditions.

"The Marshes of Glynn"

Starke, Aubrey Harrison. *Sidney Lanier: A Biographical and Critical Study*, 312-316. Reprint. New York: Russell & Russell, 1964.
Lanier's flexible use of a dactylic measure approximates the loose rhythms of Whitman. The imagery is like a "landscape tapestry" that provides a feeling of medieval mysticism and piety. Lanier not only is successful at describing the scene and the beholder's emotions but also is able to describe "the actual creation of the emotion." Praises Lanier's attentiveness to light and shadow in this, his most characteristic poem.

"The Song of the Chattahoochee"

De Bellis, Jack. *Sidney Lanier*, 105-108. New York: Twayne, 1972.
The poem is controlled by image and music more than argument. "The movement of the river through the romantic landscape to the sea is the moral imperative of responsibility" that is easily interpreted as the soul's journey through turbulent life to and for God. Lanier's prosodic skills enable him to reproduce metrically the river's movement; placement of rhymes contributes to the development of theme and feeling. Lanier's method allows him to "imply

the idea of the importance of feeling and love . . . without being excessively didactic."

"The Symphony"

De Bellis, Jack. *Sidney Lanier*, 68-96. New York: Twayne, 1972.

Traces the effect of musical experimentation on Lanier's major attempt to translate aspects of one art into another. The poem, however, is not an attempt to arrange a full orchestra or strictly follow symphonic form. Lanier used "only those instruments which symbolized 'social questions of the times.'" De Bellis gives a detailed technical analysis of the poem's "harmony of themes" and of the ways in which Lanier modulates the tone color and rhythm of each instrument or instrument group: the strings, the flute, the clarinet and horn, the oboe and bassoon. With this ingenious but seriously flawed poem of social consciousness, Lanier joined the avant-garde.

STEPHEN CRANE
(1871-1900)

General Studies

Baron, Herman. *A Concordance to the Poems of Stephen Crane.* Boston: G. K. Hall,
1974. Keyed to The Poems of Stephen Crane: A Critical Edition, 2d printing,
rev. by Joseph Katz.
The word list is noteworthy for providing contextual quotations that are more
substantial than is common in such works. Includes variants found in the notes
to Katz's edition. Following the master list (which locates usage instances by
page and line) is a list of frequency of occurrence alphabetically arranged and
another frequency list arranged by count.

Bassan, Maurice, ed. *Stephen Crane: A Collection of Critical Essays.* Englewood
Cliffs, N.J.: Prentice-Hall, 1967.
Biographical essays, general discussions of Crane's art, and analyses of individual works are included in this well-balanced, compact collection. Basson's
introduction traces Crane's extraordinarily productive yet agonized career as
well as his changing repute with the critics. Excerpts from John Berryman and
Daniel Hoffman attend to the poetry. Chronology and selected bibliography.

Beer, Thomas. *Stephen Crane: A Study in American Letters.* Reprint. New York:
Octagon Books, 1972.
First published in 1923, this was the first full biography of Crane, using
materials gathered from interviews with people who knew him as well as from
documentary sources. Gives more attention to the conditions under which
Crane wrote than to the works themselves; the style is anecdotal. Includes a
brief discussion of the collection *War Is Kind.* The introduction by Joseph
Conrad is an intimate record of his friendship with Crane, an "artistic communion" in which each writer gave the other personal and professional encour-
agement.

Bergon, Frank. *Stephen Crane's Artistry.* New York: Columbia University Press,
1975.
Like most books on Crane, this one mainly treats the fiction. However,
"Crane's Habit of Imagination" and parts of other chapters include comments
useful for the poems as well. Reviews how "much of Crane's fiction and poetry
is composed of sudden and unusual, almost spectral, gestures, characters,
sensations, and perceptions." Crane's images and symbols seem the result of
viewing the world through an unusual, deforming set of spectacles, and he
frequently refers to the act of seeing.

Berryman, John. *Stephen Crane: A Critical Biography*. Reprint. New York: Octagon Books, 1975.
An engaging treatment of Crane's life, especially his literary career. Organized by the various places where Crane lived or visited as a journalist. "Crane's Art" is handled in a separate chapter in which the poetry is viewed as the bridge between the earlier innovations of Whitman and Dickinson and the extended careers in our century of Robinson, Frost, and Pound. Examines Crane's use of assonance, off-rhyme, and generally unadorned style. First published in 1950; rev. ed. 1962.

Cady, Edwin H. *Stephen Crane*. Boston: Twayne, 1980.
Three brief biographical chapters are followed by one on Crane's character and three more on his art. *The Red Badge of Courage* is considered the turning point of Crane's development. It gets its own chapter, the surrounding ones focused as "before" and "after." Some sketchy comments on the background of *The Black Riders*. Cady praises the intensity of Crane's best poems, their surreal quality, and their subtle phonetic effects. Emphasis is on the fiction. Chronology and selected bibliography.

Cazemajou, Jean. *Stephen Crane*. Minneapolis: University of Minnesota Press, 1969.
An accessible, straightforward account of Crane's career and the significance of his achievement, this pamphlet essay is a good place to begin. The few pages on the poetry insist that Crane not only attacked false values but also exalted positive virtues. Crane's poetry shifted from abstract imaginings to work that is "more concrete and more socially oriented." Accords special praise to the prose poems. Selected bibliography.

Colvert, James B. Introduction to *The Works of Stephen Crane, Vol. 10: Poems and Literary Remains*, edited by Fredson Bowers. Charlottesville: University Press of Virginia, 1975.
Describes Crane's painterly manner and the patterns of image and symbol in his work. Crane's "imagery of a demonic nature evokes dragons, serpents, ravaged and menacing landscapes, vacant deserts, empty seascapes—visions of a world fallen and cursed." God's wrath and the Devil's malice seem to merge in an awesome battle infecting nature and the human spirit. Crane's poetry "illustrates clearly the response of a brilliant literary imagination to the turbulent and contrary flow of thought and feeling of the American nineties."

_____ . *Stephen Crane*. San Diego: Harcourt Brace Jovanovich, 1984.
A brief, accessible popular biography resting on previous research that is selected and shaped into a brisk narrative for the general reader or beginning student. Focus is on the life experiences that Crane "transmuted into an art

that expresses a compelling vision of life and marks him unmistakably as a major force in modern literature." Chronology. Heavily illustrated.

Crosland, Andrew T. *A Concordance to the Complete Poetry of Stephen Crane*. Detroit: Gale Research, 1975.
Like Baron above, except that this list of word usages is keyed to Fredson Bowers edition of Crane's Poems and Literary Remains in the University Press of Virginia edition of *The Works of Stephen Crane*. The alphabet of key words includes usage citations. Appendix A offers a word-frequency list in alphabetical order. Appendix B gives the same data in numerical order.

Gullason, Thomas A., ed. *Stephen Crane's Career: Perspectives and Evaluations*. New York: New York University Press, 1972.
A copious collection with materials on Crane's family, early estimates of his work, and essays representing various critical approaches. Discussions of novels and short stories dominate, but there is a small section on the poetry and parts of general essays shed light on the poems. Gullason provides a brief introduction to each section, reviewing critical trends. Excellent bibliography.

Hoffman, Daniel. *The Poetry of Stephen Crane*. New York: Columbia University Press, 1957.
This standard treatment of Crane's poetry validates interpretive assumptions with biographical materials. Sees Crane's philosophy and style as acts of repudiation. Crane's sense of isolation permeates his work. Hoffman's detailed analysis of themes and techniques tries to see Crane as product of late nineteenth century milieu in spite of his insistent rejection of it. Excellent chapters on "War in Heaven" and "Love on Earth." The prose is viewed as an extension of the poetry. Appendix contains previously uncollected poems.

Knapp, Bettina L. *Stephen Crane*. New York: Ungar, 1987.
A brief biography is followed by summary treatments of the major works. "Part III: The Poems" stresses Crane's montage technique and other cinematic features of his style. Knapp claims for Crane affinities with the French Symbolist poets, particularly Lautreamont and Rimbaud. His poetry "is unique as an expression of bitter outrage and hatred of God." Crane's power is in his organic rhythms and his ability to freeze moments charged with strong emotion. Images of water and horses dominate *War Is Kind*.

La France, Marston. "The Ironist's Moral Norm." In his *A Reading of Stephen Crane*. Oxford: Oxford University Press, 1971.
Describes *The Black Riders*, a planned sequence written in a "sustained creative burst," as Crane's poetic outline of his moral views. War Is Kind embroiders but does not alter these views. "The poems present the moral norm which

controls the ironic pattern in his fiction." They show Crane adapting to "a world dominated by pain, chaos, and rampant human weakness." Crane was more a stoic humanist than a Christian: He knew there was no reward for righteousness. His poems convey an unsentimentalized view of the relationships between men and women.

Ludeke, Henry. "Stephen Crane's Poetry." In his *The Democracy of Henry Adams and Other Essays*. Berne, Switzerland: A. Franke, 1950.
Argues that Crane's poems, while overshadowed by his prose, occupy an important position in the development of modernist poetry in English. Examines affinities with and possible influence of Dickinson and Whitman. Crane's poetry, though often ironic, is always direct; its very bluntness was a novelty in its time. Crane opted for simple declarations, plain vocabulary, and occasional biblical echoes in syntax and rhetoric. He was more concerned with the compressed power of the whole than with individual lines. Sees *War Is Kind* as more traditional in style than Crane's earlier collection, *The Black Riders*.

Nagel, James. *Stephen Crane and Literary Impressionism*. University Park: Pennsylvania State University Press, 1980.
Though it does not treat the poetry, this book develops insights applicable to Crane's poems. Defines literary Impressionism as a response to the French school of painting that gained prominence in the late nineteenth century. Characteristics include the notion that "reality is a matter of perception; it is unstable, ever-changing, elusive, inscrutable." Impressionism restricts or subordinates detail to theme or meaning. Good material on Crane's imagery.

Raymond, Thomas L. *Stephen Crane*. Reprint. Folcroft, Pa.: Folcroft Press, 1969.
First published in 1923, this little volume offers a paper given by Raymond at the Newark Schoolmen's Club in 1921 to celebrate the fiftieth anniversary of Crane's birth. Raymond's biographical overview is followed by a list of Crane's novels, poetry, and miscellaneous writings in order of their appearance in book form. There is also a "Stephen Crane Chronology" and a list of "notes on Stephen Crane in Books & Journals." Raymond has some brief comments on *The Black Riders*.

Solomon, Eric. *Stephen Crane in England: A Portrait of the Artist*. Columbus: Ohio State University Press, 1964.
Crane spent most of the last three years of his life in England, where he made literary friendships with H. G. Wells, Edward Garnett, Ford Madox Ford, Henry James, Joseph Conrad, and others. Solomon considers two conflicting images of Crane: "The wild young American soaking up experience and the thoughtful (still young) expatriate discussing life and art." Crane's "English persona" is a key to his "highly self-conscious literary art." Crane and these other writers had similar approaches to their work.

Stallman, R. W. *Stephen Crane: A Biography*. New York: George Braziller, 1968.
  The standard, comprehensive life of Crane and a model of literary biography.
  Key chapters are built around the development, publication, and reception of
  Crane's major works. The chapter on The Black Riders views many of the
  poems as miniatures in mood and structural design of Crane's short stories.
  Illustrated, with a checklist of writings by Crane.

Weatherford, Richard M., ed. *Stephen Crane: The Critical Heritage*. Boston: Routledge & Kegan Paul, 1973.
  Records through excerpts the reception given Crane's works by his contemporaries and near-contemporaries. Includes ten reviews of *The Black Riders* and
  four of *War Is Kind*. The reviewers, whose attitudes are mixed, include
  Thomas Wentworth Higginson and William Dean Howells. Most of the collection presents reactions to Crane's fiction. Weatherford's introduction traces the
  critical tradition through and beyond these early responses.

Westbrook, Max. "Stephen Crane's Poetry: Perspective and Arrogance." In *Stephen
  Crane's Career: Perspectives and Evaluations*, edited by Thomas A. Gullason.
  New York: New York University Press, 1972.
  Critics who assume that Crane's poetry has a single protagonist will conclude
  that his work has little thematic coherence. However, there are really two
  voices: a voice of perspective and a voice of arrogance. The voice of perspective draws Crane's sympathy and its views are affirmed. The voice of arrogance
  is mocked. Beneath these voices lies a unified sensibility. The voices provide a
  dialectic from which Crane's own coherent vision emerges.

Williams, Ames. W., and Vincent Starrett. *Stephen Crane: A Bibliography*. Glen-
  dale, Calif.: John Valentine, 1948.
  This bibliography of primary sources lists books and contributions to books,
  then "Miscellanea and Curiosa," published letters, and contemporary reviews
  of Crane's titles. This is a descriptive bibliography that provides detailed
  information on bindings, title pages, and other aspects of the physical book. A
  separate alphabetical listing of Crane's titles follows the chronological main
  list.

The Black Riders

Cox, James M. "*The Pilgrim's Progress* as a Source for Stephen Crane's *The Black
  Riders*." *American Literature* 28 (January, 1957): 478-487.
  After reviewing earlier attempts to locate sources and influences for Crane's
  sequence, Cox develops parallels between *The Black Riders* and John Bunyan's
  seventeenth century prose masterpiece. He points out similarities in structural

patterns, syntactical characteristics, and the "strong tendency toward dramatic form." Crane is never as strictly allegorical as Bunyan, but both writers' styles point toward abstraction. Cox adduces a series of shared images to clinch his argument. Our sense of Crane's irony is deepened when we realize that he is playing off the vanished world of faith represented by Bunyan.

Kindilien, Carlin T. *American Poetry in the Eighteen Nineties*, 155-160. Providence, R.I.: Brown University Press, 1956.
The opening poems indict "man's sinful nature, his pride and vanity, his self-deceit." This is conventional enough, but Crane goes on to blame God for carelessness in not providing man sufficient means to guide himself. Crane accuses God of loving cruelty and enjoying man's suffering. As in Matthew Arnold's poetry, human love is one of the few supports in a bleak, hostile universe. Crane called on man "to defy his fate and rely on the God within himself." Crane's rebellious spirit is duplicated in many works of this period.

"War Is Kind"

Marcus, Mordecai. "Structure and Irony in Stephen Crane's 'War Is Kind.' " In *Stephen Crane's Career: Perspectives and Evaluations*, edited by Thomas A. Gullason. New York: New York University Press, 1972.
The structure of the poem involves alternating stanzas of lamentation and denunciation, modes which "modulate within and between themselves." Lamentation stanzas (1, 3, and 5) address an observer who confronts a dead or dying loved one. The stanzas of denunciation focus irony upon the sufferers and the social codes that send them to death. Crane's irony is both defense and attack. The human need for self-deception is subtly qualified in this poem and elsewhere in Crane's work.

PAUL LAURENCE DUNBAR
(1872-1906)

General Studies

Brawley, Benjamin. *Paul Laurence Dunbar: Poet of His People*. Reprint. Port Washington, N.Y.: Kennikat Press, 1967.
First published in 1936, this was the first seriously researched treatment of Dunbar. Brawley describes the environment in which Dunbar was reared, noting that he had little exposure to those aspects of Negro life about which he wrote. Sees Dunbar against the period of social and economic disenfranchisement of the Negro that followed the political successes of Reconstruction. Considers Dunbar's place in the generally sentimental literary climate of the period. A career study with little critical material, this book contains a chapter on "The Poet and His Song."

Bruce, Dickson D., Jr. "On Dunbar's 'Jingles in a Broken Tongue': Dunbar's Dialect Poetry and the Afro-American Folk Tradition." In *A Singer in the Dawn: Reinterpretation of Paul Laurence Dunbar*, edited by Jay Martin. New York: Dodd, Mead, 1975.
Though there is evidence that Dunbar was driven to write dialect poetry to gain a hearing, he did not consistently denigrate his work in this genre. He was often pleased to find himself adept at "putting into poetry the life and the language of his people." Dunbar's sermon-poems convey the values of Afro-American tradition in religious discourse. The concepts of divine intervention, relativism, and determinism receive sophisticated treatment in these seemingly superficial jingles.

Cunningham, Virginia. *Paul Laurence Dunbar and His Song*. New York: Biblo and Tannen, 1969.
A comprehensive treatment of Dunbar's short life based on scrapbooks, letters, and other documents, this appreciation never is less than warm and vivid. In twenty short chapters, Cunningham creates a series of dramatic moments in which to present her subject. She examines Dunbar's precocity as a student and artist; his relationships with family and friends; and his ambiguous success in the white community. References to and quotations from the poems dot the narrative. Bibliography.

Emanuel, James A. "Racial Fire in the Poetry of Paul Laurence Dunbar." In *A Singer in the Dawn: Reinterpretation of Paul Laurence Dunbar*, edited by Jay Martin. New York: Dodd, Mead, 1975.
Emanuel observes the demand among contemporary black readers that their

artists show racial fire in order to be valued. By this standard, Dunbar's reputation suffers. His racial views seem ambiguous. His treatments of slavery "do not usually emphasize resentment on the part of the protagonist or the poet." Only one poem out of twenty on such topics has the requisite fire. Dunbar's sometimes sentimental attitudes reflect, as he knew, the outlook that sustained his people both in and out of slavery.

Gayle, Addison, Jr. *Oak and Ivy: A Biography of Paul Laurence Dunbar.* Garden City, N.Y.: Doubleday, 1971.

A compact popular biography that considers the unusual circumstances of Dunbar's education in Dayton, Ohio and the mixed blessing of his success with the cultural and literary establishment whose darling he became. Gayle suggests that "the tension between being a poet and an entertainer formed the major conflict in his life." A free man, Dunbar wrote of slavery. A shining representative of his race, he had the status of a freak for those with racist views. Dunbar was "one with an age in which compromise was the norm."

Lawson, Victor. *Dunbar Critically Examined.* Washington, D.C.: Associated Publishers, 1941.

Originally a master's thesis at Howard University, this discussion traces the "themes and tendencies" of the Romantic poets that Dunbar adopted, showing how he worked to revitalize these themes. Lawson examines "the romantic girl," "the romantic pose" and other types. Dunbar's work in dialect is called an adaptation of pastoral to Anglo-American experience; here Dunbar is seen as "a conscious and unconscious apologist of the plantation." The book concludes with a section on Dunbar's prose.

Martin, Jay, ed. *A Singer in the Dawn: Reinterpretation of Paul Laurence Dunbar.* New York: Dodd, Mead, 1975.

This selection of commentary is divided into four groupings: reminiscences, discussions of Dunbar's poetry, discussions of his fiction, and a historical essay. There are also a number of poems dedicated to Dunbar. Martin's foreword is a "biography through letters" in which significant documents do the talking. This volume grew out of the Dunbar Centenary Conference held in 1972. Nikki Giovanni's afterword stresses Dunbar's inspirational value for black writers.

Martin, Jay, and Gossie H. Hudson, eds. General Introduction to *The Paul Laurence Dunbar Reader.* New York: Dodd, Mead, 1975.

A brief appreciation of Dunbar's background, his struggles, and his versatility. Martin and Hudson believe that the full range of Dunbar's talent has been overlooked, although at least one of his works has been in print ever since his first book was published. Literary success prodded Dunbar to greater production and to public appearances. His talent was always equal to the tremendous pressures put upon him to serve his race, his nation, and humankind through his art.

Metcalf, E. W. *Paul Laurence Dunbar: A Bibliography*. Metuchen, N.J.: Scarecrow Press, 1975.
The first half of this bibliography lists works by Dunbar organized by genre: novels, poetry (first collections, then individual poems), short stories, articles, songs, dramatic works, correspondence. The second half lists works about Dunbar: monographs, articles, reviews, letters to and about, films, and so forth. Listing is chronological within each category. There is an index of books by Dunbar and another of names.

Okeke-Ezigbo, Emeka. "Paul Laurence Dunbar: Straightening the Record." *CLA Journal* 24 (June, 1981): 481-496.
Compares Dunbar's work and situation to that of James Whitcomb Riley, Robert Burns, James Russell Lowell, and Geoffrey Chaucer. Argues that Dunbar's limited success as an Afro-American poet resulted from his condescending attitude toward black folk speech. Dunbar turned away from what he could control to pursue excellence as a writer in Standard English literature. However, he was not sufficiently prepared to realize this ambition because he never mastered Standard English sufficiently: He pursued a mirage.

Revell, Peter. *Paul Laurence Dunbar*. Boston: Twayne, 1979.
Sees a pattern of vacillation in Dunbar's responses to white editorial demands and his efforts toward complete freedom of expression: Protest and capitulation were mixed throughout his career. Revell examines Dunbar's works by form, "giving particular attention to his treatment of themes from black American life." Revell seeks to discover if Dunbar, in one form or another, can "assert a black point of view." Separate chapters on "Poetry in Literary English" and "Poetry in Dialect." Chronology and selected bibliography.

Rush, Theressa Gunnels, Carol Fairbanks Myers, and Esther Spring Arata. "Dunbar, Paul Laurence." In their *Black Writers Past and Present: A Biographical and Bibliographical Dictionary*. Metuchen, N.J.: Scarecrow Press, 1975.
Includes primary and secondary sources. Biography and criticism are in one alphabetical listing of books, parts of books, and periodical articles, as well as references to other bibliographical works. Includes a short sketch of Dunbar's life and career.

Simon, Myron. "Dunbar and Dialect Poetry." In *A Singer in the Dawn: Reinterpretation of Paul Laurence Dunbar*, edited by Jay Martin. New York: Dodd, Mead, 1975.

Dunbar's work continued the two streams of American black poetry. He kept separate the stream that observed Anglo-American literary traditions and the vernacular stream that grew out of black oral tradition. Thus, "he became the prototype of the black poet with two voices." Dunbar's dialect poetry was based on such Anglo-American precedents as the work of Robert Burns and James Russell Lowell. Parallels with Lowell's career are carefully developed, as well as contrasts. Dunbar's problem was that "neither language was finally his own." He wished to find a third, more natural voice, but he never did.

Story, Ralph. "Paul Laurence Dunbar: Master Player in a Fixed Game." *CLA Journal* 27 (September, 1983): 30-55.
The fact that Dunbar wrote primarily for a white audience necessitated compromises. To be financially successful, he had to entertain; to entertain, he had to reinforce racial stereotypes. William Dean Howells' introduction to *Lyrics of Lowly Life* exhibits the benevolent racism Dunbar had to contend with. Dunbar was silent to criticism and to misguided enthusiasm; he allowed himself to become a symbolic figure, an institution. Story contends that such attitudes toward Dunbar and his work are typical of those which have shaped the careers of generations of black authors.

Turner, Darwin T. "Paul Laurence Dunbar: The Poet and the Myths." In *A Singer in the Dawn: Reinterpretation of Paul Laurence Dunbar*, edited by Jay Martin. New York: Dodd, Mead, 1975.
Reviews and rebuts six popular myths about "Dunbar's versification, his tone, his subjects, his diction, his attitudes toward his black characters, and his competence or talent." Sees Dunbar as a conscious experimenter rather than an instinctive versifier. He could evoke the whole range of emotions, not just the gentler ones. His white characters are often mistaken to be black ones, thus estimates of the extent and kind of racial stereotyping are faulty. Dunbar was an artist for the folk, but not a folk artist.

Wagner, Jean. "Paul Laurence Dunbar." In his *Black Poets of the United States*. Translated by Kenneth Douglas. Urbana: University of Illinois Press, 1973.
After a brief biographical section, Wagner addresses "Dunbar and the Plantation Tradition," "Race Consciousness and History," and "The Lyricism of Heartbreak." A balanced, learned, and lucid exposition of the major issues in Dunbar's life and work. Adjacent essays treat "The Negro in the American Tradition in Dunbar's Time" and "Dunbar's Contemporaries." Bibliographical appendix and supplement.

Wiggins, Lida Keck. "The Life of Paul Laurence Dunbar." In her *The Life and Works of Paul Laurence Dunbar*. Reprint. New York: Kraus Reprint, 1971.
A breezy, entertaining narrative told in a series of short dramatic chapters.

Wiggins collected anecdotes from people who knew Dunbar and from Dunbar himself through interviews and examination of letters. So much here presumes to reproduce conversations that the book reads more like fiction than serious biography. Nonetheless, Wiggins' personal contact with Dunbar provides significant insights, and her enthusiasm is winning. First published in 1907.

NINETEENTH
CENTURY
AMERICAN POETRY

INDEX

INDEX

INDEX